# Economics, Finances, and Business

by Meredith Curtis

MEREDITH CURTIS

Copyright © 2016 Meredith L. Curtis

All rights reserved.

Published by Powerline Productions/Kingdom Building Services, Inc.

Originally published in E-book form © 2010 by Powerline Productions/Kingdom Building Services, Inc.

Printed by CreateSpace, an Amazon Company.

All Photos and clipart © Sarah Jeffords, Josh Nolette, Sarah Joy Curtis, Meredith Curtis, Laura Nolette, and licensees/Used by permission/All rights reserved. Graphs © Julianna Curtis. Used with permission.

All rights reserved. No part of this publication may be reproduced, stored in a retrieval system, or transmitted, in any form, or by any means—digital, mechanical, photocopying, recording, or otherwise—without prior permission from the author.

ISBN-13: 978-1532972669

# ECONOMICS, FINANCES, & BUSINESS COURSE

This book is dedicated to my first economic class students who have gone on to apply what they have learned to real life!

**Julianna Curtis**

**Katie Beth Curtis**

**Jenny Rose Curtis**

**Brian Webb**

**Zack Nolette**

**Laura Nolette**

**Julianna** majored in accounting and information systems at Stetson University while living with financial integrity. She was such a help in preparing this course. Thank you, Julianna. I couldn't have done this without you. Not only did she help me with the material in the book, she ran my household so that I could write this book. Julianna has been indispensable and honored with many promotions at her jobs at Aon Hewitt and Verizon. Right now she designs computer systems for the accountants to use. She is also one of the most generous people I know!

**Katie Beth** is sowing generously into the Kingdom of God. After completing her Master's degree, she is worked as an instructor at UCF, teaching freshman English. She also started and ran her own business offering ballet and worship dance classes. Now she is a stay-at home-mom.

**Jenny Rose**, during her years at Stetson University majoring in communications and Spanish, offered music lessons and vocal training—her own business. She is now a copy editor and news podcaster for Strang Communication.

**Brian Webb** & **Zack Nolette** started their own successful computer business during college. My computer and I appreciate them! Brian graduates this spring with his engineering degree.

Zack, a marketing major, landed a great internship with AAA® during his senior year at Stetson University. This turned into a full-time job after graduation. He is a huge asset to the company, creating websites and marketing campaigns.

Brian graduated from UCF with a degree in Electrical Engineering.

**Laura** and I operate Powerline Productions, co-op together, and take lots of field trips to the beach! Laura is a writer and graphic artist.

"The earth is the Lord's and all it contains, the world, and those who dwell in it: for he founded it upon the seas, and established it upon the rivers" (Psalm 24:1-2, NASB).

"In all labor there is profit, but mere talk leads only to poverty" (Proverbs 14:23 NASB).

"All hard work brings a profit, but mere talk leads only to poverty" (Proverbs 14:23 NIV ©1984).

"One who is gracious to a poor man, lends to the Lord, and He will repay him for his good deed" (Proverbs 19:14 NASB).

## Table of Contents

Economics, Finances, & Business Overview ............ 11
What is Biblical Economics? ............ 34
Wealth of the Nations Review ............ 39
Biblical Principles of Economics & Government ............ 43
*Principles Under Scrutiny* Cartoons ............ 52
Macroeconomics & Microeconomics ............ 60
Economic Systems ............ 71
Supply and Demand ............ 78
*Whatever Happened to Penny Candy?* Review ............ 91
Economic Essay: "Why I think Counterfeiting is Illegal" ............ 101
Monthly Consumer Price Index Project ............ 102
Wealth Redistribution vs. Wealth Investment ............ 107
Finding Capital for Families & Business ............ 120
Role of Banks ............ 124
Money Mystery Review ............ 129
Foreign Exchange & Foreign Trade ............ 131
Story of Federal Reserve Bank ............ 132
Money, Fiduciary Standard, and Inflation ............ 135
Economic Essay ............ 141
Economic Basics Open Book Test ............ 142
Social Justice vs. Personal Responsibility ............ 145
*Communist Manifesto* Book Review ............ 154
Monthly Consumer Price Index Project ............ 156
Is Government our Provider? ............ 161
11 Summary Paragraphs ............ 169
Production, Retail, Credit, and Debt ............ 176
*Money Matters for Teens* Review ............ 184
Myth of the Robber Barons Review ............ 187
Why Give a Speech on Economics ............ 191
My Economic Speech ............ 193
Monthly Consumer Price Index Project ............ 194
Buying Your First Home ............ 199
Why It's Good to Pay Your Mortgage Off Early ............ 201
Economic Essay: "Why It's Wise to Pay a Mortgage off Early" ............ 202
Care Giving of Elderly ............ 204

| | |
|---|---|
| Funeral Arrangements | 209 |
| Wills & Trusts | 211 |
| Book of Your Choice Review | 214 |
| Personal, Career & Financial Security | 217 |
| Monthly Consumer Price Index Project | 218 |
| Stocks, Bonds, and Mutual Funds | 223 |
| Invest $100,000.00 in Stock Market | 225 |
| Advertising, Temptation, and Being Wise Consumers | 228 |
| Borrowing & Lending Review | 247 |
| Rich Dad Poor Dad Book Review | 250 |
| Monthly Consumer Price Index Project | 251 |
| Family Financial Goals | 257 |
| Family Financial Records | 262 |
| Living Simply | 266 |
| Living within a Budget | 269 |
| Bartering | 271 |
| Buying Your First Car | 278 |
| The Call on Your Life | 285 |
| How to Choose a Career | 287 |
| Your Ministry | 288 |
| FW Radio Interviews on Careers | 294 |
| Apprenticeship, College, & Other Pathways to a Career | 298 |
| The College Question | 299 |
| How to Choose College | 301 |
| High School Years Check List by Grade | 304 |
| Career Exploration: Personality Assessment | 308 |
| Career Exploration: Skills, Interests, & Values Assessments | 313 |
| College Majors and Careers | 314 |
| Career Exploration: Careers You Like | 319 |
| The College Application Process & Going to College Debt-Free | 323 |
| Discuss College Years with Mom & Dad | 329 |
| Monthly Consumer Price Index Project | 335 |
| Starting a Business to Glorify God & Serve People | 341 |
| Taking Initiative & Meeting Customer's Needs | 346 |
| Hard Work Has Its Rewards & Specialization | 350 |
| Profit, Perseverance, & Perfecting | 356 |
| Business Planning | 360 |

# ECONOMICS, FINANCES, & BUSINESS COURSE

| | |
|---|---|
| 14 Slogans and Logos | 364 |
| The Clipper Ship Strategy Review | 368 |
| Scheduling | 370 |
| My Schedule | 372 |
| The Ultimate Gift Movie Review | 374 |
| Monthly Consumer Price Index Project | 376 |
| How to Get Your Business Started | 381 |
| How to Make a Formal Business Plan | 386 |
| Wisdom from Proverbs I | 392 |
| Wisdom from Proverbs II | 395 |
| Business by the Book | 396 |
| Wisdom from Proverbs III | 400 |
| Ministry Fundraising | 401 |
| Economic Essay: "Seeking God First in the Area of Finances" | 402 |
| Wisdom from Proverbs IV | 405 |
| Monthly Consumer Price Index Project | 406 |
| Tweak Business Plan | 411 |
| Wisdom from Proverbs V | 412 |
| Local Church Responsibility | 413 |
| Monthly Consumer Price Index Project Summary | 414 |
| Job Interviews | 417 |
| Writing a Resume | 419 |
| Write a Letter of Recommendation | 422 |
| Fill Out a Job Application | 424 |
| Wisdom from Proverbs VI | 425 |
| Wisdom from Proverbs VII | 428 |
| Economic Essay: "Give and It Will Be Given to You" | 429 |
| Wisdom from Proverbs VIII | 430 |
| Economics Test # 1 | 438 |
| Economics Test # 2 | 444 |
| About the Author | 450 |

# Homeschooling High School to the Glory of God

If your homeschooling journey includes high school and you are looking classes or for some ideas on designing your own classes, then you are the person I am writing for. This series is for you and your family!

When my oldest daughter was 12, I began planning her high school curriculum. There were so many things on my heart for her to learn, books I wanted her to read, and dreams I had for her high school education. I designed her entire high school curriculum. This curriculum has been adapted for my next two daughters and Laura's oldest sons. They have been the guinea pigs so that their younger siblings can have the best classes possible.

My classes have been, are, and will be adapted to every child to fit their own needs and designed to take advantage of opportunities that arise, such as co-op classes, vacations, and seminars. This series is simply my philosophy of educating my high school children at home, along with curriculum we have created and used in our family over the years. Hopefully, you will be inspired to create your own classes! Or, you can adapt my classes however you would like to! After all, you are the teacher!

My goal for high school is to provide a general education that can be a springboard to any and every possible career and education path that exists for my children. That is a HUGE goal, so I may not reach it, but if I aim for nothing I'll hit nothing, so I am aiming for something BIG! With that in mind, I try to cultivate and develop gifts, talents, and goals. I don't expect my teenager to know what he/she is going to want to do for the rest of his/her life, so I try to prepare for ALL possibilities.

Here is our family's Economics, Finances, & Business Class! I hope you and your high school children will enjoy it as much as we have! May it be a blessing! Feel free to adapt this class any way you want to. After all, you are the teacher!

This is the just one of the classes in the Homeschooling to the Glory of God series. There are more classes and collections of classes available and coming soon.

Here is a list of individual courses that are available now!

- New Testament Survey
- Old Testament Survey
- Worldview: Understand the Times
- Great Commission Course
- Web Design 101
- Economics, Personal Finances, & Business
- British Literature & Writing
- American Literature & Research
- Who-Dun-It Murder Mystery Literature & Writing
- Foundations of Western Literature
- Singing 101: Make a Joyful Noise
- Real Men 101: Godly Manhood
- Real Men 102: Freedom, Courtship, Marriage, and Family
- Real Men 103: Leadership
- Real Men 104: Passing the Torch
- God's Girls Grow in Christ & Christian Character
- God's Girls Friendship, Hospitality, & Celebrations
- God's Girls Homemaking

- God's Girls Motherhood & The Christian Family
- God's Girls How to Homeschool
- God's Girls Godly Womanhood, Courtship, & Marriage

Here is a list of current books in the series!

- Teaching Literature in High School with Classes You Can Use
- Teaching Writing in High School with Classes You Can Use
- Unlocking the Mysteries of Credits, Classes, & Transcripts
- Here is a list of upcoming books in the series!
- Teaching Bible in High School with Classes You Can Use
- Teaching Character & Life Skills in High School with Classes You Can Use
- Teaching History & Geography in High School with Classes You Can Use
- Teaching Government in High School with Classes You Can Use
- Teaching Math & Science in High School with Classes You Can Use
- Teaching Art, Music, & Drama in High School with Classes You Can Use
- Teaching Economics, Business & Personal Finances in High School with Classes You Can Use
- Teaching Physical Education & Health in High School with Classes You Can Use
- Teaching Homemaking in High School with Classes You Can Use

Happy Homeschooling! And remember to Homeschool to the Glory of God!

Meredith Curtis

# Economics, Finances, & Business Overview

## Textbooks

*The Holy Bible* by God the Holy Spirit!

*Economics, Finances, & Business* by Meredith Curtis

*Principles Under Scrutiny* by Larry Burkett (also called, *Using Your Money Wisely: Biblical Principles Under Scrutiny*)

*Economics in One Lesson* by Henry Hazlitt

## Supplemental Living Books

*Wealth of the Nations* by Adam Smith

*Communist Manifesto* by Karl Marx

*What Ever Happened to Penny Candy* by Richard J. Maybury

*The Money Mystery* by Richard J. Maybury

*Money Matters for Teens Workbook* by Larry Burkett

*The Myth of the Robber Barons* by Forrest Mc Donald

*Uncle Eric Talks about Personal, Career and Financial Security* by Richard J Maybury

*The Clipper Ship Strategy* by Richard J. Maybury

*Consumer Mathematics I Lifepac 8: Business Services* (from Alpha Omega)

*Business by the Book* by Larry Burkett

*A Bargain for Frances* by Russell Hoban (picture book)

*The Little Engine that Could* by Watty Piper (picture book)

## Movies

*The Ultimate Gift*

## Optional Books

*Biblical Economics in Comics* by Vic Lockman

Article: "Ronald Reagan and the Spirit of Free Enterprise" by George Gilder

*A Banker's Confession* by Gary Sanseri

*Money Matters for Teens* by Larry Burkett

Rich Dad, Poor Dad by Robert T. Kiyosaki

## Suggestions for Book of Your Choice

*Storm Shelter* by Ron Blue

*Debt-Free Living* by Larry Burkett

*A Christian Guide to Prosperity* by Michael Fries & C. Holland Taylor

*What Color is Your Parachute?* by Richard Nelson Bolles

*The Great Niche Hunt* by David J. Frahm with Paula Rinehart

*Biblical Principles for Becoming Debt Free* by Frank Damazio & Rich Brott

*Miserly Moms* by Jonni McCoy

*Freedom of Simplicity* by Richard J. Foster

## Assignments

- List all the Bible passages you know of that deal with money, stewardship, and contentment.
- Define "Stewardship" and "Contentment." What Biblical principles relate to stewardship and contentment? Show Mom and Dad what you've found and discuss it with them. (Economic Biblical Principles Worksheet)
- Draw 18 cartoons to illustrate Biblical principles of economics.
- Make slogans and logos to illustrate Biblical principles.
- Fill out book review on all books read.
- Take Economics Open Book Test.
- Complete Money Matters for Teens Workbook.
- Fill out worksheets.
- Write economic essays and read aloud to family or co-op group.
- Give an economic speech to family or co-op group.
- List ways to save money in the following areas: housing, electric, water, car, food, clothing, home repair, furniture, appliances, insurance, impulse spending, college education, investments, traveling, hobbies, books, and entertainment.
- Make a detailed plan to move out into your own apartment
- Take several career assessment survey
- Investigate careers with the *Occupational Outlook Handbook* (released each year by the federal government)
- List expenses you foresee upcoming in your college years. List your possible sources of income. Discuss this with Mom and Dad.
- Make a list of home business ideas.
- Design a Logo and Mission Statement for your business
- Make a business plan.

# Grading

To pass class, complete ALL assignments.

Grades will be based on: 10% Open book test, 10% business plan, 20% demonstrating knowledge of written material through class discussion, 20% essays & speeches, 20% quality of work in completing assignments; 20% exam scores.

To get a C grade, quality of work = average, test scores 70% to 79%.

To get a B grade, quality of written work = good, test scores 80% to 89%.

To get an A grade, quality of written work = excellent, test scores 90% to 100%.

# Economics, Finances, & Business Assignments

**Assignment**                                                      **Completed**        **Time took**

**August week four**
Read "What is Biblical Economics?" & "Why Study Economics"
Read "What is Biblical Economics?"
Read *Wealth of the Nations* Chapters 1-10
Fill Out "*Wealth of the Nations* Review"

**September week one class**
Discuss "What is Biblical Economics?" Worksheet & "Why Study Economics"
Discuss & *Wealth of the Nations* Review (chapters 1-10)

**September week one**
Read "Biblical Principles of Economics & Government"
Read *Principles Under Scrutiny* section on Attitude
Draw 18 cartoons illustrating each Lesson!
Read *Economics in One Lesson* Chapters 1-2
Fill Out "*Economics in One Lesson* Worksheet"

**September week two class**
Read "Biblical Principles of Economics & Government"
Discuss "Why Study Economics" & *Economics in One Lesson* (chapters 1-2)
Share 18 cartoons illustrating lessons from *Principles under Scrutiny*

**September week two**
Read "Macroeconomics & Microeconomics" and "Economic Cycles" "How Economics Affects Our Personal Lives"
Fill out "Economic Cycles Worksheet"
Read *Economics in One Lesson* Chapters 3-5
Fill Out "*Economics in One Lesson* Worksheet"
Read *What ever Happened to Penny Candy?* pg.1-77

**September week three class**
Discuss "Economic Cycles" Worksheets
Discuss *Economics in One Lesson* (chapters 3-5) Worksheet

**September week three**
Read "Economic Systems"
Fill out "Economic Systems Worksheet"
Read "Supply & Demand"
Fill out "Supply & Demand Worksheet"
Read *Economics in One Lesson* Chapters 6-8
Fill Out "*Economics in One Lesson* Worksheet"
Read *What ever Happened to Penny Candy?* 78-end of book
Fill Out "*What ever Happened to Penny Candy* Book Review"
Fill out "Glossary Worksheet" using *What ever Happened to Penny Candy*

### September week four class
Discuss "Economic Systems" & "Supply & Demand" Worksheets
Discuss *Economics in One Lesson* (chapters 6-8) Worksheet
Discuss *Whatever Happened to Penny Candy* Review
Discuss Questions about *Whatever Happened to Penny Candy* Glossary

### September week four
Read *Economics in One Lesson* Chapters 9-11
Fill Out "*Economics in One Lesson* Worksheet"
Write Essay: "Why I Think Counterfeiting is Illegal?"
Complete "Monthly Consumer Price Index Project"
Optional: Read *Biblical Economics in Comics*

### October week one class
Read Counterfeiting Essay Aloud in Class or to Family
Discuss *Economics in One Lesson* (chapters 9-11)
Everybody Share the Items they Chose for Personalized Consumer Price Index Activity

### October week one
Read Wealth Redistribution vs. Wealth Investment
Fill out Wealth Worksheet
Read Economics in One Lesson Chapters 12-13
Fill Out *Economics in One Lesson* Worksheet
Read *The Money Mystery* pages 1-45

### October week two class
Discuss "Wealth Redistribution vs. Investment" Worksheet
Discuss *Economics in One Lesson* (chapters 12-13)

### October week two
Read "Finding Capital for Families" & Businesses" "Role of Banks"
Fill out "Banks, Capital, Debt, & Savings Worksheet"
Read *Economics in One Lesson* Chapters 14-15
Fill Out "*Economics in One Lesson* Worksheet"
Finish *The Money Mystery* (46-end of book)
Fill out "*Money Mystery* Review"
Optional: Read Article: "Ronald Reagan and the Spirit of Free Enterprise"
Complete "Economic Basics Open Book Test"

### October week three class
Discuss "Banks, Capital, Debt, & Savings Worksheet"
Discuss *Economics in One Lesson* (chapters 12-13)
Discuss "*Money Mystery* Review"

### October week three
Read "Foreign Trade & Exchange"
Read "Federal Reserve Bank       "
Read "Money, Fiduciary Standard, & Inflation"
Read *Economics in One Lesson* Chapters 16-18
Fill Out "*Economics in One Lesson* Worksheet"
Read *Communist Manifesto*

Write Essay: "Why It's Important to Study Economics"
Read Essay aloud in class or to family

**October week four class**
Read "Why Study Economics" Essay aloud in class or to family
Discuss "Federal Reserve Bank" & *Economics in One Lesson* (chapters 16-18)
Go Over Any More Questions on Economics Open Book Test

**October week four**
Read "Social Justice vs. Personal Responsibility"
Fill out "Social Justice vs. Personal Responsibility" Worksheet
Read *Economics in One Lesson* Chapters 19-20
Fill Out "*Economics in One Lesson* Worksheet"
Finish *Communist Manifesto*
Fill out "*Communist Manifesto* Book Review"
Complete "Monthly Consumer Price Index Project"
Study for Economics Exam

**November week one class**
Everybody share any noticeable changes Personalized Consumer Price Index Activity
Take First Economics Exam

**November week one**
Read "Is Government our Provider?"
Fill out "Is Government our Provider? Worksheet"
Read *Economics in One Lesson* Chapters 21-22
Fill Out "*Economics in One Lesson* Worksheet"
Read *Principles Under Scrutiny* section on "Family"
Write 11 summary paragraphs on *Principles Under Scrutiny* section on Family

**November week two class**
Go over Exam Answers
Discuss *Communist Manifesto*
Discuss "Social Justice vs. Personal Responsibility Worksheet"
Discuss "Is Government our Provider? Worksheet"

**November week two**
Read *Production, Retail, Credit, & Debt*
Fill out *Production, Retail, Credit, & Debt* Worksheet
Read Economics in One Lesson Chapters 23-25
Fill Out *Economics in One Lesson* Worksheet
Fill out *Economic Biblical Principles Worksheet*
Optional: Read Money Matters for Teens

**November week three class**
Discuss "Production, Retail, Credit, & Debt" Worksheet
Discuss *Economics in One Lesson* (chapters 21-25)

# ECONOMICS, FINANCES, & BUSINESS COURSE

**November week three**
*Money Matters for Teens Workbook* chapter 1 Basics
*Money Matters for Teens Workbook* chapter 2 Banks
Read *The Myth of the Robber Barons*
Complete "*The Myth of Robber Barons* Book Review"

**November week four**
Read "Why Give a Speech on Economics"
Prepare Economic Speech
Complete "Monthly Consumer Price Index Project"

**December week one class**
Discuss *The Myth of the Robber Barons*
Discuss "Monthly Consumer Price Index Project"
Give Economic Speech

**December week one**
Read *Buying Your First Home*
Read *Why it's Good to Pay Your Mortgage off Early*
Optional: Read *A Banker's Confession*
Write Essay: "Why It's Wise to Pay Mortgage off Early"
*Money Matters for Teens Workbook* chapter 3 Checks
*Money Matters for Teens Workbook* chapter 4 Checking Accounts
*Money Matters for Teens Workbook* chapter 5 Budget I

**December week two class**
Discuss *Buying Your First Home* & *Why It's Good to Pay Off Your Mortgage Early*
Discuss *Money Matters for Teens* (chapters 3-5)
Read "Why It's Wise to Pay Off Mortgage Early" Essay Aloud in Class

**December week two home**
Read "Care Giving of Elderly", "Funeral Arrangements", "Making a Will"
Fill out "Care Giving, Funeral Arrangements, & Making a Will" Worksheet
Read Book of Your Choice
Fill out Book of Your Choice Review
*Money Matters for Teens Workbook* chapter 6 Budget II
*Money Matters for Teens Workbook* chapter 7 Anatomy of a Loan
*Money Matters for Teens Workbook* chapter 8 Credit Cards

**December week three class**
Discuss *Care Giving, Funeral Arrangements, & Making a Will*
Share about Book of Your Choice

**December week three & four home**
Read *Personal, Career, & Financial Security*
Fill out *Personal, Career, & Financial Security* Book Review
Complete "Monthly Consumer Price Index Project"

**January week one class**
Discuss *Personal, Career, & Financial Security*
Discuss "Monthly Consumer Price Index Project"
Discuss *Money Matters for Teens* chapters 6-8

**January week one home**
Read Stocks, Bonds, and Mutual Funds
Invest $100,000.00
Read *Principles Under Scrutiny* Section on *Insurance & Investing*
Fill out *Insurance & Investing* worksheet
*Money Matters for Teens Workbook* chapter 9 Danger of Borrowing
*Money Matters for Teens Workbook* chapter 10 How to Give Wisely
*Money Matters for Teens Workbook* chapter 11 How to Make Money with Money
Read Rich Dad/Poor Dad

**January week two class**
Discuss Invested $100,000.00
Discuss "Insurance & Investing"
Discuss *Money Matters for Teens* chapters 7 & 8

**January week two home**
Read Advertizing, Temptation, and Being a Wise Consumer
Fill out "Consumer Worksheet"
Go Grocery Shopping with Mom's Shopping List and Money!
*Money Matters for Teens Workbook* chapter 12 How to Spend Money
*Money Matters for Teens Workbook* chapter 13 How to Buy a Car
*Money Matters for Teens Workbook* chapter 14 How to Pay for College
Read Rich Dad/Poor Dad
Monitor Your Invested $100,000.00

**January week three class**
Discuss Invested $100,000.00
Discuss Advertizing, Wise Consumer Choices, & Shopping with Mom's Money
Discuss *Money Matters for Teens* chapters 12 & 13 & 14
Analyze Commercials & Ads

**January week three home**
Read *Renting Your First Apartment*
Complete *Renting Your First Apartment* Project
Read *Principles Under Scrutiny* section on Borrowing & Lending
Fill out "Borrowing & Lending Worksheet"
*Money Matters for Teens Workbook* chapter 15 How to Get a Job
*Money Matters for Teens Workbook* chapter 16 How to Keep a Job
*Money Matters for Teens Workbook* chapter 17 World Changers!
Monitor Your Invested $100,000.00
Read *Rich Dad/Poor Dad*

**January week four class**
Discuss Invested $100,000.00
Discuss *Money Matters for Teens* chapters 15-17
Analyze Commercials & Ads

**January week four home**
Read *Rich Dad/Poor Dad*
Fill out *Rich Dad/Poor Dad* Book Review
Monitor Your Invested $100,000.00
Complete "Monthly Consumer Price Index Project"

**February week one class**
Discuss Invested $100,000.00
Discuss "Monthly Consumer Price Index Project"
Discuss *Rich Dad, Poor Dad*
Discuss *Money Matters for Teens* Workbook
Share Renting My First Apartment" Project

**February week one home**
Read "Family Financial Goals"
Fill our "Family Future Events" Worksheets
Read "Family Financial Records & Files"
Read "Living Simply" & "Living on a Budget" & "Bartering"
Fill out "Our Net Worth Worksheet"
Make a Financial Records File and Net Worth File
Make a List of Home Business ideas
Find and Read Blogs Online about Saving Money
"List of Ways to Save Money" Assignment
Discuss Tips to Save Money for a Household
Read "Buying Your First Car"
Fill out "Your First Car" Worksheet

**February week two class**
Discuss Invested $100,000.00
Discuss "Net Worth" & "Making Wise Decisions
Discuss Long-Range Savings for Cars, Appliances, Homes, Retirement
Discuss "Living with a Budget" & "Tips to Save Money for a Household"
Watch Youtube Videos about Buying a Car
Discuss Buying Your First Car Worksheet

**February week two home**
Read "The Call on Your Life" & "How to Choose a College" & "Your Ministry"
Complete "God's Call for Career & Ministry" Worksheet
Listen to and Complete "FW Radio Interviews" Assignment
Read "Apprenticeship, College, & Other Pathways to a Career"
Read "The College Questions" & "How to Choose a College"
Start Reading *The Clipper Ship Strategy*

**February week three class**
Discuss Invested $100,000.00
Career Panel

**February week three**
Read & Complete "Career Exploration: Personality Assessment"
Read & Complete "Career Exploration: Skills, Interests, & Values Assessment"
Read "College Majors and Careers"
Complete "Match Interests & Careers to Majors" Chart
Complete "Potential College Majors and Careers" Chart
Read & Complete "Career Exploration: Careers You Like"
Read "The College Application Process & Going to College Debt-Free"
Complete "Preparing for College" Worksheet
Discuss College Years with Mom & Dad
Read *The Clipper Ship Strategy*

**February week four class**
Discuss Invested $100,000.00
Share Personal Mission Statements and Pray for One Another
Discuss Results of All the Assessments
Discuss Career Possibilities, College, & College Majors
Discuss Ways to Go to College Debt-Free

**February week four**
Read *The Clipper Ship Strategy*
Complete "Monthly Consumer Price Index Project"
Study for Second Exam on Financial Management

**March week one class**
Discuss Invested $100,000.00
Discuss "Monthly Consumer Price Index Project"
Second Exam on Financial Management

**March week one**
Read "Starting A Business to Glorify God and Serve People"
Fill out "Starting a Business" Worksheet
Read "Taking Initiative & Meeting Customers' Needs"
Fill out "Initiative & Customers' Needs" Worksheet
Read "Hard Work Has Its Reward" & "Specialization"
Fill out "Hard Work & Specialization" Worksheet
Consumer Mathematics Lifepac 8: Business Services
Read The Little Engine That Could by Watty Piper
Write Your Own Children's Story that Illustrates this Economic Principle!

**March week two class**
Read your Story Aloud in Class
Discuss "Starting a Business", "Taking Initiative & Meeting Customer Needs", "Hard Work Has its Reward", & "Specialization"
Discuss Business Finances

**March week two**
Read "Profit, Perseverance & Perfecting"
Complete "Profit, Perseverance, & Perfecting Worksheet"
Read "Business Planning"
Complete "Business Planning Worksheet"
Read *Principles Under Scrutiny* Section on "Business"
Write 14 Slogans each with a Logo to Illustrate Lessons
Read The Little Engine That Could by Watty Piper
Write Your Own Children's Story that illustrates this Economic Principle!
Consumer Mathematics Lifepac 8: Business Services
Finish *The Clipper Ship Strategy*
Fill out *The Clipper Ship Strategy* Review

**March week three class**
Read your Story Aloud in Class
Discuss "Profit, Perseverance & Perfecting"
Discuss "Business Planning" & Slogans & Logos in Class
Discuss *The Clipper Ship Strategy*
Discuss Business Finances

**March week three**
Read "Scheduling"
Fill out "My Schedule"
Start Reading *Business by the Book*
Consumer Mathematics Lifepac 8: Business Services

**March week four class**
Discuss "Scheduling" in Class
Watch *The Ultimate Gift*
Fill Out *The Ultimate Gift* Movie Review
Discuss how Lessons in *The Ultimate Gift* help Someone Run a Business

**March week four**
Read *A Bargain for Frances* by Russell Hoban
Write your own children's story that Illustrates this Economic Principle!
Read *Business by the Book*
Complete "Monthly Consumer Price Index Project"
Consumer Mathematics Lifepac 8: Business Services

**April week one class**
Read your Story Aloud in Class
Discuss *Personalized Consumer Price Index*
Go Over Consumer Mathematics Lifepac 8: Business Services Lifepac Test

**April week one**
Read "How to Get Your Business Started"
Complete "How to Get Your Business Started Brainstorming"
Read "How to Make a Formal Business Plan"
Complete "How to Make a Formal Business Plan Worksheet"
Complete "Wisdom from Proverbs Worksheet"
Read *Business by the Book*

**April week two class**
Discuss Biblical Principles from Proverbs
Discuss "How to Make a Formal Business Plan"

**April week two**
Make a Business Plan
Complete "Wisdom from Proverbs Worksheet"
Finish *Business by the Book*
Complete *Business by the Book* Review

**April week three class**
Discuss Everyone's Business Plans
Discuss *Business by the Book*

**April week three**
Work on Business Plan
Complete "Wisdom from Proverbs Worksheet"
Read *Principles Under Scrutiny* Section on "Ministries & Scriptural Highlights"
Complete "Ministry Fundraising Worksheet"
Plan an Essay: Seeking First the Kingdom in the area of Finances

**April week four class**
Discuss Biblical Principles from Proverbs
Discuss "Ministry Fundraising"

**April week four**
Finish Business Plan
Complete "Wisdom from Proverbs Worksheet"
Write an Essay: "Seeking First the Kingdom in the Area of Finances"
Complete "Monthly Consumer Price Index Project"

**May week one class**
Read "Seeking Kingdom First" Essays Aloud
Discuss *Personalized Consumer Price Index*
Present Business Plan

**May week one**
Tweak Business Plan
Complete "Wisdom from Proverbs Worksheet"
Read *Principles Under Scrutiny* Section on "Church & Sharing"
Complete "Local Church Responsibility Worksheet"
Finish "Monthly Consumer Price Index Project Summary"
Write an Essay: Give & It Will Be Given to You"
Run Your Own Business for the Glory of God & to Serve People

**May week two class**
Share Any Changes to Business Plan
Present Findings from your *Personalized Consumer Price Index*

# ECONOMICS, FINANCES, & BUSINESS COURSE

**May week two**
Read "Job Interviews"
Read "Writing a Resume"
Write Your Own Resume
Write a Letter of Recommendation
Fill Out Job Application
Complete "Wisdom from Proverbs II Worksheet"
Run Your Own Business for the Glory of God & to Serve People

**May week three class**
"Mock Job Interviews" Turn in Job Application & Have Reviewed by "Potential Boss"
Interviews in Class

**May week three**
Complete "Wisdom from Proverbs III Worksheet"
Complete "Wisdom from Proverbs IV Worksheet"
Run Your Own Business for the Glory of God & to Serve People

**May week four class**
Everyone Share from their own "Wisdom from Proverbs III" Worksheet
Discuss Everyone's Personal Business Experiences
Read "Give & It Will be Given" Essays Aloud

## Economics, Finances, & Business Hours Check-Off Chart

# Welcome to Economics, Finances, & Business

Welcome to Economics, Financial Management, & Business Class! This will be a great year! Yes, it will be a lot of work, but you will learn so much about God's Word, how it applies to economic principles, money, and running your own business! You will be reading lots of wonderful books on various topics related to money.

Of all the classes that you have taken, this will be one of the most practical classes you will ever take. You will apply what you learn here for the rest of your life. All my students have loved this class!

Economics is the first topic of study you will tackle this year. You will learn lots about this often misunderstood subject. Here are some of the things you will understand by the end of this course.

- Economic Systems (Socialism, Capitalism, Mixed, Biblical)
- Macroeconomics & Microeconomics
- Capital & Wealth
- Money, Banks, Inflation
- Supply and Demand
- Foreign Trade
- Social Justice & Personal Responsibility
- Government's Role

The next part of the class will focus on Financial Management. You will learn principles and practical tips to manage your own money. Here are some of the things you will be able to do by the end of this course.

- Make a Budget
- Apply Biblical Principles such as Stewardship, Tithing, and Investing
- Pay off a House Mortgage Early
- Purchase Insurance Wisely
- Investing Wisely (including in stocks and bonds)
- Be a Wise Consumer
- Save Money & Cut Corners to Stretch your Dollars
- Barter
- Set Family and Personal Financial Goals
- Keep Financial Records
- Plan for Funeral Arrangements, Elderly Care
- Make a Will
- Buy a Car
- Choose a College Major

Finally, you will learn how to start and run your own business.

- Make a Business Plan
- Serve the Customer
- Keep Records
- Scheduling
- Make a Profit
- Work Hard and Persevere

There are a lot of books to read. Some of these books I do not agree with 100% but I appreciate some of the wisdom in them.

## Larry Burkett Books & Workbooks

Larry Burkett's Principles Under Scrutiny is amazing! It is my very favorite economics book besides The Holy Bible. This book is laid out subject by subject with Scriptures and the biblical principle it teaches. I love this book!

Larry Burkett is a man who dedicated his life to teaching Christians to obey Scriptures in the area of money and financial management. He has written numerous books and workbooks that are easy to understand and use. You will learn so much in these books and workbooks that is practical and helpful!

- *Principles Under Scrutiny* by Larry Burkett (also published as Using Your Money Wisely: Principles Under Scrutiny).
- *Money Matters for Teens* by Larry Burkett
- *Business by the Book* by Larry Burkett

## "Uncle Eric" Books

These books are excellent! They are easy to read and understand, making complex economics simple for kids and adults. Uncle Eric books are based on the Free Market, or Austrian, economic model. While not written from a Christian perspective, Richard Maybury, the author, stresses the need for morality. He believes that natural law should govern society. He sums up natural law in these two statements.

- Do all you've agreed to do
- Do not encroach on another person's property
- If you think about it, this prevents lying, cheating, stealing, fraud, murder, rape, vandalism, and trespassing. You will enjoy these books!

Learn more about these books at bluestockingpress.com/

Here are the books we will read this year.

- *Whatever Happened to Penny Candy?*
- *The Money Mystery*
- *Personal, Career, and Financial Security*
- *The Clipper Ship Strategy*

## Adam Smith's Wealth of the Nations

This is the classic book on free market economics written in 1776. Nations had been trading with one another from Ancient Times and competed for power over the seas (the transportation for trade was ships!) and wealth. The more gold and silver a nation possessed, the wealthier that nation would be. The New World had been discovered and colonized with the hope of acquiring wealth. Adam Smith suggested that the wealth of the nations was not gold and silver, but the productivity of its people and their ability to produce something to freely trade with other nations.

Adam Smith was a Scottish economist and philosopher. He believed that God was the "Invisible Hand" behind the economic cycle and that people would make decisions based on their own self-interests and the need to provide for their families. People would create products of quality to fulfill needs in the market because it would be in their best interest to produce something of excellence that others would buy.

Advocating a free market system, this book called men to freedom in the area of business. As people used their unique talents and were free to trade with others, wealth would grow unhindered. There is a strong plea for morals and ethics in doing business and engaging in trade.

This is the best book on economic principles ever written! It is not easy to understand sometimes because it was written so long ago.

You can visit our website for a list of links to free downloads of *Wealth of the Nations*. Here is a link to the page: meredithcurtis.com/economicscourse.html

## Karl Marx's Communist Manifesto

This book, published in 1888 changed the way men think of work, capital, business, and the government's role in the lives of her citizens. The Communist League commissioned this book to lay out their ideals and plan. It is an eye-opening look at the intent and goal of communism.

Written by Karl Marx (who was supported by his rich capitalist father-in-law) and Frederic Engels (son of a wealthy capitalist), this book was part of their ongoing attempt to unite socialists and work together to overthrow the bourgeoisie (nobility, middle class, and wealthy merchant classes), help the proletariat (workers) rise up, and set up a new system without private property or class distinctions. Written for a mass audience, this short book (originally a pamphlet) describes the "soon-to-be" revolution and the communist utopia that would follow.

I believe that every Christian should read this book that has so impacted our world today and is adored by college professors across the country.

Communist is non-compatible with a Christian world view and this book will explain why. For socialism to be successful, a nation must be atheistic.

You can visit our website for a list of links to a free download of *Communist Manifesto*. Here is a link to the page: meredithcurtis.com/economicscourse.html

## Henry Hazlitt's Economics in One Lesson

Published in 1946, this is an important perspective on basic economics. Henry Hazlitt is a proponent of Austrian, or Free Market economics. His book drives home the point that a good economist must look at the big picture of economic decisions. This is a helpful book on economics. I wish it was required reading in Washington D.C.

Read the book and discuss the chapters with your parents, family, or co-op. The principles taught are sound.

You can visit our website for a list of links to a free download of *Economics in One Lesson*. Here is a link to the page: meredithcurtis.com/economicscourse.html

# Directions for Economic, Finances, and Business Assignments

Here are step-by-step directions for all your assignments in the course ahead. Come back to these pages as needed for help!

## Books & Classroom Reading

You will need to set aside a lot of time for reading in this course.

Books contain a wealth of information for our study of economics. I have carefully chosen books that are living, interesting, and helpful. Some of the books changed the world! (*Communist Manifesto* and *Wealth of the Nations*) Other books are so clearly and engaging that I know you will understand difficult topics by reading these well-written books (Uncle Eric books).

Larry Burkett is such an excellent author and brother in the Lord—I hope you will enjoy his books as much as I have!

Read the books carefully. There are books review sheets to fill out for each book you read.

You will also have some other reading to do—articles that I have written to "fill in the gaps" since we are using so many sources. I have tried to explain things very carefully so that you will understand and enjoy economics.

## Worksheets & Book Review Sheets

Worksheets and book review sheets are simple tools to help you remember what you have just finished reading. Please use neat handwriting so your mother can read it when she checks your work. Also, please write in complete sentences. A good thing to do is to read everything you write aloud before you turn in any written work. It is so easy to catch mistakes this way.

## Essays

You will write a few essays in this class too. I would encourage you to post them on your blog or on facebook after you finish writing them. People just may be interested in what you have to say.

Do you need help writing an essay? If so, may I recommend *The Write Stuff Adventure: Exploring the Art of Writing* by Dean Rea—there is an excellent section on how to write an essay in this book.

## Speech

Oh, no, not a speech! Don't worry—just one. I want you to talk about what you are learning and giving one formal speech is a great assignment. You can give your speech to your family, a bunch of friends, or your homeschool coop. I have included an outline that you can fill out to make everything simple.

## Group Discussions

Please don't skip this part. If you are doing this class at home alone, please have a "date" each week with your mom and dad to discuss all that you are learning. Economics can make your brain hurt! It will be good to talk it out week by week.

As you talk about anything, you will learn more because your brain has to process information in a different way to talk. So, use this time as a time to learn even more—and, hey, why not do your "discussions" at an ice cream parlor or coffee shop.

## Business Plan

This is a challenging assignment. A business plan looks very nice, is easy to read, and lays out your business ideas in a very professional looking package. Intimidated? Don't be. You will just follow the instructions along the way to create a business plan that people can pick up and read to see what you have in mind to do. Please get help from Mom and Dad with this assignment.

It is not really hard, but, boy, will it be impressive when it is done.

## Cartoons

Political cartoons have been popular for centuries because they are funny but they have a biting message. Cartoons are a great way to express truth in a light-hearted way. You will read some Biblical principles and then illustrate these principles with cartoons. This is a fun assignment.

## Slogans & Logos

Slogans are catchy phrases that people have no trouble remembering. Likewise, logos are visual pictures that people can associate with a business or organization. Think about the Republican elephant or the Democratic donkey. You are going to come up with slogans and logos for another set of Biblical principles. Then, you can come up with your own business logo and slogan. Have fun!

## Personalized Consumer Price Index

This assignment adapted from the *Bluestocking Guide to Economics* by Jane Williams. You keep a running log of prices on specific items of your choice for the entire school year. You will find a worksheet at the end of every month pages to use for this activity. Make sure that you use the EXACT same item each month for the project to work. You are taking a look at inflation over a period of nine months. This activity is easy and interesting.

## Reading & Writing Children's Picture Books

"Aren't I too old for picture books?" you ask.

"Absolutely not!" I reply emphatically.

No one is ever too old to read a good story with lovely pictures! There are two children's stories that illustrate business principles so well that they are worth reading and discussing. *A Bargain for Frances* by Russell Hoban invites you to witness Frances learning an important economic lesson. *The Little Engine that Could* is a classic story that every business owner needs to believe in His heart. After all, we can do all things through Christ who gives us strength!

"Do I have to write a children's book too?" you ask.

"Yes!"

"But why?"

When you write a story for children you have to be able to explain something in its simplest terms AND THEN show it, rather than tell it through a story. It will help you to work through some principles to a place of deep understanding.

Ah, but I have another reason for having you write a children's book. I am hoping that some of them are really good, will get published, and can counter-balance the surplus of children's books that teach socialism.

## Investing $100,000.00

Our homeschool co-op loved this online stock game! It was easy to use and fun to play. My son loved the competition on state and national levels. It is just like playing the real stock market where you stock prices fluctuate according to the market. Of course, in this game, you are give $100,000.00 of play money to use. We played the game for three months.

Directions on the site are easy to understand and follow. Each student will need to make their own personal account.

Here is the website for the TD Bank WOW Zone Virtual Stock Market Game.

virtualstockmarket.tdbank.com/

# A Word about Economic Schools of Thought

There are three main schools of thought when it comes to economics (Captialism, Socialism, Biblcial). Most other economic theories are a combination of socialism and free market.

## Capitalism

One school of thought is called Free Market, or Austrian, Economics. This is Capitalism, and is based on individual freedom and market laws such as supply and demand. Adam Smith wrote *Wealth of the Nations* in 1776. His book is considered the best and clearest description of the Free Market system.

On the positive side, capitalism leads to wealth, lots of choices for the consumer, and freedom. On the negative side, competition can bring out greed and selfishness with the poor overlooked or forgotten completely. Capitalism needs a strong moral framework to work.

## Socialism

This school of thought assumes that the government is all-wise, all-loving, and the best one to make decisions for its people. Rather than people making economic decisions and choices, the government runs the show and citizens are just cogs in the wheel.

This system is atheistic because government plays the role of God as provider and protector. Unfortunately for socialists, God does exist and does not bless those who try to replace Him. Nations that are socialist run up huge debts and often find themselves oppressed by their government. The price of socialism is the loss of individual freedom.

## Biblical Economics

Biblical economics is much like putting Capitalism inside a nation of Christians. The basic tenets of Capitalism are found in Scripture: right to own private property, individual freedom, quality workmanship, specialization, trade, fair business practice, and more. Biblical economics looks to Scripture for God's thoughts and plans on how money is to be managed at the individual and national level.

ECONOMICS, FINANCES, & BUSINESS COURSE

# September

What is Biblical Economics?

Why Study Economics

*Wealth of the Nations* Review

Biblical Principles of Economics & Government

*Principles under Scrutiny* Cartoons

Macro & Micro Economics

Economic Systems

Supply & Demand

*Whatever Happened to Penny Candy?* Book Review

Glossary Worksheet for Penny Candy

Essay "Why is Counterfeiting Illegal"

Personalized Consumer Price Index Project

## August Week Four Home

☐ Read "What is Biblical Economics?"

☐ Read "Why Study Economics"

☐ Read *Wealth of the Nations* chapters 1-10 (in Resources section at back of book) or entire book

☐ Fill Out "Wealth of the Nations Review"

# What is Biblical Economics?

"Well Brian keeps the economy humming," I giggled to my husband when we were talking one evening. Our friend, Brian, had dropped in earlier to show us his latest purchases that included a dart gun, a music CD, and a new amp for his guitar.

Where the money came from was a mystery. He worked for Kohl's, drove a motorcycle, and lived in his own house. His checking account hovered near zero and he didn't even have a savings account!

We are told by politicians that people spending money is a sign of a "healthy economy." But is it?

What is a healthy economy in God's eyes?

And what is economics anyway?

Economics is the study of the production, distribution, and consumption of goods and services according to Webster's dictionary. Goods are products such as televisions, ships, jeans, jewelry, ice cream, or bikes. Services include hair styling, banking, cleaning, interior decorating, or teaching. People make, sell, and buy goods and services day in and day out. In the process of all this producing, selling, and buying, money is exchanged. That's why we study money, inflation, debt, and interest too.

You see, economics is simple. It is just studying what people make and do and how those things are sold. Daily life is full of buying things. We go to work and produce things (goods) or do things (services) to make money.

Money is constantly flowing from one place to another. Imagine the dollar bill in your purse. Where has it been? Where is it going? Maybe it was a little boy's allowance and he used it to buy a candy bar at 7-11. The cashier gave it as change to your daughter when she bought a Big Gulp. Your daughter used it to pay your husband back the dollar she owed Daddy, but then he needed larger bills and traded you all the ones and fives in his wallet for a twenty dollar bill.

Studying how, why, and where money goes is another part of economics.

We need money to purchase the things we need to live comfortably on this planet. Food, housing, medical care, books, travel, music, art, and clothing all cost money. The only thing free is oxygen.

In Heaven, there will be enough of everything, but here on earth there are not enough goods and services to go around. If there were, we would all own beach houses in Hawaii. So, how who will decide who gets what? That is the question that economics tries to answer. As Christians, we want the solution to be righteous, just and compassionate.

Economics is the study of who ends up with what!

# Economics and Stewardship

We need to start at the beginning to truly understand economics. God owns everything! The Lord owns it all! Everything is His!

"The earth is the Lord's and everything in it, the world, and all who live in it: for he founded it upon the seas, and established it upon the waters" (Psalm 24:1-2 NIV).

Because God created the world, He owns the world and everything in it, including you, me, your stuff, and my stuff. Everything belongs to the Lord.

God entrusts what belongs to Him to individuals and families. Our house is really God's and we are stewards of His house. Our car is really Christ's car and we are stewards of His car. Our computer belongs to Jesus, but we take care of it for Him.

This changes our perspective of our money and our stuff. Instead of grasping for more and more, we can be thankful that God would allow us the privilege of caring for His money and His stuff. We need His plan on how to handle money, property, and wealth.

Don't worry. God has a plan for us to follow so that we can be faithful stewards!

# Private Property

God's wonderful plan is for people to work hard, leading to the ownership of private property, leading to the responsibility to use that property wisely.

God gives things to individuals to care for such as property, houses, cars, clothing, and businesses. These things are considered an individual's private property. The ownership (and stewardship) of private property is the foundation of many of the Old Testament laws.

Here are some of the laws that assume private property

The command to NOT steal assumes that things belong to the owner (Exodus 20:15)

Restitution required when private property is stolen (Exodus 22)

Land given to the tribes/families of Israel (Numbers 34)

Principle of faithful in little, faithful in much (Luke 16:10)

Parable in Matthew 25 about the steward and the Owner's return

Ananius and Sapphira's right to keep the land and/or the money received from selling the land (Acts 5:1-4)

Commands to work hard (Proverbs 14:23, & 16:26)

Hard work linked to riches (Proverbs 10:4 & 28:19)

Laziness linked to poverty (Proverbs 10:4 & 28:19)

## Does God Care About Money?

I don't know how to answer that question because I cannot fully understand the heart of God. But, looking carefully at the evidence in Scripture, I notice that Jesus taught about money often in His parables and sermons. Paul had a lot to say about money too. Proverbs is full of wisdom for handling money.

God may not care a lot about money. After all, everything belongs to Him! He doesn't need money or anything money can buy. But, He certainly cares about how people handle their money. The Lord cares about how men, woman and children feel about money.

"No servant can be devoted to two masters. Either he will hate the one and be devoted to the other; or he will be devoted to the one and despise the other. You cannot serve both God and money" (Luke 16:13 NIV).

God cares who we are serving. Are we devoting our energy, time, and ambition to making lots of money or having an expensive lifestyle? Or, are we seeking after God and His Kingdom with every bit of strength we possess?

Money is a distraction for many Christians, keeping them from fulfilling their God-given destiny. Instead of walking in God's call on her life, the carnal Christian is distracted by cares of the world. Many times worries make us seek after money instead of Jesus.

## Money Reveals our Heart

Money has a way of testing our heart, revealing what our values are. What we love will come to light in our behavior and actions. When we think something is important, we will find a way to spend our money on it. If out of the overflow of the heart, the mouth speaketh, then out of the overflow of the heart, the wallet spendeth.

How we spend our money, how we react emotionally when money is tight, and how we spend a windfall of money reveals our heart towards money. Money is either a necessary tool to provide for our families and extend the Kingdom of God or money is the object of our affection and desire. The love of money is an epidemic in our culture, revealing the heart of an adulteress. Remember, we cannot serve two masters. We cannot love God AND money.

The love of money is a dangerous thing. Not only does the love of money distract us from loving the Lord, it also produces all kinds of other problems.

"For the love of money is the root of all kinds of evil. Some people, eager for money, have wandered from the faith and pierced themselves with many griefs" (I Timothy 6:10).

One sin leads to other sins. I have friends who started out on fire for God, got married, and had a godly desire to provide for their families. Soon, though, the desire to provide turned into the desire to accumulate wealth.

What a difficult balance to keep because we are commanded to prepare for the future by saving money, investing for the future.

Can we save, invest, and provide without loving money? Of course! Or Jesus wouldn't ask us to do both! Two Christians can both be living on a budget, tithing, working hard, investing for the future, and giving to the poor (doing the same thing) with one Christian loving money and the other Christian not loving money (having a different heart).

Love of money is an issue of the heart. Only you can know if you love money or see managing money as a responsibility from God. Examine your heart and ask the Holy Spirit to show you what is going on inside.

## Money is at God's Disposal

If you set your affection on God instead of money, you will never have real money problems because God will provide for every need. Needs may not be met the way we would like, but we will not go hungry. Miracles will happen in our lives as we are used by God to be a channel of blessing for others.

God owns everything, all the wealth of the entire world belongs to Him. All riches are at God's disposal to do with whatever He wishes. He also has a heart for the poor. He wants the earth's wealth to be used to bring honor to Jesus, extend the Kingdom to the ends of the earth, and meet the needs of the poor.

"He who is kind to the poor, lends to the Lord, and He will reward him for what he has done" Proverbs 19:14.

When we give money and resources to the poor, it is like lending to the Lord. He always pays off his debts. He will repay what you have given beyond what you can imagine. You can't out-give God!

God will get it to you if God can get it through you. It is God who determines whether your pockets are full or empty. He is more concerned about your character than your comfort. He will withhold finances from you if it is necessary for your character.

If we love money, it is hard to be generous. If we love the Lord, we try to manage our money in a way that pleases God, making it easy to be generous.

## Money Can Be Used to Extend the Kingdom of God

The most important thing we can do with our money is to use it for the glory of God. After all, money is simply a tool we use to do good. We glorify God by seeking His Kingdom first with all of our strength, wisdom, and wealth. We use our money to take care of our family, care for the needs of our local church, take the Gospel to the ends of the earth, and care for the poor.

When this financial truth gets down into our spirit, we will enjoy financial freedom and joy! When we obey the Lord, joy overflows!

## Learning Economics from a Biblical Perspective

The Bible speaks to every area of life: science, mathematics, homemaking, history, geography, politics, law, government, literature, art, theology, morality, philosophy, sociology, and psychology. It has a lot to say about money, how to make it, how to save it, and how to spend it.

This year, we will look at economics from a Biblical perspective, rather than a secular perspective. We will look at His plans and examine economic principles in light of Scripture.

It is God's plan for men to work hard six days a week, acquire private property, and manage that property for the glory of God.

# Why Study Economics?

The economy affects history, science, medicine, literature, arts, and individual families, like yours. It is sad that economics affects our life so much and, yet, we know so little about it. Remember last week when I said that economics is the study of who ends up with what.

Economics studies how people's wants are obtained, by whom, and to what extent. In economics, we often talk about the GNP (Gross National Product) or the GDP (Gross Domestic Product) made up of all the goods and services that are sold. The GNP or GDP includes every ice cream cone, hot dog, cell phone, hair cut, car, house, book, pedicure, or car wash.

When people (consumers) start buying more and more, the economy is growing, or expanding. Conversely, when people (consumers) buy less and less, the economy is in a recession, or depression.

The love of money (greed) and power (selfish ambition) is often the kindling that starts wars. Money is definitely needed to pay for wars and to rebuild communities and cities when wars are over. That is why a thorough study of history will include economics.

A basic standard of living is necessary for arts and music to flourish. This basic standard of living costs money and requires a stable economy to maintain it.

In the United States, we define a "healthy economy" as one where consumers are spending and borrowing lots of money and businesses are seeing their profits increasing year after year. Is this a healthy economy according to the Word of God? The Bible calls debt "foolish," so I'm sure that God doesn't see debt as healthy.

The problem with defining a growing economy by increased spending is that when consumers stop spending and save (a good thing to do according to Scripture!), then the economy is "needing to be fixed."

The economy goes in cycles of growing and recessing. This cycle, if not tampered with, is natural and normal. People go through seasons of spending and saving. A healthy economy has both seasons flowing gently from one to another. We will talk more about this cycle more in the next few months.

# Wealth of the Nations Review

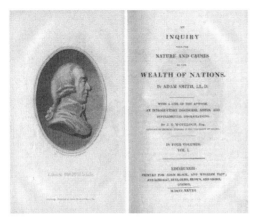

A short book review based on The Wealth of the Nations by Adam Smith. I would encourage you to read the entire book! But, if you cannot read the entire book, please read the ten chapters in the back of the book and choose your favorite five to summarize.

Choose your 5 favorite chapters and write a summary paragraph for each chapter.

**Chapter Title:** _____

**Summary Paragraph**

**Chapter Title:** _____

**Summary Paragraph**




**Chapter Title:** _____

**Summary Paragraph**

**Chapter Title:** _____

**Summary Paragraph**




**Chapter Title:** _____

**Summary Paragraph**

# September Week One Class

☐ Discuss "What is Biblical Economics?"

☐ Discuss "Why Study Economics?"

☐ Discuss *Wealth of the Nations*.

☐ Answer any questions about Course, syllabus, and assignments.

**Notes from Class**

# September Week One Home

- [ ] Read "Biblical Principles of Economics & Government" & Fill out Worksheet

- [ ] Read Larry Burkett's *Principles Under Scrutiny* section on "Attitude"

- [ ] Draw 18 Cartoons illustrating each lesson from the "Attitude" section

- [ ] Read Economics in One Lesson chapters 1-2

- [ ] Fill Out "Economics in One Lesson chapters 1-2 Worksheet"

# Biblical Principles of Economics & Government

There are clear biblical principles that apply to government and economics. Since government encroaches into the economic realm often, let's look at how these principles apply to both government and economics. The first principle is the most important one! God owns everything and He is the One in charge! We are accountable to the Lord for how we govern and how we use our money as individuals and as nations.

## Principle One: Stewardship

The Bible has something to say about all of life, including government and economics. God is our provider and boss. All authority and power resides with God. We ignore God's authority at our own peril. "Then Jesus came to them and said, "All authority in Heaven and on earth belongs to me" (Matthew 28:18 NIV ©1984). Jesus has all authority. All human authority derives from God's authority.

God also owns everything in world and all who live in it. "The earth is the Lord's and everything in it; the world and all who live in it" (Psalm 24:1 NIV ©1984).

God then delegates authority, responsibility, and wealth to people and institutions. What? Well, let me explain. God is the owner of everything and we are His stewards. We take care of His property for Him. The best biblical illustration of this is the parable that Jesus told in Matthew 24:45-51 where the master of the household puts a servant in charge of his household, possessions, and other servants while he goes away on a trip. When the master comes home, he will reward or penalize the servant based on the servant's care of others and his behavior. God places us in charge of His people and possessions. We are his stewards, accountable to him for the job we do in caring for what is entrusted to us. God entrusts property and responsibility to people. Adam and Even were commanded to subdue the earth and "rule over the fish of the sea and over the birds of the sky and over every living thing that moves on the earth" (Genesis 1:28 NASB).

The reason we have private property is that God entrusts what belongs to him to people. One of the Ten Commandments is "Thou shall not steal" (Exodus 20:15). That commandment alone demonstrates God's recognition of private property. You cannot steal from someone unless some sort of wealth or property belongs to the person. We cannot take what belongs to someone else and we are accountable for God for how we handle the property He has entrusted to us. Again, we are stewards of His property.

## Delegation of Authority/Stewardship of Authority

Just as God's delegated property to people, He has also delegated authority to people and to institutions run by people. Heavenly authority is delegated to the individual, the family, the church, and the government. Authority is given along with a responsibility, or job to do. A father has authority over his family because he has the responsibility to provide for his family and raise godly children. He has just enough authority to get the job done!

The individual has authority for self-government. He controls his speech, behavior, and choices. He is accountable to God. His responsibility is to obey God's laws, but makes the choice whether he will obey or not. That choice will lead to personal consequences.

The family has authority to raise children to serve God, educate children, and provide for family's financial needs. Families have God-given autonomy to make decisions about how they will live and raise their children. Again, God holds families accountable, especially fathers.

The church has authority from God to fulfill the Great Commission (see Matthew 28:18-20) and extend grace to the church and the lost world. Churches have authority to proclaim the Gospel and teach the Word of God. The church alone has the authority from God to collect and distribute wealth. Remember, though, that wealth is collected from volunteers. God has not given the government the authority to collect and redistribute wealth.

## God's Delegation of Authority to Government

God delegates authority to maintain justice to the government. Not a world-wide government, but sovereign nations who rule themselves as they determine. The Lord's role for the government is to reward good and punish evil.

"Everyone must submit himself to the governing authorities, for there is no authority except that which God has established. The authorities that exist have been established by God. Consequently, he who rebels against the authority is rebelling against what God has instituted, and those who do so will bring judgment on themselves. For rulers hold no terror for those who do right, but for those who do wrong. Do you want to be free from fear of the one in authority? Then do what is right and he will commend you For he is God's servant to do you good. But if you do wrong, be afraid, for he does not bear the sword for nothing. He is God's servant, an agent of wrath to bring punishment on the wrongdoer. Therefore, it is necessary to submit to the authorities, not only because of possible punishment but also because of conscience" (Romans 13:1-5 NIV ©1984).

Sovereign nations are accountable to God. Government officials are servants of God and accountable to Him. When a nation and its leaders realize they are accountable to God, it affects their laws and lifestyle, as well as the way they spend money.

With the responsibility to make and keep just laws, comes authority. How easy it is to abuse this authority. It is a wise government official who remembers he is a servant of God. It is a wise citizen who holds his or her government leaders in check.

Government is a dangerous servant and a fearful master. The power of government leaders needs to be kept in check. That is why America's Founding Fathers put checks and balances into the Constitution.

Government exists to protect the freedom of individuals. We often talk of the "left" and the "right" when we are talking about government systems. But, with fascism on the right and socialism on the left, all I see is total government control.

The balance we really need is the balance between total government control on one side and anarchy on the other side. The United States of America started with a great balance between total government control and anarchy, but over the past 100 years has moved dangerously close to the side of government control.

## The Bottom Line

Why are we accountable to God? Because He made us. He owns everything and has all authority. The Lord entrusts authority and responsibility to mankind. We are accountable to Him for how we use His wealth and authority. The world talks about money and power, but the Bible talks about wealth, authority, and responsibility. God is good, faithful, and loving, but He is also holy. He will protect and provide for us, but He will punish our sin. Man is made in the image of God and capable of great good, but also conceived in sin and capable of great evil. To protect people and prevent abuse, God puts laws in place.

# Principle Two: Law

God sets laws in motion. These laws come with consequences for obedience and disobedience. The law of gravity is a law that God has set in motion. If people ignore the law of gravity, they will hurt themselves. We reap what we sow (Galatians 6:7) God also put economic laws in place. Adam Smith calls them "the invisible hand" in Wealth of the Nations. One of the economic laws in place is the economic cycle.

## The Economic Cycle

A healthy economy goes up and down in a cycle. There are times of economic growth and times of economic down-turns, or recessions. They follow one another in a predictable pattern. During times of expansion, or growth, sales and profits go up until they reach their peak in the prosperity, or boom, stage. This is followed by a stage where things slow down with fewer sales and less profit. But, recovery follows after the recession stage. When governments step in to "help the economy along," they often prolong recessions and cause depressions. The best thing to do is to understand the predictable cycle and to work with it, not against it.

In time of expansion or prosperity, you can save money. In times of contraction, you can streamline, cut out waste, and focus on improving your product or service.

Understanding the economic cycle keeps us on our toes and allows us to thrive economically, rather than being blindsided by sudden financial disasters.

## Natural Law

God reveals Himself and His laws through nature and writes them on man's hearts. This is called natural law.

"For since the creation of the world His invisible attributes, His eternal power and divine nature, have been clearly seen, being understood through what has been made, so that they are without excuse" (Romans 1:20 NASB).

"For when Gentiles who do not have the Law do instinctively the things of the Law, these, not having the Law, are a law to themselves, in that they show the work of the Law written in their hearts, their conscience bearing witness and their thoughts alternately accusing or else defending them, on the day when, according to my gospel, God will judge the secrets of men through Christ Jesus" (Romans 2:14-16 NASB).

## Revealed Law, or Revelation

God reveals His laws through his written Word, the Bible. The Ten Commandments have been used by many nations as the foundation for judicial law. The Ten Commandments address our relationship to the Lord, His people, family, and the world around us. Many of these commandments address economics. We are commanded not to steal or to be envious of those who have more than we do. Greed, or envy is at the root of most socialist ideas, followed by stealing to "even things out." We are commanded to honor our parents and this principle is further explained in I Timothy 5 where we are to take care of parents and widows in our family. The idea of lying vs. integrity is addressed in commandment nine where we are commanded to not bear false witness. This principle addresses business contracts, buying, selling, paying taxes, truth in advertizing, and a host of other economic concern.

God's also gives punishments that fit the crime in the Old Testament. These consequences are used by God to bring people to repentance, but also to protect people hurt by the lawbreaker and the nation in a general way. A great example is the prodigal son who reaped the natural consequences of wasting his money and found himself homeless and hungry.

When we think of enforcing God's laws, we almost always think of the government. But, they are not the only ones to regulate human behavior. Individuals are to regulate their hearts, thoughts, and behavior—this is called self-government. Families are to regulate their children's behavior through education and discipline. Churches mentor members and bring church discipline to members who refuse to repent of habitual sin. Finally, the government is called to reward good and punish evil in people as it affects the nation and society.

# Principle Three: Localized Authority & Government

In Exodus 18:13-27, Moses is visited by his father-in-law, Jethro as he is leading the nation of Israel out of Egypt and into the Promised Land. Jethro, worried about his son-in-law's health, recommends that he should delegate his authority to other capable men. You see, Moses was exhausted. He had been settling every dispute for over a million people. I'm sure that was a lot of problems to handle. He did this everyday from morning until night. In accordance with Jethro's advice, Moses set men in place over thousands, hundreds, fifties and tens. They all had to love truth and hate dishonest gain. You see, greed can lead people to abuse power. Imagine you were the man in charge of ten people—that's not too bad. You could probably handle that. You would handle everything that you could, but if a bigger problem arose, you could go to the man over fifty people and he could help with decision-making. If the problem involved more people outside of the group of fifty, the man overseeing hundreds would be called in. But, you, with your ten people to manage, would handle almost everything. That is an effective to handle problems and decisions that arise—to keep it as small and localized as possible.

Decisions were made at the level of impact. That works great for managing government and money. Instead of a farmer in Nebraska setting safety standards for surfers in Hawaii, the Hawaiian surfers would choose a surfer with integrity to lead the way in setting standards. If there was a problem with bears roaming through neighborhoods and causing disturbances, the city would handle that problem with getting help from someone who lived far away. That is the way localized government works. Localized government takes decision-making to the people who are affected by those decisions.

From the time the Israelites were in Egypt, God dealt with them as both a nation and separate tribes. The tribes were based on family lineage and were given separate parcels of land when they crossed the Jericho River into the Promised Land. Sometimes only one or two tribes went to war and other times the entire nation went to war. Problems were handled and decisions made at the level of impact.

In economics, businesses would be regulated at local levels rather than national levels. Doctors would set standards of practice for doctors, plumbers would set standards of practice for plumbers, and other professions would do the same.

## Principle Four: Justice & Integrity

Until the Reformation, The Roman Catholic Church had tremendous power in Europe. This caused many problems, but there were a few good things too. One was that all the kings, queens, and rulers in Europe knew that they had to stay in favor with the Church or they could get booted off the throne. The Church was in charge! No one was above the Law of God (or the church depending on the particular law). Now, they really should have focused on being in favor with God, but that's another story. After the Reformation, there were several different denominations and no one church to keep royalty in line. At that point the "Divine Rights of Kings" theory sprang up and rulers tried to flex their muscles without anyone to question their behavior. These kings forgot the Latin saying "Lex Rex" or "Law is King." All people from peasants to princes stand equally before the Law of God. There is no favoritism and no compromise. When the majority of the people in a civilization understand this, you will have justice and integrity in behavior, speech, and national laws. Courts apply the law to cases before them, they do not make laws with their decisions.

A common respect for God's Laws creates an economic environment of integrity, honor, and freedom. People know they must keep their word. Buyers and sellers can trust one another. Two things, common in our world today, do much to destroy financial integrity.

## Inflation

Let me illustrate inflation with a story. Once upon a time, a queen was fighting a nearby country and the war was very expensive. How would she ever pay off her debt? So, she gathered up all the gold coins with her picture on them, promising her people that she would give them right back. She clipped little pieces of the coins and returned the original coins to their owners. She melted the gold clippings down and made more coins with her picture on them. But, the citizens of her kingdom realized that the coins were lighter. When Rupert and Esmeralda went to buy bread, they handed the baker five gold coins. The baker demanded coins that had not been clipped by the queen, but Rupert and Esmeralda had only clipped coins. So, the baker demanded six coins instead of five. You see, when the queen clipped her kingdom's coins, each coin was lighter and had less value. The queen devalued her currency. That is exactly what inflation is. Instead of clipping coins, the government just prints extra money, making each dollar bill already in circulation worth less.

You are probably horrified! I know inflating the money supply horrifies me, but nations, including ours, do it all the time. Each time they do it, the money in your wallet is worth less. If you think that you don't like this practice, God likes it even less.

Proverbs 20:10 say, "Differing weights and differing measure; both of them are abominable to the Lord." (NASB) God hates it when money is worth one thing one day and a different amount the next. You see, when the money supply rises, the value of the money falls, and often prices will go up. Inflation is not prices going up, but prices will go up after the government inflates the money supply.

Only two things can cause inflation, the government and counterfeiters. They both spread worthless money into the economy. Inflation is a lack of integrity. It discourages savings and encourages debt.

## Debt

There is another thing that destroys financial integrity in our day called debt. In our culture, we measure the economy in terms of how fast money is changing hands (velocity), employment rates, how much people spend, and how much people borrow. If lots of people are taking out loans, we say the economy is good. Yikes! God does not have anything good to say about loans.

Debt presumes upon the future (James 4:13-17) and causes the borrower to become a slave to the lender (Proverbs 22:7). Debt does not ask God to provide or even ask if purchasing something is God's will. Instead, debt allows us to rush in and get things we have not worked hard for. We will talk more about debt later, but please remember brother or sister in Christ, you can live debt-free! God is an amazing Provider!

If we want to measure the economy by biblical markers, a healthy economy would be one where everyone is working hard, making a profit, saving part of the profit for future needs, and investing that profit.

I am sorry to tell you that we are addicted in our culture to spending money whether we have it or not. A politician is popular if he gets lots of federal money spent in his district and "goes with the flow" of public opinion. God is pleased with politicians who vote against burdensome taxes, leave freedoms in place, honor God's laws, and protect citizens from invasion and crime. You see, government that governs least, governs best.

Before we leave the principle of integrity and justice, I want to challenge you as a citizen in a Republic. You have a leadership role in this system of government. You lead by voting good men and women into office and voting bad ones out. You also lead by speaking to your elected officials. So, for you, to have integrity, you must know political issues and the biblical principles involved and you must vote intelligently. As you learn more about biblical principles of economics and government, you will find the government doing all kinds of things that it has no authority from God to do, so keep your eyes open and don't forget to pray!

## Principle Five: Profit & Surplus

When it comes to sovereign nations, their economics should run on wealth, not debt. What is wealth? Well, I'm glad you asked. Wealth is the gold, property, money, natural resources, training, and material possessions a person or nation owns. Capital is wealth that can be used to invest, save, or make more wealth.

In Deuteronomy 28, God calls the nation of Israel to obey His commands. Obedience will bring blessings and disobedience will bring curses. This is a great chapter to read to see what God considers a blessing and what He considers a curse. In verses 12-14, the Lord mentions lending, but not borrowing, as a sign of the favor of God. "The Lord will open for you His good storehouse, the heavens, to give rain to your land in its season and to bless all the work of your hand; and you shall lend to many nations, but you shall not borrow. The Lord will make you the head and not the tail, and you only will be above, and you will not be underneath, if you listen to the commandments of the Lord your God, which I charge you today, to observe them carefully, and do not turn aside from any of the words which I command you today, to the right or to the left, to go after other gods to serve them" (Deuteronomy 28:12-14 NASB).

In the nation of Israel, God instituted the tithe for every member of the country. One tenth of produce and livestock was brought into the temple. While that carries on as tithes and offerings in the church today, we can glean some principles. It was the same percentage for everyone, so the wealthy paid more. It was not a large percentage. Some nations require their citizens to pay between 50 to 80 percent of their income in taxes. The American colonists called this burdensome taxation.

If a nation had a low percentage tax for all of its citizens and made a national budget based on what they could afford with those taxes, we would see streamlined governments with little room for waste. There is a big difference between what a person or nation can afford to do and what they want to do. If a person or nation is called to something, God will provide the finances for that thing.

God has a different method than debt for dealing with unexpected expenses. The Bible calls us to save instead of borrowing. "Prepare your work outside and make it ready for yourself in the field; afterwards, then build your house" (Proverbs 24:27 NASB). The man who wants to build a house (which will cost money) is told to get his income underway by getting his fields ready. The proceeds from his harvest can be used to build his house. If you use up all your income each month, you will have nothing for unexpected needs like car repairs, medical expenses, and new shoes. The wise store up for the future, but the foolish spend everything they have. "There is precious treasure and oil in the dwelling of the wise, but a foolish man swallows it up" (Proverbs 21:20 NASB).

Finally, the storing of money away for future needs is hard work. There is no room for laziness. "Go to the ant, O sluggard, observe her ways and be wise, which having no chief, officer, or ruler, prepares her food in the summer and gathers her provision in the harvest" (Proverbs 6:6-8 NASB).

Hard work is the way to make wealth. Hard work brings a profit, not just enough to pay the bills and meet financial needs. "In all labor there is profit, but mere talk leads only to poverty" (Proverbs 14:23 NASB). The profit from a hardworking people allows a nation to prosper. The profit from a hardworking father goes into saving for the future and investing in businesses or property that can be used to make wealth.

# Principle Six: Charity & Giving to the Poor

God loves the poor and needy. Charity, or sacrificial love that expects nothing in return, is what we are called to give to the poor and needy. God does not give government the job of caring for the poor or the right to redistribute wealth, but he does give that responsibility to families and the church. Read through the book of acts to see believers give money to the local church and watch the elders redistribute it to the poor and needy. God takes giving so seriously that He considers himself in debt to those who give to the poor. "One who is gracious to the poor lends to the Lord, and He will repay him for his good deed" (Proverbs 19:17 NASB).

In Scripture we are commanded to give to the worthy poor, not those who are lazy. "For even when we were with you, we used to give you this order: if anyone is not willing to work, then he is not to eat, either" (II Thessalonians 3:10 NASB). In I Timothy chapter five, Paul gives Timothy instructions on which widows are worthy of being helped. If we applied this advice to American welfare, many people would stop getting government welfare checks. In Jamestown and Plymouth colonies, early experiments with a form of socialism where everyone worked together and divided the bounty were tried and failed miserably. People will often take advantage of a situation where they can eat without working, or doing as little work as possible.

So, who is responsible for taking care of the poor if the government isn't? First of all, individuals should work hard if they can and provide for themselves and their families. And remember, a biblical work week was six days a week from sunup to sundown, not forty hours like we like to enjoy in America. There is nothing wrong with working two jobs. Families should also take care of widows in the family whether they are grandparents, aunts, or cousins. Businesses can set up their own gleaning laws adapted from those in the Old Testament (see Leviticus 19:9-10 and 23:22). Publix, a supermarket in our area, does this by distributing day-old bread to charities. The church fills in the gaps to help the poor and needy with no relatives to help them. Churches, families, and businesses can work together to help people find jobs and develop good working habits.

## Principle Seven: National Judgment & Revival

Everyone and every nation must give an account to God for its actions and words. God is our Judge! "God is a righteous judge" (Psalm 7:11 NASB). God is sovereign. He reigns over all! He causes nations to rise and fall. He causes nations to rise and fall.

We all know that individuals are judged. "It is appointed for man to die once and after this comes judgment" (Hebrews 9:27 NASB). Nations are judged too, but in this life, not the one to come. A nation receives blessing or curses according to how they obey God's laws, including those that have to do with money. God examines the hearts and behavior of individuals, churches, families, businesses, and government leaders.

According to Scripture, the blessing of the Lord is joy, laughter, family, feasting, celebrations, wealth, healthy livestock, land, children, grandchildren, a good reputation, and tribute brought from other nations. The judgment of God is poor leaders, young leaders, disunity, debt, famine, financial ruin, natural disasters, disease, pestilence, destruction, and fire.

God, in His mercy, will send revival if we ask Him through prayer and fasting. Nations and people need to have a truth revival (where they go back to believing the truth of God's Word) and a spiritual revival (where they repent and do what is right in obedience to God's Word). "If My people who are called by My Name humble themselves and pray and seek my face and turn from their wicked ways, then I will hear from Heaven, will forgive their sin and will heal their land" (II Chronicles 7:14 NASB). Many times revival, or the lack of revival, is in the hands of the Church. If God's people will humble themselves, repent, love God, and put biblical principles into practice in ALL areas of life, we would see a dramatic change in our culture! When we allow sin to fester in the church, the nation is hurt.

Revival leads to obedience in personal finances, self-government, family government, church government, business, local government, and national government. Revival leads to freedom.

# Biblical Principles Worksheet

List each biblical principle. Give an example for how the principle applies to government and an example of how the principle applies to economics.

I.

II.

III.

IV.

V.

VI.

VII.

# Principles Under Scrutiny Cartoons

There are 18 economic principles that you read about in the section, "Attitude," of Principles Under Scrutiny by Larry Burkett, or 17 economic principles in the section, "Attitude," of Using Your Money Wisely: Principles Under Scrutiny by Larry Burkett. For each principle, I would like you to draw a cartoon that illustrates the principle. I will give you examples below. Be creative and do your best art work. You can use drawing pencils, charcoal, or colored pencils.

**Principle # 1 is**

**Principle # 2 is**

**Principle # 3 is**

**Principle # 4 is**

**Principle # 5 is**

**Principle # 6 is**

**Principle # 7 is**

**Principle # 8 is**

**Principle # 9 is**

**Principle # 10 is**

**Principle # 11 is**

**Principle # 12 is**

**Principle # 13 is**                    **Principle # 14 is**

**Principle # 15 is**                    **Principle # 16 is**

**Principle # 17 is**                       **Principle # 18 is**

# Economics in One Lesson Worksheet

## Chapter One

What is more important: the immediate effects or the long-term effects of an economic policy and why?

Why is it dangerous to enact an economic policy that will benefit one group, but other groups? Give examples.

## Chapter Two

Does the hoodlum who threw the brick benefit society or harm society. Why?

# September Week Two Class

☐ Discuss "Biblical Principles of Economics & Government" Worksheet

☐ Share everyone's cartoons based on *Principles Under Scrutiny*, "Attitude" section

☐ Discuss "*Economics in One Lesson* chapters 1-2 Worksheet" answers

☐ Answer any questions about Course, syllabus, and assignments

☐ Discuss upcoming assignments

Notes from Class

## September Week Two Home

☐ Read "Macroeconomics & Microeconomics", "Economic Cycles", & "History & Economics" & " How Economics Affects our Personal Lives"

☐ Fill Out "Economic Cycles Worksheet"

☐ Read *Economics in One Lesson* chapters 3-5

☐ Fill Out "*Economics in One Lesson* chapters 3-5 Worksheet"

☐ Read *Whatever Happened to Penny Candy* pages 1-77

# Macroeconomics & Microeconomics

If you took a poll in your neighborhood, most people would want a bigger house, a nicer car, prettier furniture, and a fancier television. There seems to be no limit to what people want, but there is a limit to the resources available to supply the wants of people. So, if every person in the world wanted a 5,000 square foot home on a 20 acre piece of land, in a temperate climate close to a bustling city, there would not be enough homesteads to go around. That is the core of economics: the idea of scarcity. There are limited resources. So, who gets what? That is the economic question.

There are different economic theories to decide who gets what. We read Adam Smith's Wealth of the Nations (free-market economics) and we will read Karl Marx's Communist Manifesto (command economics). Free-market economic theories leave capital in the hands of the individual and allow the market to go through its cycle without interference and let the market supply and demand set prices. Command economic theories leave capital in control of the government and individuals do what they are told in relation to business, prices, and market supply. In real life, command systems don't work because people desire economic freedom, but there is no country with a free-market economy because there is no government that can keep their hands out of the economy. Inflating the money supply is done by all nations and the question these governments ask is "How much?" not "Should we inflate?" So, when politicians say they want to stop inflation, they really just want to slow it down. Inflating the money supply is part of the command, or socialist theory of economics, though some governments who inflate the money supply would be offended to be called socialist. European nations just admit it. Most nations operate in real life with some sort of mixture of the two basic theories, command and free-market.

When we talk about who gets what, free-market theorists believe that the playing field is open to all who will work hard and jump in. They believe that individuals should have freedom to buy, freedom to try, freedom to fail, and freedom to try again. In contrast command theorists believe that national governments, or one-world governments, should decide who gets what. This is a little scary considering that government is made up of men and women who are sinful creatures. Also, scary is no moral restraint on a free-market. There have to be some basic rules touching on keeping one's word (contracts), and presenting products in an honest, not deceptive way. Free-markets work best with a moral culture, especially the values found in the Word of God.

As we study economics, we will look at macroeconomics and microeconomics.

# Macroeconomics

Macroeconomics focuses on the big picture, while microeconomics focuses on the details of the big picture.

In macroeconomics, we would study economic systems (socialist, capitalist, mixed), national economies (Swiss, US, English, Japanese), international trade (trade between countries), sections of the economy (Housing, Wall Street, Farming), and how economic spheres interact (big layoff by an automotive company on the stock market). Don't let these big words throw you because the concepts are simple.

Macroeconomics looks at the economy as a whole and the factors that cause or inhibit growth. In other words, what is happening in the world that makes people buy more stuff? Macroeconomics studies how groups and nations manage the flow and distribution of wealth. Wealth includes money, land, "stuff" (possessions), houses, skills, education, and products. Does the government determine who gets what (socialism)? Do people make their own decisions and manage their own businesses (capitalism)? Supply and Demand are studied too, but as part of the overall picture.

In macroeconomics, we study the overall economy of a nation, several nations, or the world. This is the big picture.

# Microeconomics

In microeconomics, the focus is more on sectors of the economy, individual businesses, households, and the laws of supply and demand. Supply is how much of something there is. If a shoe company in Michigan has 5,000 pairs of shoes for sale, those 5,000 shoes are his supply. Demand is if people want something, how much they want it, and how much they are willing to pay for it. If there are only ten people in Michigan who want the shoe company's shoes, there is not a big demand.

Microeconomics studies consumer behavior and how individual businesses make decisions about production and cost. Why do people buy what they buy? What makes people want to buy something? What determines how much people are willing to spend on something they want? How much does a business need to charge to cover expenses and make a profit?

Microeconomics also studies influences on the economy. Microeconomics helps businesses and individuals understand the economy so they can make wise decisions. In microeconomics, we study consumers, household groups, or business sectors. Sometimes we look at specific households or individual businesses as an example.

There is a tremendous amount of overlap between macro- and microeconomics because they are not separate from one another. Nations are made up of households and businesses. Supply and demand affects nations too. Businesses are often global in nature, so that brings international trade into microeconomics.

# Financial Management

Financial Management is where we study how to manage and allocate specific capital in specific situations, to help businesses and individual families manage their wealth and make wise decisions. When we talk about business budgets or personal budgets, we are talking financial management. Under this area of study comes making a will, investing, retirement planning, education choices, and standard of living choices. This area starts with remembering that the tithe belongs to the Lord and that we are stewards of the other 90%. We want to honor Him in the way we manage our finances.

## Business Management

Each business is different, but there are general things that every business owner must know in the area of business law, marketing, production, pricing, selling, employees, and management.

So, to recap, macroeconomics deals with the big picture. Microeconomics breaks it down further into business sectors and types of households. But, to really get practical in the area of economics, you must learn to manage personal, household, and business finances, as well as how to start and run a business. Are you ready to learn? Okay, let's start with something that affects all four segments of our studies this year: economic cycles.

## Economic Cycles

A healthy economy goes up and down in a cycle. There are times of economic growth and times of economic down-turns, or recessions.

Think of your own life as an example. There are seasons of spending and seasons of saving.

Seasons of spending include buying back-to-school supplies, purchasing Christmas presents, paying for a family vacation, or acquiring a brand new computer. In all those situations, you are putting money into the economy, helping the economy grow.

Seasons of saving include saving for the family vacation, putting money aside for Christmas gifts, or pinching pennies to put extra aside for a brand new computer.

You get the picture. If you are spending money all the time, there will be no money saved up. If you need to buy something, you will have to go into debt if you do not have savings.

A healthy economy is not always growing, rather it goes through cycles of growing and recessing. This normal cycle is the result of many things, including the need for businesses and people to save money for seasons of spending. Before we look at the stages of a normal economic cycle, let's look at the factors that determine each stage.

What factors are used to determine each stage?

GNP (Gross National Product) or GDP (Gross Domestic Product) (How much stuff a nation is producing)

Interest Rates (How much interest banks are charging because so many people are in debt)

Unemployment Rates (How many people are out of work and how many people have jobs)

Consumer Spending (How much money people are spending)

In the Garden of Eden, Adam had a job, but it was an easy work—taking care of the garden and the animals. There was plenty to eat, a rent-free place to live, and wholesome fun to participate in for free. Since the fruit-incident, mankind must get a job and work hard to take care of needs (food, clothing, shelter) and wants (cars, phones, vacations, computers).

Over time, people have made things to sell to other people to make money to buy the things their own families need. Other people provide services to bring a paycheck home that will buy necessities. All this buying and selling, the flow of money, the cost of goods and services, and how much stuff is actually produced is called the economy. This economy ebbs and flows: expanding, booming, contracting, recessing, and recovering—the economic cycle.

For someone to make something to sell, he/she must look around and gather available resources (cloth, oranges). To this is added hard work. Polly turns cloth into clothing with sewing (work). Jennifer picks and boxes (work!) oranges to ship to customers in another state.

The stages in an economic cycle are Expansion, Prosperity, Contraction, Recession, and Recovery. Prolonged Recession stage can lead to a Depression. A prolonged Prosperity stage may become a "Bubble" that bursts, quickly sending the economy into a Recession stage. Government intervention will often intensify, rather than stabilize, the natural ups and downs of the economy.

# Expansion

This is a season of growing and increasing in productivity. Often business owners will increase their efficiency which, in turn, increases productivity and profit. When this is happening to many businesses at the same time, consumers start buying more stuff at cheaper prices (due to increased efficiency!)

Jennifer expands her orange shipping business by hiring more people to pack boxes to ship. She adds to her customer base too. The profits begin to grow more and more each month. Jennifer is experiencing expansion in her business.

For businesses to grow they need capital (money, resources). This capital can be obtained by saving carefully or borrowing money from a bank. Most entrepreneurs in the 1800's saved money carefully, while most entrepreneurs of today borrow money from banks to expand their businesses.

During a season of expansion in a nation, interest rates are low enough for businesses to feel comfortable borrowing money to finance expansion. Production rates are increasing and consumers are spending more. In other words, businesses are making more stuff and people are buying more stuff. This increase in production requires more employees, so businesses are more likely to hire people than fire people. Employment rates go up!

Mike and I run our businesses debt free. We save money to expand, avoiding debt. We are unusual, even among Christian business owners.

The government can create expansion in an economy by printing more money (inflation!) and decreasing interest rates. Though this causes the value of money to go down, there is a lot more money floating around, making everyone feel good. When the government creates a season of expansion and prosperity, it will inevitably burst and decline to a deeper recession than non-government created expansions.

# Prosperity

Affluence, wealth, and good cheer are in abundance in a season of prosperity. Businesses are bringing in profits and using these profits to expand their companies or start new ones. Some Christian businessmen use times like this in their business to help young men start their own businesses. Stock prices are usually high because businesses are prospering.

Jennifer purchases another orange grove debt-free when she moves from a period of expansion to one of prosperity. As the profits pour in, she is careful to tithe, save, increase her employees' pay, and purchases some needed equipment. This is a wise use of the season of prosperity.

During a season of prosperity, production rates are high and consumer spending is rampant. Businesses are flooding the market with products that people want to buy. People are spending gobs of money. Interest rates are low enough to be attractive to people so there is a lot of borrowing by businesses and individuals. Unemployment rates are very low. It is easy to find a job if you are looking and willing to work.

In an artificially (government) created season of prosperity, there will be lots of buying and selling, but little true ownership. That's because everyone is using credit cards and loans to purchase things. Often loans are easy to get, even for people who are at high risk to default. That means that banks lend to people that are likely to stop paying their loan off. When this happens the banks are stuck with a lot of cars, boats, homes, and other property—but that's another season of the cycle.

# Contraction

This is a period of economic decline for a business. Prices drop. Sales slow down, people are buying less, and families start tightening their belts. This is a time where unsuccessful businesses must make hard decisions. Inefficient business practices must change or the business could fold. Marketing practices are analyzed. New ways to improve the product are discovered.

Polly's business is struggling. She has to let two of her employees go. She gives them six months notice and allows them one day a week to look for another job. She finds a cheaper place to purchase zippers and buttons, freeing up some money to fix two of her sewing machines. She asks her employees to help her come up with improvements that will make her clothing more marketable. One of her seamstresses has an advertising plan that becomes very popular. Sales increase and she hires back the employees she had to let go. Polly made wise use of her season of contraction.

Sometimes a season of contraction happens in a business or family because they are cutting back to save for the next season of growth. Unnecessary expenses are purged and frivolous pursuits are abandoned.

In a season of contraction in a nation, production slows down or consumer spending slows down. Companies make less stuff or people buy less stuff. Unemployment rates go up as people begin to lose jobs because of a drop in their business's profits. Interest rates might rise, or banks might just be more careful about who they lend to. Someone who is a high-risk borrower might be able to get a loan in a time of expansion, but not in a time of contraction or recession. Banks are less willing to take risks on people.

Sometimes a season of contraction is just a natural response to an artificial government-induced season of prosperity. Prices just level off. Maybe housing prices went up to a level that was more than homes are really worth. A season of contraction will bring housing prices back down to a reasonable level.

# Recession

The nation is considered to be in a recession if our GNP (or GDP) declines for 2 or more consecutive quarters (3 month periods). A recession is often accompanied by a decline in the housing market, drop in stock prices, and an increase of unemployment. This is a time where unsuccessful businesses are purged. People who own businesses that fail during this season, can move their resources into more productive ones.

This is not the only time that businesses fail. Any time a business is unable to compete in the financial market, it is a way of nudging the business owner on to another, more-marketable area. Almost all very successful business owners have several failures before achieving great success. With every failure, much is learned that can be applied to the next business.

A recession is similar to a contraction, but felt more strongly by more of the population. In a recession, production slows down, profits decrease, and consumer spending decreases. People are making less money, losing their jobs, or afraid of losing their jobs, so they spend less money. Unemployment rates begin to rise.

Interest rates often go up or banks are less willing to lend money across the board, not just to high-risk borrowers.

Because it is horrible to see people lose their jobs, often the government will step in to help. The well-meaning, often times, government intervention only prolongs contraction and recession seasons of the cycle. The government has a tendency to "keep businesses" going that would be better off folding. Maybe it would be better to give business owners money to start a new business that would be more competitive in the market.

Jim owns a factory that builds boats. His company is failing. The government offers to bail him out, but Jim says, "No thank you." He fasts and prays. The Lord gives him an idea for a new business. His factory will now build bicycles. He sells most of his equipment and purchases new machinery. The bicycle manufacturing can be done in half of the space required to build boats, so Jim rents out the other half. Now he has income from the bicycles and rent. Jim made wise use of the recession season in his business.

If a recession continues, it can become a depression.

## Recovery

During recovery, things begin to improve. People start back to work who were unemployed, production increases, sales increase. Recovery is similar to expansion, but feels different because often people have "catch up" financially.

Jim and his family could not go to the dentist or buy clothes during the recession. Now that Jim's bicycle business is up and running, they have to catch up on purchases that were put off until later. Any extra money goes to buying shoes, clothing, and paying the dentist. Once they are back on their feet, the recovery season will feel like a season of expansion again.

Recovery is the time to get back on track financially, hopefully with more wisdom and take care of any needs from the recession.

## How Cycles Help

We all love seasons of expansion and prosperity. It is fun when money is rolling in, but often these seasons cause prices to jump up to unreasonable places. A season of contraction will bring those prices back down to a more reasonable level.

If we, as Christians want to avoid debt, than we need to tighten our belts and save once in awhile. We also need seasons that force us to examine our business practices, expenses, and policies. It often takes lean times to bring out creative ideas. After all, necessity is the mother of invention.

As Christians, we know that God's promises hold true in every season of the economic cycle, even when the government is intervening to help and causes more harm than good. Our provider is not hindered by economic down-turns. He owns the cattle on a thousand hills. He is able to provide in season and out of season. We are always blessed!

History is filled with people's responses to economics cycles of growth and recession. It is always important in history to study the economy and how it affects historical events.

## History and Economics

Think about the Spanish exploration of the New World. Isabel and Ferdinand needed money to fund the Spanish Inquisition. The defined being a rich nation as having lots of gold in the castle safe. They also wanted to spread their Christian faith. Dreams of gold to finance their "mission for God" spurred them to give Columbus permission to settle the New World.

Think about the colonization of North and South America. Companies, with permission from royalty, financed settlements in Jamestown, Plymouth, and many other colonial towns.

Think about the American Revolution. Colonists were outraged about taxation without representation. The English Parliament and King George were taxing Americans in very creative ways (tea taxes, stamp taxes, and more!) Why? England was heavily in debt from waging war against France on two continents. She saw America as a way out of debt, rationalizing that the colonists were "paying" for the Mother Country's protection. Economics played a part in the American Revolution.

Throughout American history, socialist programs are introduced during lean economic times. People are scared about financial matters, so they are willing to buy into social programs, thinking they will "make things better." Unfortunately, people trade their freedom for an illusion.

Not all historical events, including war, are a result of economic factors. There are many reasons that the American colonists wanted to be independent from England. They valued representative government, religious freedom, and a republic form of government. So, don't fall into the lie that economic reasons are the cause of everything. But, money and the desire for money, have played a large part in history.

## War and Economics

To understand the causes, progression, and results of many wars throughout history, you must look at economy. Lean economic times have caused countries to look at other nations and desire their wealth, leading to a military invasion. Which wins is often determined by economic issues. Wars cost a lot of money to fight. When a war is finished, a country often finds itself in debt, like England did after the 7 Years' War (French and Indian War), which leads them to make economic policies. England imposed high taxes on the American colonists, arousing fury among those who already wanted to be free from England's rule.

Sometimes, in contrast, good economic times, have created a desire for even more. Germany before World War I was enjoying the good fruit of a free market economy, but their leader, Kaiser Wilhelm was not content. Itching for more power, he jumped into a conflict between Austria-Hungry and Serbia. Germany's economy was ruined after World War I and became saddled with a debt that was not paid off until 2010, 90 years after the war ended.

War is never a good for a fighting nation economically. There is so much destruction, loss of life, and loss of property. The cost cannot be calculated. The only profitable business is for those not in the war to supply arms and equipment to those fighting the war.

# How Economics Affects Our Personal Lives

Economics doesn't just affect nations and leaders, it affects families and individuals.

## Business

To start a successful business, you must understand your target market, competition, and other economic principles. Without clear economic understanding, you are steering blind toward the future. For example, you may believe in free market capitalism, but if you live in the United States in the early 21st century where there is no longer a free market system, but rather a mixed, mostly socialist, set up, you will have to take into account the taxes, regulations, and prohibitions on your business. Can you still make a profit in a socialist economy? Yes, but it is harder.

## Health & Medicine

Unfortunately, health and medicine are big business. Drug companies are good investments for stock investors because these companies are making a tidy profit. Government money is poured into research, further lining these companies' pockets. Insurance companies drive the price of medical care up too. It is important for you to understand how the economy works so that you can figure out where the money is going and why.

## Personal and Family Finances

Economic principles can help you to prosper as a family. Understanding how debt works will help you avoid it, along with learning biblical principles. You will need to make changes in your family finances depending on what is happening in the economy at large. I put $4,000.00, little by little scrimping and saving, into a mutual fund for Jenny Rose for her college education. To my dismay, it had dwindled down to $1,300.00. I was devastated and resolved to pay closer attention to the economy and to learn more about mutual funds and other forms of investing. Avoid this kind of mistake.

# Economic Cycles Worksheet

Label the economic cycles in the chart. The first is done for you.

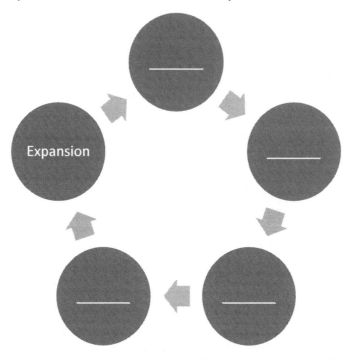

List each cycle, explain what happens during the cycle, and give an example of how it affects a family or business.

How is the economic cycle helpful?

# Economics in One Lesson Worksheet

## Chapter Three

Are there financial benefits to massive destruction?

Why does effective economic demand require purchasing power?

What is the difference between an increase in demand and a diversion in demand?

How are supply and demand two sides of the same coin?

True or False: Wanton destruction of anything with real value is always a net loss.

## Chapter Four

Why do people have so much faith in government spending and how is that harmful?

Why is it harmful to the economy and the taxpayer for the government to create projects to provide employment?

How does creating jobs for some destroy jobs for others?

What is the psychological advantage for the politician when the government creates projects?

## Chapter Five

How do heavy taxes on businesses discourage production?

How do heavy taxes on individuals discourage production?

# September Week Three Class

☐ Discuss "Macroeconomics & Microeconomics" & "Economic Cycles" & "History & Economics" & "How Economics Affects Our Personal Lives"

☐ Discuss "Economic Cycles" Worksheet

☐ Discuss "*Economics in One Lesson* chapters 3-5 Worksheet" answers

Notes from Class

# September Week Three Home

- [ ] Read "Economic Systems" & "Supply & Demand"

- [ ] Fill Out "Economic Systems Worksheet" & "Supply & Demand Worksheet"

- [ ] Read *Economics in One Lesson* chapters 6-8

- [ ] Fill Out "*Economics in One Lesson* chapters 6-8 Worksheet"

- [ ] Read *Whatever Happened to Penny Candy?* pages 78 to end of book

- [ ] Fill out "*Whatever Happened to Penny Candy?* Book Review"

- [ ] Fill out "Glossary Worksheet" using *Whatever Happened to Penny Candy*'s Glossary

# Economic Systems

## The Three Islands

"Time for vacation!" Dad announced one evening at dinner. "We have three weeks to relax and have fun."

"Are you sure we can afford it, Dear?" Mom inquired.

"Don't worry, Sweetheart. I just got a big bonus. The project I've been working so hard on turned into a huge success. The boss is pretty happy with me right now."

Three weeks of vacation turns into a big adventure because your father wants to visit three different island nations for vacation. They are right next to each other, but each one is different in the way they run their government and economic system.

You pack your suitcases and join Mom, Dad, and your siblings on the adventure. Your first stop is Command Island.

# Command Island

"Is this all there is?" your younger brother asks you as your family descends the stairs from the airplane to the tarmac. There are armed guards in rows making a walkway for your family and the rest of the passengers to walk through to the dilapidated building that you guess is Command Island's one and only airport.

"Well, Honey, don't worry, we'll get settled in one of the hotels and relax." You can overhear your mom talking to your dad and patting his arm.

"Right," your dad answers, trying to cheer up, "We'll find a hotel and get settled."

"Only one hotel on the island," another passenger informs your dad.

"What?!" your whole family asks in unison.

"One hotel, one restaurant, one taxi service, one public beach, one movie theatre, and one golf course." The passenger shakes his head. "Not a fun place for a vacation. I'm here on business….well, trying to get permission to build another hotel. So far, the answer is no. The government doesn't want anything to compete with their hotel or any of their businesses."

"The government owns the hotel?" you ask, surprised.

"And the taxi service, and the movie theatre, and the restaurant, and the golf course."

"How does the government have any time to do what it's supposed to do?" your little sister asks.

"Sssshhhh." The man puts his finger to his lips and motions for your sister to stop talking. "You can't speak against the government here," he whispers.

Your vacation for the first week ends up pretty boring. The hotel pool is empty because the workers didn't feel like coming in this week to fix it. They get paid no matter what they do. The hotel is comfortable, but drab. The waitress makes your father mad at the first meal, but there is nowhere else to eat, even though the food is awful. Your dad does enjoy the golf course, though, except for the fact that he can't use his own clubs. He has to use the clubs that are provided so that everything will be fair. Oh, and there are no winners or losers in the golf game.

# Combo Island

"So, glad we're off Command Island," you whisper to your little sister as you walk through into the much nicer airport, one of two on the island.

Your whole family shows their passports and fills out 5 pages of paperwork. The next stop is hailing a taxi.

"How much will I owe you?" Dad asks the driver who has all kinds of permits posted above his rearview mirror.

"That depends on the ages and occupations of each of you," he replies. "The government requires that we give a 50% discount for college students, children between the ages of 12 and 15, fire fighters, and garbage men. Then, there is also a 3% sales tax and a 1% education tax added to the fair."

"Oh, okay," dad mumbles in confusion.

He does manage to arrive at an amount of money to pay the taxi driver. He and mom choose one of the four hotels and your family settles in after another complicated method of paying for a hotel room. There are 7 different taxes added to the hotel bill. There is also a government questionnaire that needs to be filled out with questions regarding personal history, family ancestry, health condition, and possible need for subsidization for the hotel bill. Dad says that he doesn't want government help, so he has to fill out another form rejecting the government subsidization. Dad also had to show that everyone in the family has health insurance, life insurance, and sky diving insurance.

Your family only has health insurance, so there is talk of being deported, but Dad is able to fill out 17 forms to buy temporary life and sky diving insurance for each family member for one week. He is told that he can fill out more forms to get 50% off what he paid reimbursed. I won't talk about what happens next because Dad gets a little angry and Mom cries.

There were ten restaurants on the island, so you chose a little Chinese place that has a scrumptious buffet. Unfortunately, you have to be examined by a doctor first to see if you are healthy enough to eat the food. The children eat free, but parents pay double.

When your family finishes eating its government-approved food and reads and signs the form with the Combo Island Surgeon General warning of the effects of buffets on weight, they are exhausted and just want to go home and sleep.

Wanting to avoid the confusion with the taxi fair, your family decides to walk to the hotel. This evidently is taboo because the next day is spent with a government counselor, who spends the rest of the vacation tagging along.

You are thankful when the week is up.

# Freedom Island

"Wow!" you say aloud when you walk into the airport on Freedom Island. It is a hustling, bustling place full of friendly smiles and bright colors.

Several taxi cabs are lined up outside of baggage claim, each charging different prices, according to the size and comfort of the taxi cabs or their own personal decision. Dad manages to get a great deal on a comfortable taxi van and your family piles in.

"Where to?" the taxi driver asks, pleasantly.

"How many hotels do we have to choose from?" Mom asks.

"Oh, there are over 100 hotels, motels, and bed and breakfasts on this island. Big ones, little ones. Fancy ones, plain ones. There are also two resorts."

You are amazed. Dad and the driver negotiate a price that is agreeable to both of them so that your family can drive around and see the entire island. There are tons of shops, golf courses, miniature golf, bumper cars, video arcades, two paint ball fields, tennis courts, and several public beaches.

Dad and Mom decide against a fancy resort or expensive hotel, choosing instead a moderately priced hotel with a lovely pool and hot tub. This way there is more money to spend on all the fun activities on the island.

That night you are part of a family meeting where you each give input (with Dad and Mom making the final decision) about where and how you will spend your vacation money.

Mom wants to shop. Your brothers want to go to the Water Park. You want to hit the video arcade and your sister wants to visit the petting zoo. Dad, of course, wants to golf and go deep sea fishing. The great news is that if you eat at moderately priced restaurants for every meal, except one special evening, you can do it all.

## Free Market

A Free Market System, or Capitalism, or Price System, or Market System is based on supply and demand. If someone wants to buy something, someone somewhere will make it and sell it.

Capitalism says, "People will behave in their own best interest."

If someone has capital (money, land, talents), he will use it to make more money to provide for his needs and his family's needs. He might start a business if he has enough money, farm if he has enough land, or provide a service or product with his talent. In the process, he will provide products and services for other people that those people want or need. He will also employ people to help him in his endeavors, providing jobs.

Capitalism fosters hard work to provide for oneself and one's family. The Free Market system of economics finds a strong champion in Adam Smith, author of Wealth of the Nations.

The 2010 Index of Economic Freedom, a joint effort of the Wall Street Journal and the Heritage Foundation, listed the Top Ten Free Markets of 2010. Based on Adam Smith's idea that protecting individual freedom results in greater prosperity for everyone, they used as their criteria: business freedom, monetary freedom, trade freedom, fiscal freedom, government freedom, investment freedom, financial freedom, property rights, freedom from corruption, and labor freedom.

heritage.org/index/Default.aspx

### Here are the Top Ten Free Markets of 2010:

- Hong Kong
- Singapore
- Australia
- New Zealand
- Ireland
- Switzerland
- Canada
- United States
- Denmark
- Chili

This list has changed since 2010. Here is the list for 2015.

- Hong Kong
- Singapore
- New Zealand
- Australia
- Switzerland
- Canada
- Chili
- Estonia

- Ireland
- Mauritius

Do you notice the changes? The United States is no longer in the top ten nations. I suppose it has to do with the many changes that have been made in our nation to restrict economic freedom and dictate our economic choices.

# Socialism

A Socialist System, or Command System, is based on government control. The government decides who will make what, how much will be made, and how much it will cost.

Socialism says, "The government knows best."

In a Socialist System, the government will take over an entire industry (this is called nationalizing companies or nationalizing industries). In May 2009, Venezuela nationalized a gas compression plant and five steel and iron briquette companies. The government simply took over the companies and the owners no longer own the companies. Venezuela has been nationalizing companies since Chavez took office. In June 2010, the Venezuelan government issued a statement that they would nationalize an American company, Helmerich & Payne, who had been working in Venezuela for 52 years. This company expects to get paid by the Venezuelan government for the work it has been doing for the government. There is a $100 million dollar tab that Helmerich & Payne want paid and Venezuela doesn't want to pay it. Well, that's one way to get rid of a tab you don't want to pay! The Bible calls this stealing, by the way.

Or the government might operate certain parts of the industry. Or, the government will provide their own services alongside other businesses in an industry. In 2010, the United States Congress passed a bill providing government health insurance alongside private insurance plans. The government is not really in competition with these private companies because the government is never concerned about making a profit. In fact, government industries often lose money each year, sucking up billions of taxes paid by hard-working citizens.

Welfare programs are always provided by the government in a Socialist Market. Though the Bible commands families and the church to take care of one another, a socialist government will care for her people from cradle to grave through welfare programs such as Food Stamps, Social Security, Medicare, Medicaid, HUD programs (housing), Head Start (education of toddlers), Work Study (jobs), Federal Grants for Research or Education, School Loans, and more!

If someone doesn't feel like working, it's okay in a socialist country because they can always let the government take care of them. Of course, these programs cost lots of money which is provided by people who do choose to work. The high taxes paid by the working class are very harmful to the economy.

Karl Marx, who wrote the Communist Manifesto, makes it clear in his book that Socialism can only work if you get rid of God and religion, which he defines as the opiate of the people. God and socialism cannot co-exist because the Bible tells us to look to Christ to meet our needs, while socialism tells us to look to the government. "And my God will supply all your needs according to His riches in Glory in Christ Jesus" (Philippians 4:19 NASB). The Bible tells us that if a man doesn't work hard, he shouldn't eat, while socialism tells us that everyone should be provided for, whether they choose to work or not. "For even when we were with you, we gave you this rule: 'If a man will not work, he shall not eat.' We hear that some among you are idle. They are not busy; they are busybodies. Such people we command and urge in the Lord Jesus Christ to settle down and earn the bread they eat. And as for you, brothers, never tire of doing what is right" (II Thessalonians 3:10-13 NIV©1979)

## Mixed Economy

A Mixed System is a combination of the Capitalist System and the Socialist System.

Mixed Systems say, "We aren't really sure what to do, so we will try to combine two completely different philosophies that are the antithesis of each other and see if it works."

John Maynard Keynes (1883-1946) believed that Capitalism would fail unless government got involved. We often use the term Keynesianism to describe government involvement in Capitalism. That doesn't mean that John would agree with what we are describing or that it is something that he advocated. Sometimes communist nations mix in a little free-market economics to their policies to try to make a little money.

A Mixed System relies on plenty of government assistance to stimulate and slow down the economy. The government encourages its citizens to buy certain things and businesses to make certain things or provide certain services. The idea is that the government really knows best and should help see that everything stays stable and everyone is taken care of.

In a Mixed System, people can have their own businesses, but they are heavily regulated and taxed. Incentives are given to promote specific financial behaviors (such as being able to write off interest payments on your tax return if you take out a loan to buy a house—this encourages people to borrow money to buy a house!)

Another thing that governments do in a mixed economy is to provide government subsidies. Farm subsidies are supposed to help the "poor little family farm," but in truth they go to the big farm corporations.

The government subsidizes Amtrak because the passenger fares do not cover the cost of running the railroad company. Is it helpful to bail out a company? The goal of a company is to make a profit. There are other ways to make money that Amtrak could do, rather than receiving government help. They could sell advertizing located in the train and along the tracks. As long as the government fills the gap between cost and income, Amtrak will not be motivated to make a profit. Sometimes the government keeps a company afloat that needs to fold. Often in a financial crisis, a business will shake off "dry rot." It gets rid of things that are costing money, but not helping to produce a profit. Some companies will die if they can't compete in the market, but the owners often will start other companies that can compete. In the long run, companies that cannot compete in the market are better off folding.

## Biblical Principle of Freedom!

The Bible gives us freedom of choice with consequences that follow that choice. We can obey God with certain consequences or disobey God with certain consequences.

Freedom means that we can choose how we will live, what we will do for a living, what we will buy, or where we will live. You can spend your money as you see fit, realizing that there are consequences for the choices you make. I can spend all my money on food if I want to and live in a shack. I can put my children in private school or homeschool them. We are free!

What is the difference between Biblical economics and capitalism is moral restraint. Capitalism will fail without godly values. We will talk about Biblical capitalism in this course.

ECONOMICS, FINANCES, & BUSINESS COURSE

# Economic Systems Worksheet

You are going on a two week vacation. Which island would you like to visit and why?

What economic system is Command Island?

What are the things that clue you in to the economic system of Command Island?

What economic system is Combo Island?

What are the things that clue you in to the economic system of Combo Island?

What economic system is Freedom Island?

What are the things that clue you in to the economic system of Freedom Island?

What is the difference between Capitalism and Biblical Economics?

Why is the Mixed System such a failure?

# Supply and Demand

Biblical capitalism is based on the law of supply and demand. If everyone in your hometown woke up tomorrow and wanted to eat coffee-flavored grits for breakfast, several business people would get busy and meet that need. Within a short amount of time, you would have enough coffee-flavored grits to meet the need/wants of the consumers in your home town.

**Supply**, availability of a product or service, and **demand**, desire of consumers for the product or service, interact with one another to set the price. If the supply is low and the demand is high, the price will go up. If the supply is high and the demand is low, the price will go down. Of course, it is more complicated than that, but that is the basic idea of the law of supply and demand. Now, let's dig a little deeper.

What if the stores charged $15.00 for a small package of coffee-flavored grits? Well, some people would buy the grits, but many people would decide that it was just too expensive. The stores would lower the price of the grits so that more people would buy it. But, the stores can't lower their prices too much, or they won't make enough money to cover the cost of the coffee-flavored grits and they will go out of business.

The equilibrium price, or market clearing price, is the price that satisfies the buyer and the seller. The buyer feels happy with the price he is paying to buy his coffee-flavored grits and the seller feels the he is selling enough coffee-flavored grits at a high enough price to be making a satisfying profit. The equilibrium quantity is the amount of coffee-flavored grits that will be sold at the equilibrium price.

Supply and demand is tied closely to Opportunity Cost. Opportunity cost is what you pay or give up to do, or buy, something. You can't watch television and write a paper at the same time. If you are going to watch television, you will give up the opportunity to write your paper. The opportunity cost of watching television is writing your paper. You can't buy both a $100,000.00 home and a $110,000.00 vacation home if you only have $110,000.00. Buying one will cost you the opportunity of purchasing the other one.

People use opportunity cost (often unconsciously) to determine how much they are willing to pay, or sell, the product or service. Therefore, opportunity cost is used in creating the equilibrium price.

Graphs are an important tool that economists use to illustrate supply and demand. The demand curve shows how much people will buy at each price while the supply curve shows how much suppliers will supply at each price.

Let's make some graphs of our own.

Let's pretend that buyers will buy 200 pounds of coffee-flavored grits at $0.50/pound, but if the price goes up to $0.90/pound, they will only buy 120 pounds of coffee-flavored grits. If the price is raised again to $1.10/pound, consumers will only buy 75 pounds of coffee-flavored grits and if it goes all the way up to $1.50/pound, consumers will only buy 40 pounds of coffee-flavored grits. The higher the price, the less is purchased; or the higher the price, the lower the demand. I have filled in this graph with the numbers we have just talked about.

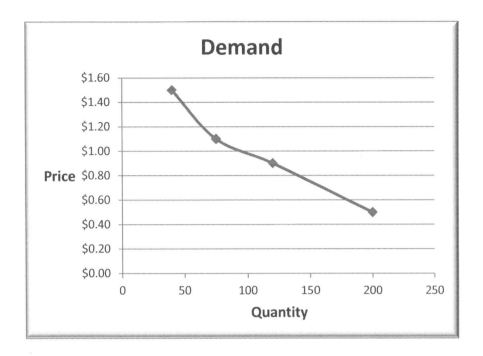

Now, let's take a look at the seller's perspective. If the sellers can get $1.50/pound for the coffee-flavored grits, then all the stores will carry the grits. They will produce and sell all 200 pounds. If the price drops to $1.10/pound, then some stores will quit selling the grits and will only produce 150 pounds of coffee-flavored grits to sell. If the price drops to $0.90, the sellers will not be as motivated, so production will drop off to 90 pounds of coffee-flavored grits. When the price drops to $0.50/pound, most of the producers/sellers will go into another business and the ones who are left will produce only 30 pounds of coffee-flavored grits. I have filled in this graph with the information I just gave you.

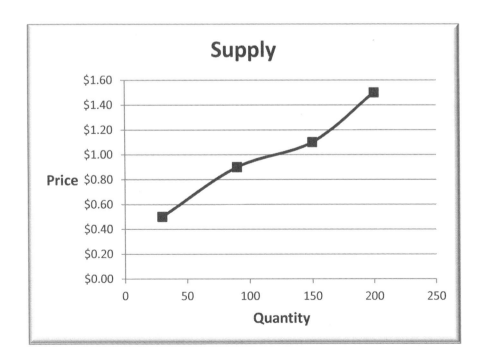

When economists want to show the price at equilibrium, they combine the two graphs. These two graphs are just for coffee-flavored grits. When all the products in the economy are included in the graph, it is called Aggregate Demand and Aggregate Supply. Aggregate Demand and Aggregate Supply include everything that is bought and sold in an economy, from rakes, shovels, cars, houses, and jewelry to guitar lessons and haircuts. Aggregate Supply and Aggregate Demand are similar to normal supply and demand but on a bigger scale. The equilibrium price of Aggregate Demand and Aggregate Supply is the Price Level. The equilibrium quantity is the same as the Gross Domestic Product (GDP) or Gross National Product (GNP).

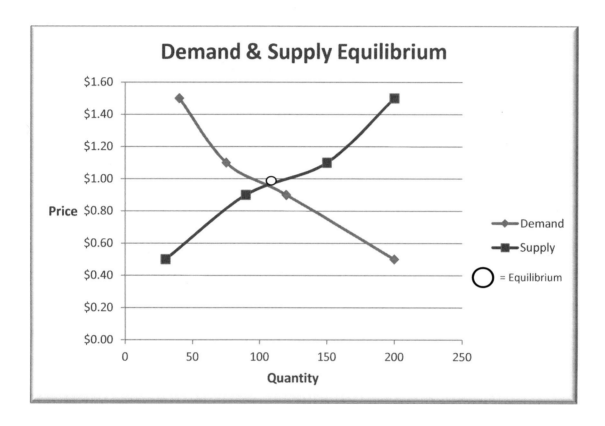

# Price Controls

Sometimes the government, with the idea of helping its citizens, will use price controls. Price floors and price ceilings are price controls. Let me explain.

In Lake Mary, FL, where I live, what if some people could not afford to buy coffee-flavored grits and they were really sad. The newspaper did an article on it to arouse public sympathy. So the state of Florida decided to help out with a price ceiling, setting a maximum price that stores could charge for coffee-flavored grits.

There are three problems with price ceilings.

Shortages. The price ceiling will make the production of coffee-flavored grits not worth the time and effort for some of the sellers because they cannot make as much of a profit. Soon, there will be a shortage of coffee-flavored grits.

Black Market. Some sellers will sell coffee-flavored grits at illegal prices to people who can afford it—a black market. Black markets are very prevalent in communist countries.

Quality Reduction. Some sellers will simply reduce the quality of their coffee-flavored grits so that they can still make a profit.

In all these situations, the consumers end up losing out!

One form of price ceilings that I have seen is rent control. This sounds so sweet of the government to step in and help poor people have affordable housing, but it back-fires. The government tells apartment owners that they cannot charge more than a certain amount of money for rent. If the owners can't afford to cover expenses with the cheaper rent, they will use the apartment for something else. Then, there is a housing shortage. Cities with rent control often have housing shortages.

Sometimes, the government wants to help an industry and will establish a price floor. The price floor is the lowest price a seller can sell a product. If this price floor is above the equilibrium price, then people will not buy the product. Soon, there is a surplus.

Price controls don't work because of the laws of supply and demand. If people do not feel that their reward is worth the Opportunity Cost, they will not do something. It is not worth the effort. If a seller cannot charge the price he feels will be worth the effort he is putting in, he will not produce the same quality product—it will not be worth it to him. If consumers don't feel the product is worth the price, they won't purchase it. Many times, a consumer will be willing to purchase a superior product on the black market.

Socialist/communist nations and countries with mixed economies use price controls all the time. Yes, you are right—price controls don't work for them, but they keep doing it. I don't know why either!

Let's make it practical. Pretend that you mow lawns. There is a price control in your city that will only allow you to charge $10.00 a lawn. There are many different size lawns in your neighborhood from very small to five acre lawns. You will probably find that it is only worth your effort to mow the smaller lawns. You will refuse to mow the bigger lawns. There will be a shortage of lawn guys who will mow big lawns.

Now, consider the reverse. Now, the city wants to help you lawn guys. There is a price floor. Consumers cannot pay less than $50.00 for their lawn to be mowed. What will your customers do? I bet they will let their lawns grow as long as possible before they have you cut them. You might make more money, but you will be putting in lots more time to cut and more wear and tear on your mower. Some people would just decide to mow their own lawns.

## God's Plan

Supply and demand works because of human nature. People will act in a reasonable way to do what is best for themselves and their family (rationality assumption). Rationality assumption works until people become selfish and greedy. (We will talk about this in a few minutes!)

Supply and demands works within a framework of individual freedom. This freedom is balanced with submitting to authority. The Bible gives authority to families, churches, and government.

God has authority over individuals, families, churches, and governments

Parents have God-given authority over their children

The Church has God-given authority and responsibility to care for its members

Government has God-given authority to reward good and punish evil-doers

Governments often overstep their bounds of God-given authority to care for their citizen's welfare. We trade individual freedom for Government welfare programs, a very poor trade.

Supply and Demand works because of the Scriptural principle of individuality. Each person God makes has unique talents, strengths, ambitions, and goals. There is not a cookie-cutter job, home, school, meal plan, health plan, or career track that works for everyone. God made us to be free to pursue our calling in Him!

## The Problem with Capitalism & Government Solutions

In the world's system, solutions to problems are always based on government. In pure capitalism, based on freedom for industries, government ultimately gets involved because of the sin nature of man.

Capitalism can lead to greed and oppression of the poor. In the climb to the top, people will often step on others with disregard. Sometimes business owners do not pay workers what they are worth. Monopolies can make it hard for the small business owner to compete. Conversely, when a communist nation turns to capitalism, its citizens are not used to working hard to provide for themselves.

Monopolies are businesses that can control prices in their industries without fear of competition. It happens when there is only one supplier in an industry or it is the biggest business by far. Microsoft is a good example of this. A monopoly will often buy out a smaller competitor to stay in control. Governments try to control or prevent monopolies with regulations.

So, governments step in with laws to regulate human nature and businesses. Unfortunately, these laws often hinder growth and harm businesses.

Regulations are laws to keep businesses responsible and honest. They are usually designed to protect the consumer. We have millions of regulations in the United States of America including minimum wage, nutrition labels, warning labels, tariffs, affirmative action, safety testing, and so much more. In fact, regulations are so numerous that the average business owner does not even know all the regulations that apply to him.

When you have as many regulations as we have in America, business owners are frustrated, workers are frustrated, consumers are frustrated, and the economy is sluggish.

Many times, in order to combat the "evils of capitalism," the government turns to socialism. By taking over industries (nationalization), the government thinks it can provide for everyone from the very poor to the very rich. That is a funny joke! See, there is a big difference between a business and the government.

A business exists to MAKE A PROFIT! Out of this profit, jobs are created, capital is produced, and wealth is created. A by-product of a successful business is jobs and the creation of goods and services that people need. The incentive to MAKE A PROFIT causes business owners and managers to make wise decisions, cut off excess pork, work lean and mean, and get the most for the money they invest.

The government exists to GET RE-ELECTED and keep their POWER. They don't care if they make a profit or lose money. The government, without having the same goal as a business, is not in a position to compete with businesses in the private sector. Government programs and industries are bloated, inefficient, and full of foolish expenses and practices. Bureaucracies are the foundation of government. A bureaucracy is the large group of people who perform the duties of an agency or government. This is often an overlap of job description and confusing chains of command.

Another difference between private business and government is that government employees' jobs and paychecks are guaranteed. It is hard, if not impossible, to fire a government employee. Workers in the private sector have to work hard to keep their jobs. More effort, harder work → better product, better services.

Competition brings prices down. When businesses compete against each other, they strive to produce the best product at the cheapest price so that the consumer will choose their product. Government industries have no competition.

Talk to people who have worked for the private sector and the government. Ask them to tell you about working in each place.

## Fiscal and Monetary Policy in a Mixed Economy

Many governments try to have their cake and eat it too. We call this the Mixed System of economics. A little bit of socialism (more government POWER) mixed with a little bit of capitalism (more MONEY!). The idea of mixing the two is to provide choice and quality of products and services for the citizens, while using government intervention to keep the economy growing at an even pace, not too fast and not too slow.

Fiscal and Monetary Policy is the action taken by the government in an attempt to manipulate the economy and the consumers for their own good. This usually involves debt and inflation, both scorned by Scripture.

The GNP (Gross National Product), or GDP (Gross Domestic Product), is made up of government spending, consumer spending, investment, and exports.

Fiscal Policy is spending that the government does in order to "help" the economy and boost or lesson the GNP, or GDP. An Expansionary Policy increases the money spent in government programs such as welfare, unemployment, insurance benefits, and pork barrel programs. When the economy is not doing well, the government will borrow money to spend money on welfare and pork barrel spending programs. When the economy turns around and people are making more money, thus paying more taxes, the idea is that people will pay the debt back. (Of course, the Bible calls debt foolishness!) Contractionary Policy is decreasing government spending.

Monetary Policy tampers with the money supply, or cash, in the economy. Expansionary Policy increases the money supply to increase the GNP, or GDP (more money floating around means more money being spent by consumers!). Contractionary Policy decreases the money supply, or cash, in the economy.

Pork Barrel Spending is wasteful government spending voted for by politicians to please their constituents, or lobbyists. Fixing roads that don't need to be fixed, building an airport where one is not needed, and gold plated toilet seats in the pentagon are all examples of pork barrel spending.

The government uses economic indicators to determine how the economy is doing. Economic Indicators are statistics that economists look at to determine how the economy is doing. The government looks at certain economic indicators to determine how to "guide" the economy including unemployment rates, new housing construction, manufacturing and trade inventories and sales, rental vacancy rate, homeownership rate, and U.S. international trade balance. You can look these figures up on government websites. They are a matter of public record compiled by the U.S. Department of Commerce's U.S. Census Bureau and released each month.

Economists also look at the GDP (Gross Domestic Product), Money Supply (the federal bank is always inflating the money supply—it's just a matter of how much), and the S&P 500 Stock Index.

Lagging indicators show what has already happened in the economy. Lagging indicators included GDP, income, wages, unemployment rate, inflation rate, interest rates, and balance of trade. If people are making money and spending it, the economy has been humming along. If sales are down, it shows that the economy is in a slump. Unemployment rates are a lagging indicator because if a company has been doing well, they will have to let people go. Unemployment follows a downward trend in the economy. If someone has been sick, they might lose weight, still feel tired, or have gotten behind in their school work. Lagging Indicators look at the results of how the economy has been doing.

Coincident indicators show the current economic shape. Personal income, retail sales, number of employees on company payrolls, and industrial production happen right as changes in the economy are taking place. If someone is sick, they will have a temperature while they are sick. Coincident indicators "take the temperature" of the economy.

Leading indicators are interpreted in an attempt to figure out what the economy will do next. Leading indicators including the stock market's performance, manufacturing activity, inventory levels, retail sales, building permits, and number of new business start-ups. If business are starting up, making thinks, and accumulating inventory, then it often indicates the economy will grow. If businesses are slowing down production, it might indicate the economy will slow down. When someone has been sick and not eating or getting out of bed, hunger or a desire to walk to the family room might indicate that they are getting better. Leading indicators give economists clues to the future health of the economy.

Please realize that there is no guarantee with Leading Indicators. They can steer economists wrong. No one can really predict what the economy will do because it is about how people will buy, build, and borrow.

Here are the problems with government fiscal and monetary policy.

The government needs money to carry out its schemes. It gets money from working people or people with assets (land, homes, etc.).

Once it takes away money from people (through taxes, licenses, etc,), these people have less money and less freedom.

Because we cannot predict the future (James 4:13-16), these policies are awkward at best and dangerous at worst.

The government is notoriously inefficient. Once it has our money, the government spends it in shameful, wasteful ways through bloated and inefficient programs.

## The Problem with Communism

Communism seeks to create the perfect, utopian one-world government/nation. The government socializes everything (education, business, press, family). The myth is that if the government takes over, it can eliminate evil and do good. This does not take into account the sin nature of mankind, who is prone to evil including greed, hunger for power, selfish ambition, and selfishness. Government is made up of people who are prone to evil.

Ronald Reagan said, "The only place socialism will work is Heaven and we won't need it there."

Religion is considered competition to the government, so it is discouraged or outlawed. Government will provide, protect, and own you, rather than the God who created you. The idea behind communism is that people, freed from the struggle to provide for their material needs, will emerge as good, kind, and wise causing evil to disappear.

Of course, we know that this is not true. Apart from Christ, we can do nothing.

Communism has failed miserably to achieve her aims and, instead, has produced a wealth of pain and suffering. The leaders in communist countries become power-hungry, ruthless dictators. Power corrupts and absolute power corrupts absolutely.

When you give up your freedom for welfare programs, you lose much more than you gain!

The Solution is Biblical Economics!

What is a Biblical economic system? God's plan includes the efficiency and freedom of the capitalist/free market system with moral restraints. Economic prosperity combined with help to those who cannot provide for themselves. The Bible prevents employers from mistreating their employees, while allowing freedom for workers and owners to work out their own relationships. Personal freedom to work, live, choose, and fail is enjoyed as each person, with God's help, runs the race marked out for him/her.

## Private Property

"Then Peter said, "Ananias, how is it that Satan has so filled your heart that you have lied to the Holy Spirit and have kept for yourself some of the money you received for the land? Didn't it belong to you before it was sold? And after it was sold, wasn't the money at your disposal? What made you think of doing such a thing? You have not lied to men but to God" (Acts 5:3-4 NIV ©1979).

"Every man will sit under his own vine and under his own fig tree, and no one will make them afraid, for the LORD Almighty has spoken" (Micah 4:4 NIV ©1979).

"Build houses and settle down; plant gardens and eat what they produce. Marry and have sons and daughters; find wives for your sons and give your daughters in marriage, so that they too may have sons and daughters. Increase in number there; do not decrease. Also, seek the peace and prosperity of the city to which I have carried you into exile. Pray to the LORD for it, because if it prospers, you too will prosper" (Jeremiah 29:5-7 NIV ©1979).

"He who oppresses the poor to increase his wealth and he who gives gifts to the rich—both come to poverty" (Proverbs 22:16 NIV ©1979).

## Treatment of Employees

"So in everything, do to others what you would have them do to you, for this sums up the Law and the Prophets" (Matthew 7:12 NIV ©1979).

"Do not take along any gold or silver or copper in your belts; take no bag for the journey, or extra tunic, or sandals or a staff; for the worker is worth his keep" (Matthew 10:10 NIV ©1979).

"Woe to him who builds his palace by unrighteousness, his upper rooms by injustice, making his countrymen work for nothing, not paying them for their labor" (Jeremiah 22:13 NIV ©1979).

"Masters (bosses, business owners), provide your slaves (employees, independent contractors) with what is right and fair, because you know that you also have a Master in heaven" (Colossians 4:1 NIV ©1979).

"Slaves, obey your earthly masters with respect and fear, and with sincerity of heart, just as you would obey Christ. Obey them not only to win their favor when their eye is on you, but like slaves of Christ, doing the will of God from your heart. Serve wholeheartedly, as if you were serving the Lord, not men, because you know that the Lord will reward everyone for whatever good he does, whether he is slave or free. And masters, treat your slaves in the same way. Do not threaten them, since you know that he who is both their Master and yours is in heaven, and there is no favoritism with him" (Ephesians 6:5-8 NIV ©1979).

## Paying Employees

"Do not defraud your neighbor or rob him. Do not hold back the wages of a hired man overnight" (Leviticus 19:13 NIV ©1979).

"Now listen, you rich people, weep and wail because of the misery that is coming upon you. Your wealth has rotted, and moths have eaten your clothes. Your gold and silver are corroded. Their corrosion will testify against you and eat your flesh like fire. You have hoarded wealth in the last days. Look! The wages you failed to pay the workmen who mowed your fields are crying out against you. The cries of the harvesters have reached the ears of the Lord Almighty. You have lived on earth in luxury and self-indulgence. You have fattened yourselves in the day of slaughter. You have condemned and murdered innocent men, who were not opposing you" (James 5:1-6 NIV ©1979).

"The elders who direct the affairs of the church well are worthy of double honor, especially those whose work is preaching and teaching." For the Scripture says, "Do not muzzle the ox while it is treading out the grain," and "The worker deserves his wages" (I Timothy 5:17-18 NIV ©1979).

## Personal Freedom to Follow God's Will

"For we are God's workmanship, created in Christ Jesus to do good works, which God prepared in advance for us to do" (Ephesians 2:10 NIV ©1979).

"Again, it will be like a man going on a journey, who called his servants and entrusted his property to them. To one he gave five talents of money, to another two talents, and to another one talent, each according to his ability. Then he went on his journey. The man who had received the five talents went at once and put his money to work and gained five more. So also, the one with the two talents gained two more" (Matthew 25:14-17 NIV ©1979).

"For by the grace given me I say to every one of you: Do not think of yourself more highly than you ought, but rather think of yourself with sober judgment, in accordance with the measure of faith God has given you. Just as each of us has one body with many members, and these members do not all have the same function, so in Christ we who are many form one body, and each member belongs to all the others. We have different gifts, according to the grace given us" (Romans 12:3-6 NIV ©1979).

## Government's Role

"Submit yourselves for the Lord's sake to every authority instituted among men: whether to the king, as the supreme authority, or to governors, who are sent by him to punish those who do wrong and to commend those who do right. For it is God's will that by doing good you should silence the ignorant talk of foolish men. Live as free men, but do not use your freedom as a cover-up for evil; live as servants of God. Show proper respect to everyone: Love the brotherhood of believers, fear God, honor the king" (I Peter 2:13-17 NIV ©1979).

ECONOMICS, FINANCES, & BUSINESS COURSE

# Supply & Demand Worksheet

Explain the law of supply and demand.

What is another name for the equilibrium price?

What is the equilibrium price?

Give an example in your own life of opportunity cost?

How do price controls cause shortages?

How do price controls fuel the black market?

How do price controls decrease quality of products?

What four things make up the GNP (Gross National Product), or GDP (Gross Domestic Product)?

Define the following Economic indicators and give an example of each one:

Lagging Indicators (definition):

Lagging Indicators (example):

Coincident Indicators (definition):

Coincident Indicators (example):

Leading Indicators (definition):

Leading Indicators (example):

What are the four problems with government fiscal and monetary policy?

Let's talk about Government Fiscal Policy. Place the following government behaviors in the proper column in the table below: welfare, unemployment benefits, pork barrel spending programs, borrowing money, increasing the money supply (inflation), cutting government programs, decreasing government spending, fixing roads that don't need to be fixed, or decreasing money supply. Everything is either Expansionary Policy or Contractionary Policy.

| Expansionary Policy | Contractionary Policy |
|---|---|
|  |  |

Write out one Scripture for every Biblical Economic principle we talked about.

Private Property

Treatment of Employees

Paying Employees

Government's Role.

# Fill in this Lake Lulu Ugandan Cashews Supply & Demand Equilibrium Chart.

There are several nut and candy stores in the town of Lake Lulu. These store owners hear about delicious Ugandan cashews that are three times bigger than normal cashews and delicious. Marketing research is done and here are the results.

Let's pretend that buyers will buy 900 pounds of Ugandan cashews at $7.00/pound, but if the price goes up to $8.00/pound, they will only buy 700 pounds of Ugandan cashews. If the price is raised again to $9.50/pound, consumers will only buy 500 pounds of Ugandan cashews and if it goes all the way up to $10.50/pound, consumers will only buy 100 pounds of Ugandan cashews. Fill in the graph below with these numbers using a blue line for demand.

Here is seller's perspective. If the sellers can get $10.50/pound for Ugandan cashews, then all the stores will carry the cashews. They will import and sell 900 pounds of cashews. If the price drops to $9.50/pound, then some stores will quit selling the cashews and will only import 700 pounds of Ugandan cashews to sell. If the price drops to $8.00, the sellers will not be as motivated, so importation will drop off to 500 pounds of Ugandan cashews. When the price drops to $7.00/pound, most of the importers/sellers will go into another business and the ones who are left will import only 100 pounds of Ugandan cashews. Chart the supply with a red colored pencil.

Where do the two lines meet? That is the Lake Lulu Ugandan Cashews Supply/Demand Equilibrium.

# Economics in One Lesson Worksheet

## Chapter Six

Why is "government encouragement" to business as harmful as government hostility?

What are the two types of government-backed loans to farmers?

What is the danger of high-risk loans to the economy?

Is it right for taxpayers to be forced to pay for loans to farmers and other business owners? Why or why not?

## Chapter Seven

Give some examples of machines increasing the need for workers in various industries.

How do machines affect the number of workers in the work force?

What should someone do whose job is now done by a machine?

## Chapter Eight

Why are some people afraid of efficiency?

Why do "Spread-the-Work Schemes" fail in the end?

ECONOMICS, FINANCES, & BUSINESS COURSE

# *Whatever Happened to Penny Candy?* Review

A short review on Whatever Happened to Penny Candy? by Richard J Maybury!

How has what we call money changed over the years?

What is T.A.N.S.T.A.A.F.L.?

What is counterfeiting?

What is Gresham's Law?

What is inflation?

What is the difference between a dollar, money, and legal tender?

What is the wage and price spiral—how does it affect the economy in the long run?

What is runaway inflation? How does it correct itself?

Explain velocity and the demand for money?

What are the three stages of velocity in runaway inflation?

What's so bad about federal debt?

What happens when the government adjusts the economy?

What is a free market system?

What is a government controlled system?

Which is the USA?

What warnings does history hold for our nation?

ECONOMICS, FINANCES, & BUSINESS COURSE

# Glossary Worksheet

Define the following words using *Whatever Happened to Penny Candy?* (There is a glossary in the book—just copy the definitions!)

Bank Note:

Base Metal:

Black Market:

Business:

Business Cycle:

Circulation:

Clad Coin:

Clipping Coins:

Coin:

Counterfeit:

Currency:

Debasing:

Deflation:

Denarius:

Depression:

Double-Diget Inflation:

Economics:

Economist:

Exchange:

Federal Reserve Note:

Fiat Money:

Fineness:

Gresham's Law:

Hallmark:

Hard Money:

Inflation:

Law of Economics:

Legal Tender Law:

# ECONOMICS, FINANCES, & BUSINESS COURSE

Legal Tender Money:

Mint:

Money:

Precious Metal:

Price:

Public Works:

Recession:

Reeding:

Revolution:

Runaway Inflation:

Soft Money:

Stagflation:

Subsidy:

TANSTAAFL:

Tax:

Token:

Velocity:

Wage:

Welfare:

Wealth:

Withdrawls:

# September Week Four Class

☐ Discuss "Economic Systems" Worksheet

☐ Discuss "Supply & Demand" Worksheet

☐ Discuss "*Economics in One Lesson* chapters 6-8 Worksheet" answers

☐ Discuss *Whatever Happened to Penny Candy* Review

☐ Answer any questions about Penny Candy Glossary

Notes from Class

# September Week Four Home

☐  Read Economics in One Lesson chapters 9-11

☐  Fill Out "*Economics in One Lesson* chapters 9-11 Worksheet"

☐  Write an Essay: "Why I Think Counterfeiting is Illegal"

☐  Do "Monthly Consumer Price Index Activity"

☐  Optional: Read Biblical Economics in Comics

# Economics in One Lesson Worksheet

## Chapter Nine

How would a balanced budget, or a nation who pays her way without debt, absorb soldiers into the work force after a war?

Why do people want to hold on to un-necessary government workers and how does this harm the economy?

## Chapter Ten

What is the difference between full production and full employment?

Which is more important: full production and full employment? Why?

## Chapter Eleven

Why does the author say that present day tariff and trade policies are worse than they were in the seventeenth and eighteenth century?

How is free trade an aspect of the specialization of labor?

What would the short-term effects be of getting rid of protective tariffs?

What would the long-terms effects be of getting rid of protective tariffs?

How do tariffs benefit the producer at the expense of the consumer?

What are your thoughts on free trade (no tariffs)?

ECONOMICS, FINANCES, & BUSINESS COURSE

# Economic Essay: "Why I think Counterfeiting is Illegal"

Here is my Outline

**Introduction**

**First Point =**

**Second Point =**

**Third Point =**

**Fourth Point =** (you may not have a 4th point!)

**Conclusion**

# Monthly Consumer Price Index Project

This is an ongoing project for the duration of this class. You will have to go shopping once a month and record prices of each item. Once you choose an item, write it in on your monthly Consumer Price Index Project page. You will need to record the make, model, brand, and size—price the EXACT same item each month. You can go "shopping online." Go to the same store each month. This is a fun project and will provide interesting results at the end of the year.

## Durable Items

(These items are things that you purchase that have life spans of more than 1 year. Examples would be televisions, computers, refrigerators, radios, computers, calculators, washing machines, i-pods, shoes, clothing, chairs, beds, curtains, tables, blenders)

**Durable Item Shopping Bag for Month of** _____

| Durable Item | Store | Brand | Weight or Size | Color | Type/Model | Price |
|---|---|---|---|---|---|---|
| SLR Camera w Lens | Sam's | Nikon | 10 MP 3" LCK 3X Zoom SD/SDHC | | D3000 #23341 | $445.00 |
| | | | | | | |
| | | | | | | |
| | | | | | | |
| | | | | | | |
| | | | | | | |
| | | | | | | |
| | | | | | | |
| | | | | | | |
| | | | | | | |
| | | | | | | |

**Shopping Bag Cost for Durable Item =**

**Non-Durable Items for Month of** _____

# ECONOMICS, FINANCES, & BUSINESS COURSE

(These items are things that you purchase that have life spans of less than 1 year. Examples would be toothpaste, aluminum foil, food, drinks, make-up, gasoline, oil, nail polish, after shave, napkins, fast food, mouthwash, deodorant, candy, vitamins, medicine, contact solution)

**Non-Durable Item Shopping Bag**

| Durable Item | Store | Brand | Weight or Size | Color | Type/Model | Price |
|---|---|---|---|---|---|---|
| Wheat Thins | Target | Nabisco | 10 oz. | | Low-fat Salted | $2.00 |
| | | | | | | |
| | | | | | | |
| | | | | | | |
| | | | | | | |
| | | | | | | |
| | | | | | | |
| | | | | | | |
| | | | | | | |
| | | | | | | |
| | | | | | | |

**Shopping Bag Cost for Non-Durable Item =**

## Service Items for Month of _____

(These are services your family purchases. Examples of services would be haircuts, oil changes, pedicures, lawn mowing, massage, car wash, doctor visit, dental visit, X-ray at hospital, ER visit, gym membership, lawyer consult, accountant consult, taxes, tutoring, college tuition)

Service Items Shopping Bag

| Durable Item | Store | Brand/Kind | Length of Time/Amount | Purpose | Type/Model | Price |
|---|---|---|---|---|---|---|
| Massage | Shear Bliss | | 1 hour | Relaxation | Deep Tissue | $85.00 |
| | | | | | | |
| | | | | | | |
| | | | | | | |
| | | | | | | |
| | | | | | | |
| | | | | | | |
| | | | | | | |
| | | | | | | |
| | | | | | | |
| | | | | | | |

**Shopping Bag Cost for Service Items =**

ECONOMICS, FINANCES, & BUSINESS COURSE

# October

Wealth Redistribution or Investment

Wealth Worksheet

*Money Mystery* Review

Capital for Families & Business

Banks, Capital, Debt, & Savings Worksheet

Foreign Trade, Federal Reserve Bank, Money, Inflation

Economic Basics Open Book Test

Social Justice or Personal Responsibility

*Communist Manifesto* Review

Personalized Consumer Price Index Project

# October Week One Class

☐ Read Essays Aloud.

☐ Discuss "*Economics in One Lesson* chapters 9-11 Worksheet" answers

☐ Everybody share products & prices chosen for "Monthly Consumer Price Index Project"

☐ Answer any questions about Upcoming Assignments

**Notes from Class**

ECONOMICS, FINANCES, & BUSINESS COURSE

# October Week One Home

☐ Read "Wealth Distribution vs. Wealth Investment"

☐ Fill Out "Wealth Worksheet"

☐ Read *Economics in One Lesson* chapters 12-13

☐ Fill Out "Economics in One Lesson chapters 12-13 Worksheet"

☐ Read *Money Mystery* pages 1-45

# Wealth Redistribution vs. Wealth Investment

Johnny was in history class with 30 other students. He worked hard and finished all his homework. He could have studied a little more for the test, but he did manage to make a B. Carla was another story. She talked throughout the lectures and never turned in any homework. She made an F on the test, which didn't surprise Johnny at all.

"What did you get on the test?" Andy asked Johnny, interrupting his thoughts about his B.

"I got a B. I wish I would have studied a little more, but I got on facebook," he admitted, sheepishly. "How about you?"

"I got an A. But, man, I spent the entire weekend cracking the books. I even unplugged my computer. I like Facebook too!"

They both laughed. Johnny decided he would study more next time. There was still time to bring his grade up.

"I have an announcement." the teacher stood up, signaling that class was beginning. "How many of you are happy with your grades?"

Very few hands went up. Johnny shrugged and finally raised his hand too.

"I've decided to give you new grades," the teacher announced.

Those who had not raised their hands looked up expectantly. Would they get better grades?

"I just feel so bad for people who got bad grades that I decided to take all the test scores, add them up, and divide by 31. This will give us an average grade. Everyone will get the same grade.

If you were Johnny, how would you feel about this?

How do you think Andy feels about sharing his test score with the whole class when he gave up the computer for the weekend to study?

How will Carla like the teacher's new method of giving grades?

If the teacher keeps up this practice, how motivated will the smarter kids be to study?

There was a delightful practice in the early church. Folks who had extra money, homes, or property would sell it and give the money to the apostles. The apostles would distribute the money to the poor among them. In this way, every need was met and love, flowing freely, made the Gospel attractive.

The early Christians shared their wealth with their brothers and sisters in Christ. They were not forced to, but, rather, freely gave. Some did and some did not. When Ananias sold his land and held some back (while pretending to give it all!), he was struck dead because he lied to the Holy Spirit. The apostles said to him, "Wasn't this your land, and after you sold it, wasn't this your money to do whatever you wanted with it?" It was clearly his choice to give or not give. (Read the full story in Acts 5)

Today, we are going to talk about wealth, wealth redistribution, and wealth investment. There is a lot of controversy over this topic, so let's tackle it.

## What is Wealth?

First of all, what is wealth? Wealth, according to economists, is anything that has value: money, stocks, cars, houses, real estate, planes, art, clothing, education, and land. People that have more wealth are considered rich, while people that have less, or no, wealth are considered poor.

## Poverty

The Bible has a lot to say about taking care of the poor. God tells us to have compassion on the poor, to give to the poor. We are told that when we give to the poor, we are actually making a loan to God, and He will repay it. (Proverbs 19:17)

The world is filled with rich people and poor people. This is because we live in a fallen world. Jesus said, in Matthew 26:11 and Mark 14:7 that the poor will always be with us. In Heaven, there will be no poverty. Until Jesus comes back and there is a new Heaven and a new earth, we will have poor people in the world.

Sometimes, people are poor because they don't work. Sometimes, people are poor because of circumstances beyond their control. Physical conditions, mental illnesses, and unforeseen events can plunge people into poverty. We should never judge the poor. I have experienced years of poverty while my husband and I were both working very hard.

Poverty in many nations is the absence of wealth. But, in the United States, we have an income level that is designated the poverty level where income below that level is considered poverty. Here are the 2009 Poverty Guidelines for the 48 Continental States and Washington, D.C. Alaska and Hawaii have separate guidelines because the cost of living is higher there.

| How Many Persons in Your Family? | Poverty Guideline |
|---|---|
| 1 | $10,830.00 |
| 2 | $14,570.00 |
| 3 | $18,310.00 |
| 4 | $22,050.00 |
| 5 | $25,790.00 |
| 6 | $29,530.00 |
| 7 | $33,270.00 |
| 8 | $37,010.00 |
| More than 8 persons? | Add $3,740.000 for each additional person |

Here are the 2016 Poverty Guidelines for the 48 Continental States and Washington, D.C. Alaska and Hawaii have separate guidelines because the cost of living is higher there.

| How Many Persons in Family | Poverty Guideline |
|---|---|
| 1 | $11,880.00 |
| 2 | $16,020.00 |
| 3 | $20,160.00 |
| 4 | $24,300.00 |
| 5 | $28,440.00 |
| 6 | $32,580.00 |
| 7 | $36,730.00 |
| 8 | $40,890.00 |
| More than 8 persons? | Add $4,1600.00 for each additional person |

## How Wealth is Distributed

In America, many people who live in poverty have cell phones, drive cars, own computers, and eat fast food, while in other nations, poverty means not having food to eat. Keep this in mind when we are talking about poverty. Poverty means different things in different places. In our nation, poverty affects education, nutrition, health, career, and work ethic. Well meaning welfare programs have some families on a cycle of poverty that lasts generations.

Everyone agrees that we should help the poor, but how to do it is the question. Let's start with the first question: How should wealth be distributed?

Wealth can be distributed three ways.

- To each according to need
- To each the same
- To each according to productivity

In a family, we could distribute to each according to need. If Sally needs braces, money goes to get Sally braces. If Johnny needs pencils and paper for school, money is spent to get him pencils and paper. Mom needs a maternity shirt because she is pregnant, so money is spent to buy her a maternity shirt.

In a family, we could distribute to each the same. Sally gets braces, pencils, paper, and a maternity shirt. Johnny gets braces, pencils, paper, and a maternity shirt. Mom gets braces, pencils, paper, and a maternity shirt. It doesn't matter if they need things or not—everyone is treated the same.

It would be hard in a family to distribute each according to productivity because children are of all different ages and capable of different levels of productivity. Everyone should WORK HARD in a family because everyone has their needs met in a family. So let's look at families in a town.

In one town, if Sally's Daddy can fix cars faster than Beth's Daddy with the same quality of workmanship, Sally's Daddy will make more money. The value of a person's work and the quality of a person's work will determine how much money a person makes.

Distributing wealth to families according to their productivity causes productivity and quality to go up. If everyone gets the same no matter how hard they work, quality and productivity go down. Why do you best without reward? Why work hard for the same results?

## How the Government Redistributes Wealth

The government in the United States of America has taken upon itself the job of redistributing wealth. The government has to take wealth from some people to redistribute wealth to other people. How does the government do that?

- Through taxes (the government takes some or a lot)
- Through forcing workers to work for the government—whatever work is produced is owned by the government (the government takes it all)

## Taxes & Government Revenue

Taxes are the way government collects wealth so that it can pay for its services (programs), government workers' salaries, and wealth redistribution. Wealth collected through taxes is called revenue.

So who decides how much each person will pay in taxes? The government, of course.

There are three ways the government can decide how much people will pay.

- Proportional Tax, or Flat Tax
- Progressive Tax
- Regressive Tax

**Proportional Tax**, or **Flat Tax**, is a percentage that stays the same for all people, no matter how much or how little they make. Joe, who makes $22,000.00 a year, pays the same percentage of his income in taxes as Fred, who makes $70,000.00 a year. If the tax rate is 20%, Joe will pay $4,400.00 and Fred will pay $14,000.00 in taxes. Notice that Fred pays a lot more money than Joe because he makes more.

**Progressive Taxes** tax at a higher percentage as a person's income level goes up. Each level of the tax percentage is called a Marginal Tax Rate (MTR). The higher marginal tax rate applies only to the income in that bracket. Confused? Yes, it is confusing. Let me just show you a chart of Graduated Income Tax, rather than try to explain how it works.

| Progressive Tax System | MTR of 10% on income between $00.00-$10,000.00 | MTR of 20% on income between $10.00-$20,000.00 | MTR of 30% on income between $20.00-$30,000.00 | Total Taxes Paid |
|---|---|---|---|---|
| $10,000 Wage Earner | $1,000 Paid in Taxes | ///// | ///// | $1,000.00 Paid in Taxes |
| $20,000 Wage Earner | $1,000 Paid in Taxes | $2,000 Paid in Taxes | ///// | $3,000 Paid in Taxes |
| $30,000 Wage Earner | $1,000 Paid in Taxes | $2,000 Paid in Taxes | $3,000 Paid in Taxes | $6,00 Paid in Taxes |

# ECONOMICS, FINANCES, & BUSINESS COURSE

The United States had very few taxes in the beginning. The government did tax liquor, sugar, tobacco, bonds, and slaves. To pay for the War of 1812, the nation imposed a temporary sales tax on gold, silverware, jewelry, and watches. In 1817, this tax ended and the government supported itself with tariffs on imports.

In 1862, to pay for the Civil War, Congress voted for the nation's first income tax. The tax rate was 3%. In 1872, the income tax was declared unconstitutional by the Supreme Court. The government then got money from the taxes on liquor and tobacco.

In 1913, the 16th Amendment gave us income tax permanently. Here is a chart showing the very top Marginal Tax Rate—the highest rate anyone in the country had to pay.

| Tax Years | Top Marginal Tax Rate (MTR) | Taxable Income over… |
|---|---|---|
| 1913-1915 | 7% | $500,000.00 |
| 1916 | 15% | $2,000,000.00 |
| 1917 | 67% | $2,000,000.00 |
| 1918 | 77% | $1,000,000.00 |
| 1919-1921 | 73% | $1,000,000.00 |
| 1922 | 58% | $200,000.00 |
| 1923 | 43.5% | $21932-193500,000.00 |
| 1924 | 46% | $500,000.00 |
| 1925-1931 | 24-25% | $100,000.00 |
| 1932-1935 | 63% | $1,000,000.00 |
| 1936-1941 | 79-81% | $5,000,000.00 |
| 1942-1947 | 82-94% | $200,000.00 |
| 1948-1950 | 82-84% | $400,000.00 |
| 1951-1963 | 91-92% | $400,000.00 |
| 1964-1976 | 70-77% | $200,000.00 |
| 1977-1978 | 70% | $203,300.00 |
| 1979-1981 | 70% | $215,400.00 |
| 1982 | 50% | $85,600.00 |
| 1983 | 50% | $109,400.00 |
| 1984 | 50% | $100,000.00 |
| 1987 | 38.5% | $90,000.00 |
| 1988 | 28% | $29,750.00 |
| 1991 | 31% | $82,150.00 |
| 1993 | 39.6% | $89,150.00 |
| 1994 | 39.6% | $250,000.00 |
| 2003 | 35% | $311,950.00 |

Keep in mind that rich people can afford to pay lawyers and accountants who show them how to "HIDE" their income in tax shelters, and in other ways. Very rich people often don't end up paying these high rates. The people who usually pay a lot of taxes, without being able to afford to hide their money are the middle class.

Regressive Taxes are the exact opposite of Progressive Taxes. As someone's income goes up, the taxes go down. This is not a popular way to tax. Please fill in the chart for Regressive Taxes. The percentages will be reversed. Notice the difference in what everyone pays.

| Regressive Tax System | MTR of 30% on income between $00.00-$10,000.00 | MTR of 20% on income between $10.00-$20,000.00 | MTR of 10% on income between $20.00-$30,000.00 | Total Taxes Paid |
|---|---|---|---|---|
| $10,000 Wage Earner | Paid in Taxes | ///// | ///// | Paid in Taxes |
| $20,000 Wage Earner | Paid in Taxes | Paid in Taxes | ///// | Paid in Taxes |
| $30,000 Wage Earner | Paid in Taxes | Paid in Taxes | Taxes Paid | Paid in Taxes |

The government takes great delight in gathering taxes and coming up with new ways to tax its citizens. Here are some of the most common taxes the government collects.

**Sales Tax** is a tax imposed on finished products when they are sold. In Florida, we pay sales tax and county tax. Our sales tax in Seminole County (in 2010) is 7%, but in Volusia County it's only 6.5%. We pay sales tax on cars, clothing, school supplies, fast food, electronics, and tons of other things. If I buy a new dress for $25.00 at the Seminole Mall, I will have to pay $26.75, adding the tax in. If I go to the beach and stay in a hotel, I will pay sales tax on the price of the room and a resort tax as well.

**Income Tax** is a tax on the wages/income that a person receives for working at his job. We just finished talking about income tax. "Income" is a term that is used to include interest on savings accounts, tips, financial gifts, alimony, awards, bonuses, gains from sale of property, jury duty fees, pensions, prizes, scholarships, unemployment compensation, gambling winnings, hobby income, punitive damages from a lawsuit, reimbursement for moving expenses, debts forgiven, employee stock options, death benefits, stock dividends, gains from illegal activities, embezzled funds, estate income, trust income, royalties, and travel allowance.

**Business Tax**, like an income tax, this is a tax on the profit a business.

**Property Tax** is when the government taxes the value of land and the dwelling (house or other building) on that land. The government is, in essence, saying that the land belongs to the government, not the owner of the land, by taxing the land. Land that is undeveloped will often have an animal or two grazing on it. This is so that the owner can pay property tax on farm land, rather than commercial. Farm land is taxed at a lower rate than commercial land.

**Inheritance Tax**, or **Estate Tax**, is a tax on wealth that is passed from one person to his/her heirs when he/she dies. This is what England used to get land away from the rich in the early 20th Century. To pay the huge estate tax, the heirs would have to sell their land.

**Capital Gains Tax** is a tax on the increase in value of a person's wealth. For example, if I buy a house for $100,000.00 and I sell it five years later for $400,000.00, then I have a capital gain of $300,000.00 which I will have to pay taxes on.

# Tax Deductions and Exemptions

The government does give exemptions and deductions that adjust the amount of income that you have to pay taxes on.

You start out with your gross income and take deductions (business expenses, alimony payments, student loan interest) to get your Adjusted Gross Income.

Every tax payer in the United States gets an exemption for his/or herself and their dependants. You subtract an amount of money for each person in your household from your adjusted gross income to get your taxable income.

Tax credits are monies that are added back in/or subtracted from your tax liability. The Earned Income Tax Credit is for people who make lower income (in 2010 less than $38,000.00) [it is very complicated, based on how many children you have and other things]. These taxpayers are able to subtract a certain amount of money from the taxes they owe. If the number after subtracting is a negative number, the government will pay them. Many lower income families don't just not pay taxes, they get money back that they did not put in. Interesting way of doing business. Of course, the government is not a business. You can guarantee a business would do things differently. There are also credits that cannot be negative.

Are you confused yet? Maybe this will help.

$_____ Gross Income

$_____ -Deductions

[_____] =Adjusted Gross Income

$_____ -Itemized Deductions or Standardized Deductions

$_____ -Exemptions

[_____] =Taxable Income

%_____ x Tax Rate

[_____] =Gross Tax Liability

$_____ -Tax Credits and Prepayment

[_____] = Tax Due or Refund

Government gives certain deductions to encourage certain behaviors. For example, Student Loan interest and Mortgage Interest are both deductions you can take on your income taxes. This encourages people to borrow money to go to school and to borrow money to buy a home.

## Biblical Wealth Accumulation & Distribution versus Taxes

The Bible has a different method than taxes, taxes, taxes. God, in fact, "taxed" His people, but He called it a tithe. It supported the work at the temple and the workers of the temple. It was 10% for all people, no matter how rich or poor they were. There were no deductions or exemptions. Interesting how God always keeps everything simple.

10% to the Lord and 10% to the government would seem very reasonable to me personally. Of course, the government would have to do a lot of slashing, especially of pork barrel spending.

Is it okay for governments to tax people? Should we pay our taxes? Jesus answered this question when he was asked by His disciples if they should pay taxes to the ungodly Roman government.

"Then the Pharisees went and plotted together how they might trap Him in what He said. And they sent their disciples to Him, along with the Herodians, saying, 'Teacher, we know that you are truthful and teach the way of God in truth, and defer to no one; for You are not partial to any. Tell us then, what do You think? Is it lawful to give a poll-tax to Caesar, or not?' But Jesus perceived their malice, and said, 'Why are you testing Me, you hypocrites? Show me the coin used for the poll-tax.' And they brought Him a denarius. And He said to them, 'Whose likeness and inscription is this?' They said to Him, 'Caesar's.' Then He said to them, 'Then render to Caesar the things that are Caesar's; and to God the things that are God's.' And hearing this, they were amazed, and leaving Him, they went away" (Matthew 22:15-22 NASB).

The biggest problem with our tax system right now is that it is excessive. When people are asked to pay close to or more than half of what they earn, something is wrong. Borrowing, or going into debt, is encouraged by our tax system, while saving money for the future is discouraged by our tax system. This is the complete opposite of what Scripture teaches.

We should pay taxes, but use your political power (by voting, campaigning, lobbying) to decrease taxes. I vote against every tax increase on principle because the government is so wasteful with my tax money (of which it receives plenty!) that I don't want to supply them with any more money to waste.

Should the government be able to decide that it wants to do something or give money to a certain group of people and force citizens to pay for it by taxing them? I don't think so. Because our government is involved in so many activities that are out of its jurisdiction, or scope of authority, we have no real power to decide where our money is going. I hate the fact that my tax dollars help fund abortion.

The government likes to pretend that it is Robin Hood by stealing from the rich to give to the poor, but it is still stealing, breaking the 8th commandment.

Excessive taxes, especially progressive taxes punish success and hard work. If someone works hard and earns more money, he must pay a higher percentage of what he earns. This discourages people from working hard, especially if one can get hand-outs from the government for free.

If you think of workers as runners running a race and taxes as the weights they have to carry, our tax system forces runners to carry heavier and heavier weights the faster they run. If we want to see the economy thrive, we should set the runners up to run to win the race, without all the shackles that hold them back.

How are the poor to be taken care of? How are people's needs to be met? Does God have a plan?

Yes, God's plan is for men to work hard and accumulate wealth. From this accumulation of wealth, men meet the needs of their families and give to those in need. We are told in the Word of God not to love money, or pursue it balanced with the idea of storing up for future needs.

# Contentment

"But godliness actually is a means of great gain when accompanied by contentment. For we brought nothing into the world, so we cannot take anything out of it either. But if we have food and covering, with these we shall be content. But those who want to get rich fall into temptation and a snare and many foolish and harmful desires which plunge men into ruin and destruction. For the love of money is the root of all sorts of evil, and some by longing for it have wandered away from the faith and pierced themselves with many griefs" (I Timothy 6:6-10 NASB).

"For I know how to get along with humble means, and I also know how to live in prosperity; in any and every circumstance I have learned the secret of being filled and going hungry, both of having abundance and suffering need. I can do all things through Him who strengthens me" (Philippians 4:12-13 NASB).

Our possessions, our STUFF, are not to be the focus of your life or my life. JESUS is to be the focus of our lives. Whether or not someone has more STUFF than we do should not be a big deal to anyone. God cares for us and will meet all our needs through His GLORIOUS RICHES in Christ Jesus (Philippians 4:19).

# Storing Up Wealth

"There is a precious treasure and oil in the dwelling of the wise, But a foolish man swallows it up" (Proverbs 21:20 NASB).

"Go to the ant, O sluggard, observe her ways and be wise, which having no chief, officer, or ruler, prepares her food in summer and gathers her provision in the harvest. How long will you lie down, O sluggard? When will you arise from your sleep? 'A little sleep, a little slumber, a little folding of the hands to rest'—your poverty will come in like a vagabond and your need like an armed man" (Proverbs 6:6-11 NASB).

We are to store up our extra wealth for future needs such as college tuition, retirement, a new car, a new dishwasher, a new computer, a sudden illness, car repairs, new clothing—you get the point. We should not be surprised when the car breaks down. Cars break down. We should save for those things that cost us money in life.

## Storing Up Wealth for the Next Generation

"You still the hunger of those you cherish; their sons have plenty, and they store up wealth for their children" (Psalm 17:14 NIV ©1979).

"A good man leaves an inheritance for his children's children, but a sinner's wealth is stored up for the righteous" (Proverbs 13:22 NIV ©1979).

We should also save for the next generation, our children and their children, our grandchildren. Godly men and women save money and leave an inheritance. Taxing an inheritance reduces a family's ability to provide for future generations. Capital is needed to start a business. An inheritance can be invested to produce even more wealth, providing jobs beyond the family.

The Bible also talks about land ownership in the Old Testament. God gave land to different families/tribes in Israel. This land was to stay in the family. Land could not be taken away permanently from someone, even if they became poor and had to sell their land. In the Year of Jubilee, the land was returned to the family. The Year of Jubilee happened every 50 years. During the Year of Jubilee, all debts were cancelled and land was returned to its original owners.

You NEVER see in Scripture the government taking away land from the owner and using it for itself. Land belongs to God and is loaned, or entrusted, to families to make a living. Property tax violates the principle of private property. It assumes the somewhere the government has rights or ownership of the land. Do you know that if people don't pay their property tax, the government will confiscate the land? That is appalling to me. I think of an older man or woman, who has paid off his/her home, but is now barely able to make ends meet. If he/she cannot pay the government taxes for land that BELONGS to him/her, they lose the home and land.

## Using Stored Up Wealth

Wealth that is accumulated can be used to do good. Not only will a family be able to provide for its own needs as they arise, even if they are unexpected, but the family will be able to give to those who are in need. Families can give food, money, and items (appliances, furniture, clothing, computers) to the poor. People in the 1800's who were wealthy donated buildings, libraries, concert halls, universities, research grants, and all kinds of amazing things to help society. Godly men and women took gifts to the poor of food and money. People gave their time to care for orphans, widows, elderly, and the infirm.

Giving to others is to start with those in our old family, especially widows and orphans. Relatives can move in and be cared for when wealth is accumulated. The reason the oldest son got a double portion in the Old Testament times was that the oldest son took care of his parents when they were old with the double portion.

I laugh when I watch rich rock stars and actresses appeal to Congress for money, wondering why they don't give some of their own millions. I so appreciate Angeline Jolie for her heart to give to the poor (but don't agree with her morals).

The early church spent its money on leaders and the poor. The needs of the poor were met consistently. The first job of the deacons was to make sure that both the Jewish and Grecian widows were being taken care of. Another very important thing that you can do with accumulated wealth is to INVEST it in a business or other financial venture to create more wealth, jobs for other people, and help for the needy.

ECONOMICS, FINANCES, & BUSINESS COURSE

# Wealth Worksheet

How does the Government raise revenue?

What is Progressive Income Tax?

What is MTR?

How does MTR work?

Name 6 different taxes the government levies.

What is the problem with Property Tax?

What is Wealth Accumulation?

What is wealth accumulation used for?

Give 2 Scriptures about storing up/or accumulating wealth.

Give 2 Scriptures about leaving an inheritance for your children.

# Economics in One Lesson Worksheet

## Chapter Twelve

Can a nation grow rich by giving money or things away?

Why can't a nation or business get rich by making risky or bad loans?

What is an export subsidy?

## Chapter Thirteen

What are parity prices?

What was the argument for parity prices for agriculture?

How do parity prices hurt the consumer?

How do parity prices hurt the economy?

What are your thoughts about government policies that destroy food and crops while people are starving in other nations?

# October Week Two Class

☐ Discuss "Wealth Redistribution vs. Investment" Worksheet

☐ Discuss "*Economics in One Lesson* chapters 12-13 Worksheet" answers

**Notes from Class**

## October Week Two Home

☐ Read "Finding Capital for Families & Business" & "Role of Banks"

☐ Fill Out "Banks, Capital, Debt, & Savings Worksheet"

☐ Read *Economics in One Lesson* chapters 14-15

☐ *Fill Out "Economics* in One Lesson chapters 14-15 Worksheet"

☐ Read *The Money Mystery* pages 46 to end of book

☐ Fill out "*The Money Mystery Book* Review"

☐ Optional: Read Article "Ronald Reagan and the Spirit of Free Enterprise"

☐ Complete "Economics Open Book Test"

# Finding Capital for Families & Business

At any given moment, someone you love needs cash. Grandma needs new glasses, not covered by her insurance plan. Dad needs capital to expand his business. Mom needs to have her sewing machine fixed. Uncle Tom is out of work, unemployment has run out, and he has to pay his bills. Your cousins need a new family car because the old one is at death's door. And Aunt Millie is expecting twins…they need to fix up the spare bedroom as a nursery. Grandpa wants to add another truck to his successful pest control company.

Where will this money, or capital, come from? Capital is the saved-up or borrowed financial wealth used to start or expand a business. Capital can be more than just money. Capital can be natural resources, social networks, or other things, but for this discussion, we will consider capital as cash.

Families need cash to buy things, pay for healthcare, replace worn-out appliances, take vacations, and pay for education. Where will the money come from? What if they don't have enough saved?

Governments need money to fight wars, provide welfare programs, and pay for their pork barrel spending. How will they get all the money they need? What if there is not enough money that comes in from taxes?

## The World turns to Debt

The average American Christian is carrying a balance on their credit card. That means that they owe money to Master Card or Visa or Discover.

When Zack pays for gasoline with a credit card, he is entering into debt. When Karen uses a mortgage to buy a house, she is entering into debt. When Xerox takes out a loan to pay for a copy machine, Xerox is entering into debt.

Some Christian families save up their money for almost all of their purchases, including cars and homes. Other Christian families save up money for everything except a home. But, sadly, many Christian families swipe the plastic at will, racking up charges on their credit cards at a rate that is astronomical.

## Government Turns to Debt

When the government can't pay its bills, it uses a nifty kind of debt called government bonds. Municipal bonds are issued by a city to borrow money. Investors purchase these bonds and the city is in debt to the holders of the bond. Treasury bonds and savings bonds are issued by the federal government. Investors purchase these bonds and the nation is in debt to the federal government. So, the government is in debt to the investor and has to pay back the loan plus interest.

When the government takes less money in than it pours out, the government is running a deficit. When it takes in more than it receives, it has a surplus. If a deficit occurs year after year, the government begins to accrue, or build up, a big national debt.

In 2010, the national debt was $13.6 TRILLION dollars. The American government's estimated income for 2010 is 2.381 trillion. Can you spell d-e-f-i-c-i-t? Big difference between income and out go, isn't it? 164 billion is the amount of money that America pays for INTEREST on her debt. That is not touching the principle—that is just the interest. Hmmm, is that why America is having trouble finding creditors (people who want to lend us money)?

## Interest Rates

What does it mean to be in debt? Well, a person or company with wealth lends you some of that wealth. You agree to pay back the wealth at a later time. Oh, did I mention that you don't just agree to pay back the same amount of wealth back, but you must pay back interest too. That is why the person or company lends to you in the first place. They want to make money.

The original value of wealth that has to be paid back is the principle. The interest rate is a percentage of the principle. The interest is tacked on to the principle. Though loan sharks make you pay the principle and interest back right away or else, most people and businesses give you more time. You usually make monthly payments that include a bit of principle and a lot of interest. The closer you get to paying off the loan, the more of the payment goes to principle, rather than interest.

Interest rates that are low add less money to the principle than interest rates that are high. But, either way, interest rates double or, sometimes, triple the cost of the item you are purchasing.

## Christians Turn to God

God wants us to come to Him with our needs. He asks us to cry out to Him when there is not enough money to pay the bills, buy food, or make other purchases. There are four solutions for us when we need capital:

- Hard Work
- Contentment with Delayed Gratification
- Saving (accumulating wealth)
- Giving (tithing, offerings, gifts to the poor)

God has many harsh things to say about debt. He wants Christians to live debt-free, working hard, and trusting God to provide.

Here are some principles to learn and remember.

Debt is servanthood (Proverbs 22:7)

Get out of debt quickly (Proverbs 6:1-5)

Pay off debts (Psalm 37:21, Romans 13:8)

Don't assume that in the future you will be able to pay off a debt (Proverbs 27:1 & James 4:13-17)

Lend generously (Deuteronomy 15:7-10, Proverbs 3:27-28, Luke 6:30-34)

Don't charge interest when you loan people money—this is why Christians could not be money-lenders or bankers (Deuteronomy 23:19-20, Proverbs 3:27-28, Matthew 5:42, Luke 6:30-34)

Forgive debts (Matthew 6:12)

Being a lender is a blessing, being a debtor is a curse (Deuteronomy 28:12, 43, 44)

Sometimes debt is referred to as usury. Usury is considered by some to be exorbitant interest, but the early church fathers considered it interest of any kind. Collateral is what is used to guarantee that a loan will be paid back. You might give a lender something you own until you can pay the loan back. In Bible times, someone might give his cloak, but the Bible asks lenders to be kind about collateral too.

## What about Businesses?

Today, businesses use debt extensively, but this was not always the case. 100 years ago, if Fred wanted to start a corner grocery store, he would work hard and save every penny he could. He would skimp and save, sometimes even postponing marriage, so that he could scrap capital together to purchase a building and the stock for his store.

Starting up a business takes capital. Any business takes some money up front to get it going. When my husband, Mike, was in seminary the money we had in savings to live off of was running out. We were in a dilemma…there was not enough money to supplement his part-time job so that he could finish school. We took the rest of our savings and Mike bought some equipment to start a lawn business. He had to buy a trailer (that our station wagon could pull) to hold the equipment, some lawn equipment, and business cards. It was a bold and scary step. We could have lost all of our money. We did a lot of praying and fasting. The business was a success. Mike made enough for us to live on while he finished school. We have started other businesses in our marriage…all with our own savings.

Sometimes we feel like odd ducks because we refuse to borrow money, but let me tell you, our life is headache-free compared to other businessmen we know.

## Christians Invest with Wealth they have Accumulated

Where did the savings come from to start Mike's lawn business? Where did the money come from for him to go to school?

Well, the first 3 years we were married, we lived on ½ off our income. We stayed on a strict budget and refused to touch our savings. Month after month we did without so that we could put ½ of our income in savings. We had a goal (seminary for Mike) and it was important to us. We did not go to the movies or eat out at a restaurant for 3 years…yes, I am serious. You can do without a lot more than you think you can do without. We live in a society that tells us to spend, spend, spend. But, if we are always spending, we cannot work hard and diligently accumulate wealth.

What are some ways to gather capital to start a business or expand a business?

- Personal savings
- Sale of personal property (house, car, jewelry, electronics, land)
- Inheritance
- Gifts from family members, brothers in the Lord
- Investment money
- Selling stock

Sometimes when a business man is successful, he will invest in another man's business. Fred's grocery store grew large and prosperous. He saved the profits and expanded to 3 more stores in other cities. Now, Fred decided it was time to invest in other Christian brothers and their businesses. Fred met Jim, a young watch maker who wanted to start a watch repair shop. Fred invested some of his money in Jim's business. Jim did not have to pay Fred back, instead, Jim would pay Fred a percentage of his profits. An investor is a co-owner.

## How Debt affects a Business

Debt is an expensive way to run a business. The cost of the product goes up because the expense of the interest adds to the cost of production. Added to this is the stress of owing creditors who can rightfully seize your property if you default on your loan.

Debt does things backwards. Save first, gather money, wait on God, and then, buy something. This applies to businesses and individuals.

# Role of Banks

We refer to savings banks, bank and trust companies, and savings and loan associations as banks. All of these financial institutions are privately owned and do two things. They loan money and accept deposits.

## Loan Money

Banks loan money to individuals, couples, and businesses. Loans are paid out to the borrower and repaid by the borrower to the lender with interest. Fred does not go into debt, but his neighbor, Phil, borrows money from the local bank. He actually has several loans from the local bank: a first mortgage, a second mortgage, a car loan, a business loan, and a college loan for his daughter. Phil shells out a lot of interest to the bank, keeping them merrily afloat.

## Credit

We often hear talk about your credit rating. What is credit, anyway? Credit is the amount of money a bank would be willing to lend you based on your financial state and credibility. The amount a bank would be willing to lend to you is based on many factors. These factors give you a credit rating. Now keep in mind that banks want to lend to people who will pay their loans back, but they also want to lend to people who like to borrow money. You have higher credit rating if you have borrowed and paid back money. But, you have to go into debt to do that. It is a game that banks and credit card companies play to get you into the world of debt (which the Bible calls slavery). Don't fall for it!

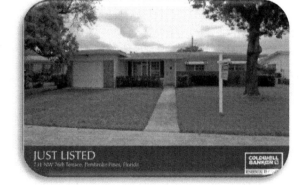

Do you pay your bills on time?

Do you pay back your loans?

Do you pay off your credit cards?

How much debt are you currently in?

## Accept Deposits

Banks accept deposits of money from people with the mutual agreement that people can get their money back whenever they want it or on an agreed-upon future date. Fred has a savings account and a checking account at the local bank. He gets letters each month asking from them asking if Fred would like to borrow money. Fred throws the letters away.

Why does Fred have a savings account in a local bank? Because when Fred deposits his money in the bank, he allows the bank to "use" his money to do business. In return for the use of his money, the bank pays Fred interest on his account. In 2010, interest rates are very low, so depositing your money in a savings account can feel like a worthless thing, but there have been many years where the interest paid to savings account has been much higher.

Many years ago, when my grandparents moved back from Venezuela (where they had worked for U.S. Steele) to the United States, interest rates were very high (over 10%). They put their money into savings accounts and Certificates of Deposit (CDs) and within a few years had doubled their money with the wonder of compound interest.

Compound interest works like this. You deposit money and make interest on the money. The next time you make interest on your money, you make interest on the money PLUS the interest you've already earned. You deposit $100.00 at 10% compound interest. The first time you get interest, you get $10.00 (10%). The second time, you have a balance of $110.00, so you get an interest payment of $11.00 instead of just $10.00 interest. Now, you have a balance of $121.00 and your interest payment will be $12.10. You can see how this can really grow your account, especially at higher interest rates

Fred pays his bills with checks from the local bank. He used to have a debit card, but kept forgetting to write down in his check book register every time he used it so he ripped the debit card up too.

The Rule of 72 tells us how many years money will take to double at a particular interest rate. Divide the number 72 by an interest rate and discover how many years it will take money to double at that interest rate. Here's an example. $4,000.00 at 3% interest—divide 72 by 3 and you get 24 years. It will take 24 years to double your investment and get $8,000.00. But, imagine that you have an interest rate of 12%. Divide 72 by 12 and get 6 years. In 6 years you can double your investment at a 12% interest rate.

Banks also offer credit cards (more debt!), IRAs (individual retirement accounts), and ATMs (Automatic Teller Machines).

## How Banks Make Money

Banks make money in three ways.

- From the Spread (difference between the interest rates they receive for loans and the interest rates they give for deposits)
- Earning interest on the securities they hold
- Customer fees (checking account fees, loan servicing, sale of financial products)

## How Banks "Create" Money

The following will probably frighten you....I'm warning you ahead of time.

Banks are required by the Federal Reserve System to keep cash on hand in their vault. The Federal Reserve System requires Primary Reserves and Secondary Reserves for each bank (financial institution). The primary reserves are cash, deposits due from other banks, and reserves required by the Federal Reserve System. Secondary reserves are securities that banks purchase. These securities can be sold to meet short-term needs for cash. The securities are almost always government bonds. Primary and secondary reserves are kept in the bank's own vault or at the closest Federal Reserve Bank. Any money the bank has on hand, after it meets its Federal Reserve Bank requirements, is called excess reserves.

Banks "create" money with their excess reserves. This is how banks do it.

Fred deposits $1,000.00 in his bank (which has a 20% reserve requirement). His bank keeps $200.00 in the vault, but lends $800.00 to Phil for a washing machine at Sears. Sears puts the $800.00 in Sears' bank, which keeps $160.00 in reserve (as required), but lends out $640.00. That $640.00 is invested in a 3rd bank and the cycle continues. The original deposit of $1,000.00 became $2,440.00 on deposit in 3 different banks—ONLY ON PAPER! (Or should I say on computer!)

Now, here is the interesting part. The Federal Reserve can contract or expand the money supply using banks. "How?" you ask. All it has to do is raise or lower the banks' reserve requirements. A sharp increase in required reserves will cause a reduction in the amount of money available to loan out.

## Marriage of Government & Banks

Government and banks are tied together in a frightening way. Banks have a lot of power for good or bad in people's lives because money is so important for families and businesses. In the beginning of our nation, Alexander Hamilton advocated a strong national bank, while Thomas Jefferson believed that banks should be independent. Hamilton won the debate.

Though there are many banks throughout the nation. Both the federal and state governments issue bank charters and regulate banks. The Federal Reserve controls the money supply at the federal level. Banks finance the national debt and make money off of it because they purchase securities, mostly government bonds.

The United States government encourages and requires all kinds of lending from banks. They enforce non-discrimination policies that sometimes require banks to lend to people who are poor credit risks (likely to NOT pay off their loans). There is a constant tug and pull between government and banks that should concern us all.

# Banks, Capital, Debt, & Savings Worksheet

What is Capital?

How can Capital be obtained to start a business?

How do banks make money?

Name some reasons that people go into debt.

Share 5 Biblical Principles about debt.

What is interest? How does it affect the amount of money that you owe when you borrow money?

Define Compound Interest? Use an example.

How can Compound Interest help you build capital/accumulate wealth?

# Economics in One Lesson Worksheet

## Chapter Fourteen

Why do people want to save "X industry"?

What are the two main schemes for saving "X industries"?

Describe how Congress saved the silver industry and the coal industry. What harm did they bring?

Why does "X Industry" benefit only at the expense of other industries?

What happens to taxpayers when the government artificially keeps an industry alive?

Can all industries be expanding at the same time?

## Chapter Fifteen

What is the "production-for-use-and-not-for-profit" school of economic thought?

What are the fallacies of the "production-for-use-and-not-for-profit" school of economic thought?

What lesson do we learn from Robinson Crusoe and Swiss Family Robinson?

How are prices fixed in a free-market society?

Why is there always a tendency for the price of a commodity and its marginal price of production to equal one another? Does this mean there is a cause-and-effect relationship?

How do consumers "cast their votes"?

ECONOMICS, FINANCES, & BUSINESS COURSE

# Money Mystery Review

A short review on *The Money Mystery* by Richard J Maybury!

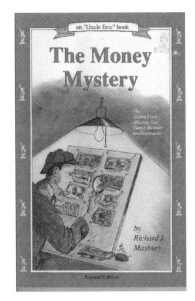

Why is the study of economic history so important?

Give examples of how the economy affected the political and social climate from the book?

Explain velocity and the demand for money.

What happens when the government "adjusts" the economy?

What is a free market system?

What is a government controlled system?

Which is the USA?

What warnings does history hold for our nation?

# October Week Three Class

☐ Discuss "Banks, Capital, Debt, & Savings Worksheet"

☐ Go over answers to "*Economics in One Lesson*" chapters 14-15

☐ Discuss *The Money Mystery* and *The Money Mystery* Book Review

**Notes from Class**

# October Week Three Home

☐ Read "Foreign Trade & Exchange", "Federal Reserve Bank" & "Money, Fiduciary Standard, & Inflation"

☐ Read *Economics in One Lesson* chapters 16-18

☐ Fill Out "*Economics in One Lesson* chapters 16-18 Worksheet"

☐ Read *Communist Manifesto* (at least half of book)

☐ Fill out "*The Money Mystery* Book Review"

☐ Write Essay: "Why It's Important to Study Economics"

☐ Read Essay aloud in class or to family

# Foreign Exchange & Foreign Trade

Our car was manufactured in an American factory owned by a Japanese manufacturer with headquarters in Aichi, Japan. When I go grocery shopping, I can buy food imported from Europe or South America. American movies and books are sold all over the world. People from different countries buy and sell to one another. When we sell or buy goods from a company in a different country, we are taking part in foreign trade. To purchase an item in Mexico, I must use pesos. This leads us to engage in foreign exchange.

## Foreign Exchange

Every country has its own currency. If you want to buy Swiss Army knives from a Swiss merchant, you must pay him in Swiss currency. That way, he can buy what he needs to buy in Switzerland to make his knives.

Each nation sells its own goods and payment for those goods is received in that nation's currency. If people all over the world want their goods and services, their currency will be in great demand and the supply will dwindle, so people will pay more and more to get their currency (law of supply and demand).

A London Factory begins making coffee-flavored grits and it has great success. People all over the world are buying coffee-flavored grits. Where can people get the British currency they need to purchase coffee-flavored grits? People will trade more of their own nation's money to get British money to purchase the grits.

Let's back up a minute. From the 1840's to 1971, there was a policy for currency and exchange rates that was fixed. The United States was the world's banker (all foreign nations had their central banks hold American dollars in reserve. The United States dollar was backed by gold and silver. In 1971, the United States dollar was no longer backed by gold and silver. The United States stopped playing world banker. Currencies began to float freely against each other based on what the market was up to.

## Foreign Trade

Foreign Trade is simply the trading (buying and selling) of goods and services between two or more different countries. Imports and exports are the essence of foreign trade. An import is an item coming into your country from another country, while an export is an item going out of your country to another country.

Brazil exports coffee and we import Brazilian coffee. Japan exports stereo equipment and we import Japanese stereo equipment. Switzerland exports army knives and we import Swiss army knives.

Some nations are really good at producing a quality product at a cost-efficient price. This is why other nations want to buy it.

Sometimes, products produced in one country are very similar to the same products produced in another country. These products (commodities) are grouped together in one mass market and sold. This would be trading commodities. Oil and grain are good examples of trading commodities.

Many countries have industries that they want to protect. These industries would have a hard time competing with foreign goods, so the government imposes a tariff, or tax on certain foreign goods. While this does generate revenue for the nation, its purpose is to protect its own industries that are not producing up to the same quality of similar foreign industries.

# Story of Federal Reserve Bank

We were looking for the Osborn Convention Center in Jacksonville where I was speaking at a homeschool convention.

"This is where it should be," Laura said, pointing to a large white building. We had already circled the building twice.

"I don't see anyone here," I replied. I had expected a large crowd of people outside the building. "And why are the entrances blocked off?"

"Not only blocked off. There are spikes that could really hurt your car," my son, Jimmy, added.

"Let me get out and talk to the people in the lobby. They can give us information."

I hopped out of Laura's Honda Odyssey van and strode up to where I thought the entrance would be. But no doors. Finally I pressed my face up against the glass window to look inside the lobby. Three armed guards. Interesting that security was so tight for a homeschool convention.

"Ma'am, step away from the building. Step away from the building," a loud voice startled me. The walls seemed to be speaking.

"Can you help me? I'm lost. I'm looking for the Osborn Convention Center."

"Ma'am are you with the dark blue Odyssey with license plate number…" The voice rattled off Laura's license plate number and described the occupants of the van.

"Ummm. Yes." What had I stumbled upon?

"Ma'am, this is the Federal Reserve Building. Would you please step away from the building, get back in your car, and drive away before we detain you."

I ran back to the car.

"Let's get out of here! This is not the convention center. We've stumbled on the Jacksonville Branch of the Federal Reserve Banking System."

The Federal Reserve System plays a vital role in our nation's economy. It is the central bank of the United States, acting as a bank for the federal government and a bank for other banks. Its supposed purpose is to monitor and stabilize the money supply and regulate American banks. There are twelve Federal Reserve Banks under the oversight/authority of a Board of Governors. These banks are located in Boston, New York, Philadelphia, Cleveland, Richmond, Atlanta, Chicago, St. Louis, Minneapolis, Kansas City, Dallas, and San Francisco.

The Federal Reserve Bank Act was voted on by Congress and signed into law by Woodrow Wilson. Wilson was also a proponent of the League of Nations, a socialist ideal. During his administration, we also received the 16th Amendment (Income Tax).

The Federal Reserve Bank Act gave the Federal Reserve Bank a life span of 20 years, but it's still in existence. Who was President of the United States when its term expired? Franklin D. Roosevelt.

## Board of Governors

Overseeing the Federal Reserve System is a Board of Governors with seven members. These members are appointed by the President and confirmed by the Senate. The full term for each member is fourteen years with staggered terms so that one term expires each even-numbered year.

The Chairman and Vice-Chairman run the board and are appointed for four year terms, but may serve two terms. They work in Washington D.C.

Here is a list of all the Board of Governors members and directors since the Fed's creation in 1914.

http://www.federalreserve.gov/aboutthefed/bios/board/

In 2010, the board members were Ben S. Bernanke, Chairman, Donald L. Kohn, Vice-Chairman, Kevin M. Warsh, Elizabeth A. Duke, and Daniel K. Tarullo. There were 3 vacancies in July 2010.

In 2016, the board members are Janet L. Yellen, Chairman, Stanley Fischer, Vice-Chairman, Daniel K. Tarullo, Jerome H. Powell, and Lael Brainard.

## What Does the Federal Reserve Bank Do?

The Federal Reserve System carries out the government's economic policies, working hand and glove with the government. Though it does not receive money directly from Congress, it makes money from interest on Government Securities/Bonds. I would hardly call this an "Independent Banking System."

Here are some of the things that the Federal Reserve Bank/System does.

- Manipulates the Money Supply

- "Creates" money, increases or decreases the illusionary supply of "money" in circulation
- Sets interest rates for private banks
- Maintains inflation/determines level of inflation
- Tells private banks how much cash they need to keep in reserves
- Stores private banks' reserves at their branches
- Regulates private banks
- Provides banking services to the US government: checks, electronic payments, distributes coins & paper money to private banking institutions
- Gives approval or rejects private banks who want to be involved in foreign trade or be established in other nations
- Conducts research on the U. S. economy
- Conducts research on regional economies
- "Educates" the public on its role through publications, speeches, seminars, and web sites

The Federal Reserve Bank controls the interest rates. When the Fed lowers interest rates, people are more likely to borrow money and save less. (Truthfully, most Americans don't save at all!) When the Fed raises interest rates, it encourages people to save more and borrow less.

The Federal Reserve Bank keeps inflation happening in our nation by slowly (or sometimes rapidly) increasing the supply of money in the economy. This causes prices to rise and the cash we have on hand to be worth less. Inflation hurts people who are trying to save money.

## What is the Federal Open Market Committee?

The Federal Open Market Committee (FOMC) has 12 members (7 Board of Governor members, 1 Federal Reserve Bank of New York president, and 4 of the other Reserve Bank Presidents). The committee holds 8 meetings a year. If you watch the news, you have probably heard about these meetings and wondered what on earth they were. The committee talks about what is going on in the nation financially and how the economy is doing. Then, they decide what course of action to take. For example, not enough people are borrowing money (state of economy), so the committee decides to lower interest rates (their Monetary Policy). Monetary Policy is the action taken by the central bank of a nation in an attempt to help or hinder the economy.

## Is the Federal Reserve Bank Good or Bad?

Our nation's economy is built on the principle of debt and borrowing money from banks at interest rates set by the Federal Reserve Bank, who works hand and glove with the Federal Government. To run a nation on the principle of debt, you have to maintain continuous inflation, so that it is enticing to borrow money.

The Board of Governors has a tremendous amount of wealth and power in their hands, yet they are not elected officials and are subject only to occasional scrutiny by Congress.

The most effective way to destroy a nation is to debase/devalue its currency (inflation). That is what the Federal Reserve Bank does on a regular basis. Is it harmful or helpful to our nation? What do you think?

ECONOMICS, FINANCES, & BUSINESS COURSE

(Copyright Gospel Communications International, Inc - www.reverendfun.com )

# Money, Fiduciary Standard, and Inflation

Cain and Abel may have bartered back before the offering disaster where God accepted Abel's sacrifice, but not Cain's offering. Abel was a shepherd and offered up a burnt offering (lamb) to the Lord. Cain, a farmer, offered some of his veggies and grains. God was pleased with Abel, but not with Cain. In anger, Cain killed Abel.

But before that terrible day, the young men may have bartered.

"I'll give you 5 pounds of barley flour, a bushel of corn, and an apple pie for the wool that is sheared off of five sheep," Cain offered.

"Make it 6 pounds of barley flour, 2 bushels of corn, and a strawberry pie for the wool of 3 lambs," Abel countered.

"5 pounds of barley flour, 2 bushels of corn, and a strawberry pie for the wool of 3 sheep, not lambs. That is my final offer." Cain stood firm with his arms crossed.

"Deal," Abel accepted, holding his hand out for a quick shake.

Bartering is still used today, especially during economic lean times.

As the population grew, everyone had something different to barter with.

"This is getting confusing," Enoch, started to complain, but stopped himself. "When I was a kid, there was such a wide variety of stuff available on market day, but what I need isn't here. I need milk for making pudding, but Maljuba is out of cow's milk and goat's milk. Should I leave the winter boots with him and pick up the milk later. Or maybe I should trade the blueberries instead. I could trade with Ayubago. I could give her some blueberries and she could give me some yogurt. If I do leave the boots with Malijuba, will he forget to give me the milk next week on market day?...I wish the Lord would just beam me up." Enoch did the shopping, or bartering for his family. He also took out the trash without being asked and brought home roses for his wife each evening—a truly righteous man!

It probably was long before Enoch was on the scene that men and women decided to use a system that would be easier to use than bartering. My guess is that a system of money was developed before the flood and many coins were buried under the deluge.

# Money

Money is something tangible that is used for exchanging goods and services. Instead of bartering with one another, you trade a common item of value. You purchase things from one another using money. Money is a way that people can agree on the value of material goods and services. This piece of money (coin, shell, sheep, paper) is worth so many ears of corn, pounds of blueberries, pairs of boots, or tea bags.

Money can be coins, paper money, shells, jewels, spices, animal skins, gold, silver, and any other agreed upon form of exchange. Cattle (sheep, cows, camels) are an old form of money. That is why wealth is often described in terms of how many herds a rich man had (see Job 1:1-3). Cowrie shells were widely used as money in Asia and the Pacific Islands.

Back in 700 BC, the King of Lydia started printing coins for his kingdom. Surrounding nations soon followed suit. These coins were made of silver, gold, and bronze. Now, it's very possible that other kings minted coins before this King, but this is the first coin that we have record of. Archeologists may discover older coins than Lydian coins.

During colonial times in our nation, Americans used French, English, and Spanish coins to purchase items. After the America Revolution, we had to pay off debts that accrued during the war. So we came up with our own currency. Do you remember Paul Revere? He was a silversmith and designed the first coins. In 1793, the Philadelphia Mint produced American coins for the United States.

Gold has often been used for money throughout history. Gold was measured out or gold coins were given to pay for an item or service. Gold works so well because it has intrinsic value. Most people, if offered gold, would take it. Almost all people on this planet agree that gold is valuable.

# Gold or Silver Standard

Instead of having people carry around gold nuggets or coins, a government can mint coins or print currency that represents gold or silver. So, each coin or paper bill is worth a certain amount of gold or silver. This is called the "Gold Standard" or "Silver Standard." Each coin or dollar is "backed up" by a certain amount of gold, kept in a safe place by the government.

In the United States of America, we do not "back up" our coins and dollars any more with gold or silver. Instead, we use the "Fiduciary Standard."

# Fiduciary Standard

This system is built on trust, not the true value of the money being minted, or printed. Instead of gold or silver establishing the value of coins and dollars, what establishes the value of our money is the trust people around the world have in the United States government. Yikes! That's a little scary!

Pull a dollar bill out of your wallet and read it carefully. It says, "This note is legal tender for all debts, public and private," but it doesn't say, "This note is worth three ounces of gold." Your coin doesn't say, "This coin is worth one ounce of silver." I would prefer that my coins and dollars could be exchanged for gold and silver, if need be.

It feels like a big game of "Let's pretend." The government is basically saying, "Look, we all know that this is just a piece of paper, but let's pretend that it's worth a dollar."

If everybody stops pretending that the piece of paper is worth a dollar, then it won't matter what the government says because the bill will become worthless.

Why on earth does the government do this? Here are two reasons:

It takes the pressure off the government from having to keep gold and silver in Ft. Knox to back up its currency.

It allows the government to print as much money as it wants to print. Yes, it's true. The government can print as many dollar bills as it wants to print because we are only pretending that it is worth the value it claims to have.

The fiduciary standard allows the government to print money whenever it wants to "stimulate the economy," leading to inflation. Let's talk a little bit about inflation now.

## Inflation

To explain inflation, let's first talk about counterfeiting. This is how inflation began.

Back in Ancient times, people began to counterfeit coins in an interesting way. King Andrew was minting silver coins for his kingdom to pay his soldiers. He was running low on silver, so he did an immoral thing. He clipped little bits of silver off the coins he'd already made to use to make more coins. This way King Andrew was able to make more coins. More coins were circulating in his kingdom. When these new clipped coins began to circulate in his kingdom with the other silver coins, people preferred the unclipped coins to the clipped coins because they had more silver in them, making them more valuable.

Since he was the king, the soldiers could not arrest King Andrew for devaluing (lowering the value) of the coins. In fact, King Andrew made his citizens use his coins, though there was less silver in them. The people, forced to use them, decided that because they were worth less, they would raise the price on items they were selling to make up for the amount of silver that had been clipped out.

Shepherd Samuel wanted six clipped coins for his sheep now instead of five regular coins. Fisherman Fred demanded three clipped coins instead of two regular coins for his flounder. Baker Betty handed out five loaves of bread for one clipped coin instead of the seven loaves of bread she used to distribute for one regular coin.

So, even though there was more money in King Andrew's kingdom, it now took more money to purchase all that people needed to purchase. More money, but that money had less purchasing power. That is inflation.

Inflation is an increase in the amount of money in circulation and is accompanied by a decrease in the value of that money. As a result, prices go up.

When we think of inflation, we think of rising prices, but we don't realize that the prices rise because of the increased amount of money circulating.

## Debasing the Money Supply

What King Andrew did by clipping coins is called debasing currency. Another way to debase currency is to mix cheaper metals in with the gold, silver, or bronze before minting the coins. To present a mixture of lead and silver to people as a silver coin is deceptive. To hold up a "gold coin" that has tin mixed in with the gold is fraudulent. That is what these ancient people did.

God compares this practice to personal sin in the book of Ezekiel. He is describing the practice of mixing cheaper metals in with the expensive gold and silver to deceive people. God is not deceived when the Israelites mix godly practices (gold and silver) with ungodly practices (cheaper metals). He intends to judge this behavior.

"Then the word of the LORD came to me: 'Son of man, the house of Israel has become dross to me; all of them are the copper, tin, iron and lead left inside a furnace. They are but the dross of silver. Therefore this is what the Sovereign LORD says: 'Because you have all become dross, I will gather you into Jerusalem. As men gather silver, copper, iron, lead and tin into a furnace to melt it with a fiery blast, so will I gather you in my anger and my wrath and put you inside the city and melt you. I will gather you and I will blow on you with my fiery wrath, and you will be melted inside her. As silver is melted in a furnace, so you will be melted inside her, and you will know that I the LORD have poured out my wrath upon you,'" Ezekiel 18:17-22 NIV.

Again, in Isaiah 1:25, God compares Israel's sin to the practice of debasing coins by mixing valuable metals with cheaper metals, such as tin. "I will turn my hand against you; I will thoroughly purge away your dross and remove all your impurities."

These ancient practices are practiced differently today. How many of you have watched a crime drama or movie about a counterfeiting ring. Or maybe you have read an article in the newspaper when a successful counterfeiting ring is finally caught.

You and I would never consider printing up fake money and spending it. We know in our heart of hearts that it is not just illegal, but morally wrong. But, did you ever wonder why it is morally wrong? What is the big deal about printing our own money and spending it? Doesn't spending money "jump-start" the economy? Is it simply that God wants us to work hard to earn our money? Or does counterfeiting harm other people?

Let's imagine that you and I decide to become counterfeiters. We hook up with a disgruntled former employee of the Philadelphia Mint who can get us paper, printing presses, and everything else we need. Soon our little operation is humming along merrily and we had millions of dollars (in twenties and fifties) to spend on whatever our heart desires.

In our small town of Crooksville, we are happily spending money on boots, shoes, ice cream, candy, books, music CDs, DVDs, computers, televisions, furniture, clothing, hats, cars, bikes, and electronics. We even purchase a boat. The economy in Crooksville moves into a time of expansion and prosperity because of all the money we are infusing into the local economy.

Bob's Boots increases their inventory and takes out a loan for an addition to his store. Ed and Ellen hire a new employee for their booming electronics store. Candace can hardly keep chocolate on the shelf at her candy store. She is considering taking out a loan to advertize on television.

But, things eventually catch up to us and the FBI arrests our little counterfeiting ring.

**Inflation is an increase in the money supply.**

The problem with inflation is that it creates an illusion. The Free Market will penalize inefficiency and reward efficient businesses. Inflation creates the illusion that all businesses are prospering.

When dollars have less purchasing power, businesses must raise their prices to still make a profit. Or they can decrease the size (quantity) or downgrade the quality of their product. This is actually a form of raising prices, since you are getting "less" for the same amount of money, but consumers balk less at getting less than at paying more.

Ask your mom about this practice. She probably does a lot of grocery shopping. So, ask her about sizes of products. A "pound can" is now 14 ½ ounces instead of 16. What used to be a half gallon of ice cream is now sold in 1 ½ quart containers. Interesting? This price increase in the form of downsizing is one way that businesses deal with inflation.

Inflation also rewards debt and punishes savings. If you borrow money, you will pay the loan back with dollars that have less purchasing power. If you save money, the money you sock away will have less purchasing power in two or three years.

Yet, as Bible-believing Christians, we know that God calls debt foolish. How can a procedure that encourages debt be good or wise?

"Remove the dross from the silver, and out comes material for the silversmith; remove the wicked from the king's presence, and his throne will be established through righteousness," Proverbs 25:4-5 NIV.

## Government's Impact on the Economy

When the economy is sluggish, the government practices legal counterfeiting by inflating the money supply. This influx of money can appear to improve the economy, but prices go up quickly and the average person is less well off after inflation than before. Often a middle-class family's income will not go up, but prices rise making it difficult for these families to make ends meet.

# Economics in One Lesson Worksheet

## Chapter Sixteen

Why does the government loan money to farmers to hold their crops off the market (or purchase their crops and destroy them) and how does this harm the economy?

Does restricting production help or harm the economy? Why?

## Chapter Seventeen

What are the two consequences when the government "fixes" a price below the market value?

How does price fixing lead to rationing?

How does rationing lead to a black market?

## Chapter Eighteen

What is rent control?

How does it harm the economy?

How can rent control seem to help in the short run, but cause destruction in the long run?

ECONOMICS, FINANCES, & BUSINESS COURSE

# Economic Essay

By now, I hope you realize why studying economics is so important. It's time to spread the news. You will write an essay on "Why It's Important to Study Economics" to inspire your friends and family members to study economics themselves.

Here is my Outline

**Introduction**

**First Point =**

**Second Point =**

**Third Point =**

**Fourth Point =** (you may not have a 4th point!)

**Conclusion**

# Economic Basics Open Book Test

Define the following words and phrases!

**Law of supply & demand:**

**Specialization of Labor:**

**Wealth:**

**Money:**

**Economy:**

**Economic system:**

**Capitalism:**

**Socialism:**

**GNP:**

# ECONOMICS, FINANCES, & BUSINESS COURSE

**Economic Cycle:**

**Answer the following questions!**

How is government financed?

What are Taxes?

What causes inflation?

In what way is the government involved with the banking system? How does this affect the economy?

Which is more important: production or work?

# October Week Four Class

- [ ] Read "Why Study Economics" Essays Aloud in Class

- [ ] Discuss "Federal Reserve Bank"

- [ ] Go over *Economics in One Lesson* Questions chapters 16-18

- [ ] Go Over Any More Questions on Economics Open Book Test

- [ ] Prepare for First Economics Exam

Notes from Class

ECONOMICS, FINANCES, & BUSINESS COURSE

# October Week Four Home

☐ Read "Social Justice vs. Personal Responsibility"

☐ Fill Out "Social Justice vs. Personal Responsibility" worksheet

☐ Read *Economics in One Lesson* chapters 19-20

☐ Fill Out "*Economics in One Lesson* chapters 19-20 Worksheet"

☐ Finish *Communist Manifesto*

☐ Fill out "*Communist Manifesto* Book Review"

☐ Complete "Monthly Consumer Price Index Project"

☐ Study for Economics Exam

# Social Justice vs. Personal Responsibility

It was the summer of 2010 and the economy was not in a good state.

"They won't hire me?" Bruce admitted after I asked him about the job interview.

"What?! They loved your resume. I don't get it," I replied.

"There are no openings in the area I wanted. The only opening was in the warehouse."

"And you didn't want to work there?" I asked, surprised.

"Oh, no. I did want to work in the warehouse. I practically begged to work in the warehouse. I told them that I have experience in working in a warehouse." Bruce ran his fingers through his hair, a habit he had when he was upset.

"Why wouldn't they hire you for the warehouse job?" I probed, even though I knew Bruce was upset.

"They said that I'm overqualified. They want to hire someone who will stay and be fulfilled…."

Bruce rambled on, sharing what the personnel lady had shared with him. I felt sick inside. He had a family that depended on his income and his wife was pregnant again.

Later that evening, I told Mike about Bruce and his fruitless job hunt.

"Well, maybe we can hire him to retile the kitchen," Mike said, patting my arm. "Don't worry. We will do whatever we can to help."

What should we do when hardworking people can't find a job? Why are people unemployed?

# Unemployment

Economists are concerned about unemployment. The rate of unemployment is a statistic that economists look at to determine the overall health of the economy. If you watch the news, you will hear a lot about unemployment rates.

But unemployment statistics are not the most important thing we need to think about. Behind those statistics are men and women who have families to support, who are hurting and scared, and who often become discouraged and give up.

## Unemployment Terminology

Let's start with learning the economic terms applied to employees and job hunters. An Unemployed Person is someone who is available to work, wants to work, and is part of the Labor Force. The Labor Force is all the employed and unemployed workers in an economy. Not everyone who does not have a job is considered unemployed. Here are some people who do not have a paying job, but are not considered unemployed:

- Students who choose not to work
- Homemakers
- Retirees
- Financially wealthy people who choose not to work
- People physically unable to work
- People mentally or emotionally unable to work

These people are not part of the labor force. Now, don't forget that all God's people are commanded to work hard, including retirees, homemakers, and financially wealthy people who choose not to work for a paycheck. Homemakers work hard caring for their home and families without an income. Wealthy people may work hard for a charity. But, the labor force is referring to those who can, do, and/or want to work for a paycheck.

There are many different reasons that someone is unemployed.

- People quit their job
- People get fired
- People get laid off because the company is not doing well financially
- People leave jobs for health reasons and now want to come back
- People leave jobs to care for a new baby and now want to come back

- People leave jobs to go to school and come back when they graduate
- People are new to the job market

Andy, a Job Leaver, quit his job, hoping to find another that paid more money to cover all his loans. Job losers get laid off or fired. Fred was Laid Off for six months because of a financial crisis at his company. He was thankful that he had money in savings to live off of and he also did some odd jobs for friends at church. Steve, a RE-entrant, left work for a few years because he was on dialysis and had a kidney transplant. Steve was unable to work, but re-entered the job market, hoping to find work when he recovered physically from the transplant surgery. Mike was a New Entrant, who had just graduated from high school and was ready to find a job. Billy, a Discouraged Worker, has not been able to find a job, so he has given up and is sleeping on his older brother's couch.

There are several types of unemployment.

**Frictional Unemployment** (job losers and job leavers in between jobs)

**Seasonal Unemployment** (workers who have seasonal jobs during the off-season such as lifeguards and ski instructors)

**Cyclical Unemployment** (when the unemployment rate is affected by recessions and expansion in the economy)

Structural Unemployment (when an entire industry is phased out with everyone in that industry out of a job)

## Is Government the Solution to Unemployment?

Unemployment is a common excuse governments use to grow in size and power. Socialists like to say that it is unfair for one person to be employed and another person to be unemployed. The underlying principle of "fairness" means that everything should be equal so that if one person has a job and one person doesn't, the person with the job should give some of their money to the person not working. The government does two things to provide "fairness' to those who unemployed.

The government provides Unemployment Insurance (paid for by former employers. Paychecks for people who are laid off—a percentage of their former income). The United States federal government also provides Job Training (tax dollars or federal debt pay for a worker to go to school or be trained by a government agency).

Government meddling in the economy actually causes unemployment. It is very expensive to hire employees because of the employee benefits that government requires. We have to pay unemployment insurance on employees who do not even qualify to receive unemployment. We have friends who have quit hiring employees because of all the government red tape (regulations). High taxes on businesses take money away from a business that could be used to pay salaries. Minimum wage laws drive costs up because a business owner has to pay a teenager or retiree (who doesn't want or need as much money) the same as a father providing for his family.

Is the government well meaning? I really don't know. Government is made up of people who want to be re-elected. They do this by offering their constituents the allusion that they can get something for nothing. But, nothing in this world is free, except our salvation through Christ.

If government would stop interfering with so many rules and regulations, businesses would be able to spend more money paying employees and hiring more workers.

## God's Solution for Unemployment

Unemployment is a common excuse governments use to grow in size and power. Instead, we should handle unemployment with God's principles, found in Scripture.

We are to save for the day of disaster. We are to work hard so that we have a profit (that can be stored away). We are to invest in our Heavenly Bank Account by tithing and giving so that funds are available when we are in need. We are to seek the Kingdom first, knowing that God will take care of all of our needs. We are to give to our brothers and sisters in need.

## Work Hard & Avoid Idleness

"Now we command you, brethren, in the name of our Lord Jesus Christ, that you keep away from every brother who leads an unruly life and not according to the tradition which you received from us. For you yourselves know how you ought to follow our example, because we did not act in an undisciplined manner among you, nor did we eat anyone's bread without paying for it, but with labor and hardship we kept working night and day so that we would not be a burden to any of you; not because not because we do not have the right to this, but in order to offer ourselves as a model for you, so that you would follow our example. For even when we were with you, we used to give you this order: if anyone is not willing to work, then he is not to eat, either. For we hear that some among you are leading an undisciplined life, doing no work at all, but acting like busybodies. Now such persons we command and exhort in the Lord Jesus Christ to work in a quiet fashion and eat their own bread. But as for you, brethren do not grow weary of doing good" (II Thessalonians 3:6-13 NASB).

If a man doesn't work, he is not to eat. Does this mean we don't help people who are unemployed? Of course not! But, we need to help them by providing opportunities for them to work, as well as giving financial gifts.

When someone is unemployed, their job is to find another job and it should be tackled aggressively, not just a few hours a week. Here are some things that unemployed men and women can do. The church should help them in all these areas.

- Update or make a resume that will appeal to employers
- Grow in character qualities such as hard work, dependability, honesty, diligence
- Improve/Grow in skills, abilities, and knowledge
- Apply for jobs daily—work hard at looking for a job!
- Use network to ask for help with job hunt and ask for more contacts with people who can help with the job hunt
- Pray and Fast
- Improve Schedule and Budget
- Consider starting own business
- Look for side jobs to bring in extra money

## Who Helps the Poor and Needy

We all know someone that has gone through or is in hard times. My friend, Peggy, was in a wheelchair after a car accident. She needed help to get around, bathe, and eat. Susie lost her husband and had to provide for 5 children by herself. Bill's home was destroyed in a hurricane, even though he managed to flee to safety. Bill and his family lost everything. Jamie struggled with mental illness, living on the streets of Miami, pushing a shopping cart.

Who will help these people? Shouldn't it be the government's job to step in and do something?

Many people really believe that government can solve problems and make life better for people. Is the government really compassionate, wanting to help people? I can't answer that. My opinion of politicians is that most of them like power and want to stay in office. Promising all kinds of things to the masses is a great way to get votes.

I don't know of too many government programs that work in eliminating poverty. In fact, most Americans would agree that welfare doesn't work. So what is the solution? Pour more money at it! I find it amusing that the government solution is to pour more money at everything and keep doing what doesn't work in the first place.

## Does Poverty Cause Crime?

One way that politicians get us to vote for more government spending is to sell the idea that poverty causes crime. The idea is that people who can barely make ends meet will turn to crime to get ahead. So, because the government is supposed to protect its citizens from crime, the government should attack the cause of crime, poverty. The solution: welfare and other government programs.

While extreme poverty can lead to crime sometimes, crime is not a problem of the poor alone. If this were true, then all the rich people would be upright, honorable, and holy. A lot of rich people I know are just as sinful as poor people. Yes, they might commit different crimes—fraud and embezzlement instead of breaking and entering—but, they are both stealing!

## Government Programs to Fight Poverty

Here are some government programs in place spending trillions of tax-payer's money to run. Yes, that's right, working Americans are coerced to pay for these programs, whether they like them or not.

- Welfare
- Worker's Compensation (paychecks to people who get hurt on the job)
- Medicare (medical care for the elderly)
- Emergency Relief (gives help during disasters)
- Subsidized Housing (pays all or part of rent for poor people)
- Social Security (workers are coerced to pay for this government subsidized retirement plan)

These programs are well-known, but how about some more programs that are less well known. Online, I googled, "help from government." I went to one of the government websites, gave my state, and checked off the kind of help I wanted. A very long list of available programs came up. Here are some of the programs that caught my eye.

- Mortgage Insurance for Disaster Victims
- AIDS Research Loan Repayment Program
- Adjustable Rate Mortgage Insurance
- Adoption Assistance
- Advanced Education Nursing Traineeships
- Alcohol National Research Service Awards
- Alcohol Research Career Development Awards
- American Jazz Masters Fellowships
- Assistance for Indian Children with Severe Disabilities
- Assistance for Victims of Trafficking
- Assistance to Torture Victims

- Basic FHA Loan (Home Mortgage Insurance—HUD/FHA)
- Bioinformatics and Computational Biology Research and Research Training
- Biological Response to Environmental Health Hazards
- Bureau of Indian Affairs (BIA) Financial Assistance and Social Services
- Business Physical Disaster Loans
- Chafee Foster Care Independent Living

Those are just a few that looked interesting to me! And I just got to the C's. You get my point. The government is involved in all kinds of things to HELP people.

All of these programs cost lots and lots of money that people like you and me are working very hard to earn. Unfortunately, most of these programs are filled with government waste.

## Coercion & Government Waste

Government programs to help the poor and needy are not optional. They are coerced from us in the form of mandatory taxes. They are also paid for by the debt. I do not mind helping the poor, needy, and elderly. But, I would prefer to do so through a Christian organization, rather than a wasteful bureaucracy. There are things that the government thinks are good things that I think are evil. For example, I believe that abortion is murder. Yet, my tax dollars pay for abortions and testing on aborted baby fetuses.

A business is concerned about being lean and effective so that it can make a profit. The government has no such goal. It spends more and more money and if it runs out of money, the government simply prints more money or goes into debt.

Here is some of the fruit of government help.

- Welfare has not eliminated poverty. The percentage of Americans living at poverty level stays roughly the same.
- The welfare system is full of government waste. We might do better to take all the money spent on welfare and divide it up among the poor families. They would be able to pay bills, start businesses, and take vacations. Instead, we have a massive bureaucracy that eats up most of the money before it gets to the people it is supposed to help.
- Welfare does not lift people out of poverty. Instead, we see generations in the same family on welfare.
- Welfare discourages hard work.
- Welfare encourages dependency on the government.
- Welfare encourages the breakdown of the family

## Biblical Principle of Compassion & Charity

Jesus is full of compassion. As His followers, we must be filled with compassion for those who are in need. His love should fill us to overflowing. Compassion in our hearts leads to charity in our lives.

Charity is Voluntary

Charity is voluntary, flowing out of love and compassion. Remember the story of the Good Samaritan? Each person was free to give as much as he could give. Some did choose not to give and that will happen, but charities are much more effective than government programs in helping effectively.

Here are some charities that are making a difference in America and around the world.

- Local Churches (take care of the poor within and outside their congregations, give to shelters, charities, and missions, educate workers)
- Rescue Missions (provide food, clothing, shelter, training, and rehabilitation)
- The Red Cross (medical care and emergency services)
- Crisis Pregnancy Centers (save lives of unborn babies, help woman through pregnancy and afterward, offer financial and spiritual help)
- World Vision (poor around the world, help with national disasters)
- Charitable Hospitals (medical care operates on "as-you-can-pay")
- Harvest Time International (provides food, clothing, medical supplies around the world)
- Compassion International (help to poor & needy around the world)
- Samaritan's Purse (food, medical care, and relief around the world)
- Salvation Army (disaster relief, poverty relief, youth, trafficking, rehabilitation)

The list could go on and on with the names of orphanages, women's shelters, food distribution programs, prison visitation programs, drug rehabilitation programs, family counseling programs, and organizations providing assistance to every kind of human difficulty. Christ's Church is busy about the work of caring for the needy—more efficiently and more effectively.

## Gleaning

They were back in Israel after a long journey. There was no money left and enough food for one more meal. Ruth tried not to think of her hometown in Moab, but she felt a little scared. She had promised her mother-in-law, Naomi, that she would never leave her, she had chosen to follow the God of Israel, and had trusted Him to take care of the two of them. Had God brought them this far to die?

"I will go get a job," Ruth announced the next morning. She was putting on a brave front, but inside she doubted that anyone would hire a foreigner.

That morning, Naomi patiently explained the gleaning laws to Ruth. Ruth relaxed and set off for the field of Boaz, a member of Naomi's family. She would glean in his field and there would be plenty of food for both women.

## What is Gleaning?

"When you reap the harvest of your land, do not reap to the very edges of your field or gather the gleanings of your harvest. Do not go over your vineyard a second time or pick up the grapes that have fallen. Leave them for the poor and the alien. I am the Lord your God," Leviticus 19:9-10 NIV.

The gleaning law fascinates me! It is so creative and makes so much sense. What a great way to take care of the poor and unemployed.

Imagine that you are a farmer or a vineyard owner. You are gathering in your harvest, trying to get every piece of fruit, grain, or crop that you can. You end up missing some. And, some of your harvest falls while you are transporting it to the storehouse.

What should you do? It would be a lot of work to go back over the field, especially because you just went through the whole field or vineyard. So, you leave it for the poor.

The poor, unemployed, and foreigners can now come through and gather what is left. The poor people follow behind the workers and pick up what is left behind.

Here is what is so wonderful about the gleaning law.

- The poor are given food
- They work to provide it (it is not getting something for nothing)
- The poor are required to work
- The farmer doesn't have to collect the food for them
- There is no paperwork or forms to fill out
- The field or vineyard is left clean and tidy

What a great idea that the Lord had when he made up the gleaning law. It fulfills all His commands ("He who doesn't work doesn't eat" and "Take care of the poor"). God is so wise and amazing.

## Fruit of the Gleaning Law

Ruth was gleaning in Boaz's field during the barley harvest. She earned the respect of the Israelites with her cheerful attitude and hard work. Naomi's friends told her that Ruth was worth ten sons!

The gleaning law keeps self-respect intact for the recipient of the harvest. He/she works and receives payment for his/her labor. How simple.

The owner doesn't feel like he/she is being taken advantage of because his/her needs are met too. The field is clean and tidy. Real work is done.

## The Gleaning Law in Modern Times

Can this principle be applied today? I think so! Of course, it would be harder to apply in a society that loves filling out massive amounts of paperwork in triplicate, but it could be done.

The goal of gleaning is to build responsibility and a sense of accomplishment on the part of the poor person.

Some charities already use this principle by collecting used items from people, repairing them, and selling them in "Thrift" or "Second-hand" stores. Poor people work to repair and sell items.

Leftover food in grocery stores could be received by those who would be willing to stock shelves or sweep floors when the work day is over. Leftover food in restaurants could be received by those willing to wash dishes and help clean up the restaurant.

Torn or ripped clothing could be taken home by folks who would straighten clothing racks and sweep the floors.

Of course, farmers of all kinds could allow the poor to glean their fields.

Dumpster diving is illegal, but folks could put nice things out by the road a few days early for garbage pick-up with a sign, "Free." Free item tables at garage sales.

Well, the possibilities are endless and I hope you get the point. There are creative ways to show compassion to the poor while leaving their dignity intact.

# Economics in One Lesson Worksheet

## Chapter Nineteen

Is a wage really a price? Why?

What is the first thing that happens when a minimum wage law is passed?

How do minimum wage laws lead to higher prices for consumers and unemployment?

The best way to raise wages is to raise marginal labor productivity! How can you raise marginal labor productivity?

## Chapter Twenty

How do unions feel about workers' labor productivity?

What is the legitimate function of a union?

When do strikes stop being legitimate?

What are some delusions people have about unions?

How have unions hurt workers? How have they helped?

# *Communist Manifesto* Book Review

By Karl Marx and Frederic Engels

The authors believe that all of history is a struggle between two things. What are these two things?

What is capital?

Who do the authors say possess capital now?

Who should possess the capital? How will this be done?

List the Ten Things or Measures that Workers (Proletariat) can vote in to move their nation into communism without a struggle.

1.

2.

3.

4.

5.

6.

7.

8.

9.

10.

What is an industrial army?

What things do you see being implemented in the United States?

What do the authors think about people relating to God? Do they advocate a religion?

What is the final statement in the book?

What did you learn from reading this book?

# Monthly Consumer Price Index Project

This is an ongoing project for the duration of this class. You will have to go shopping once a month and record prices of each item. Once you choose an item, write it in on your monthly Consumer Price Index Project page. You will need to record the make, model, brand, and size—price the EXACT same item each month. You can go "shopping online." Go to the same store each month. This is a fun project and will provide interesting results at the end of the year.

## Durable Items

(These items are things that you purchase that have life spans of more than 1 year. Examples would be televisions, computers, refrigerators, radios, computers, calculators, washing machines, i-pods, shoes, clothing, chairs, beds, curtains, tables, blenders)

**Durable Item Shopping Bag for Month of** _____

| Durable Item | Store | Brand | Weight or Size | Color | Type/Model | Price |
|---|---|---|---|---|---|---|
| SLR Camera w Lens | Sam's | Nikon | 10 MP 3" LCK 3X Zoom SD/SDHC | | D3000 #23341 | $445.00 |
| | | | | | | |
| | | | | | | |
| | | | | | | |
| | | | | | | |
| | | | | | | |
| | | | | | | |
| | | | | | | |
| | | | | | | |
| | | | | | | |
| | | | | | | |

**Shopping Bag Cost for Durable Item =**

**Non-Durable Items for Month of** _____

# ECONOMICS, FINANCES, & BUSINESS COURSE

(These items are things that you purchase that have life spans of less than 1 year. Examples would be toothpaste, aluminum foil, food, drinks, make-up, gasoline, oil, nail polish, after shave, napkins, fast food, mouthwash, deodorant, candy, vitamins, medicine, contact solution)

**Non-Durable Item Shopping Bag**

| Durable Item | Store | Brand | Weight or Size | Color | Type/Model | Price |
|---|---|---|---|---|---|---|
| Wheat Thins | Target | Nabisco | 10 oz. | | Low-fat Salted | $2.00 |
| | | | | | | |
| | | | | | | |
| | | | | | | |
| | | | | | | |
| | | | | | | |
| | | | | | | |
| | | | | | | |
| | | | | | | |
| | | | | | | |
| | | | | | | |

**Shopping Bag Cost for Non-Durable Item =**

**Service Items for Month of** _____

(These are services your family purchases. Examples of services would be haircuts, oil changes, pedicures, lawn mowing, massage, car wash, doctor visit, dental visit, X-ray at hospital, ER visit, gym membership, lawyer consult, accountant consult, taxes, tutoring, college tuition)

Service Items Shopping Bag

| Durable Item | Store | Brand/Kind | Length of Time/Amount | Purpose | Type/Model | Price |
|---|---|---|---|---|---|---|
| Massage | Shear Bliss | | 1 hour | Relaxation | Deep Tissue | $85.00 |
| | | | | | | |
| | | | | | | |
| | | | | | | |
| | | | | | | |
| | | | | | | |
| | | | | | | |
| | | | | | | |
| | | | | | | |
| | | | | | | |
| | | | | | | |

**Shopping Bag Cost for Service Items =**

ECONOMICS, FINANCES, & BUSINESS COURSE

# November

Is the Government our Provider?

Is the Government our Provider? Worksheet

*Money Matters for Teens* Review

Production, Retail, Credit, & Debt

Production, Retail, Credit, & Debt Worksheet

Economic Biblical Principles Worksheet

*The Myth of Robber Barons* Review

Economics Speech

Personalized Consumer Price Index Project

# November Week One Class

☐ Share Noticeable Changes in the Personalized Consumer Price Index Activity

☐ First Economics Exam (See Resources Section of this book)

Notes from Class

ECONOMICS, FINANCES, & BUSINESS COURSE

# November Week One Home

☐ Read "Is Government Our Provider"

☐ Fill Out "Is Government Our Provider Worksheet"

☐ Read *Economics in One Lesson* chapters 21-22

☐ Fill Out "*Economics in One Lesson* chapters 21-22 Worksheet"

☐ Read *Principles Under Scrutiny* section on "Family"

☐ Write 11 Summary Paragraphs on Lessons on "Family" from *Principles Under Scrutiny*

# Is Government our Provider?

Many people really believe that government can solve problems and make life better for people. I am not one of those people. I don't believe that the Bible gives governments the responsibility or authority to provide and care for the medical and social needs of families and individuals who live in its nations.

The government cannot wipe out poverty? Do you know why?

Remember when I told you earlier that Jesus said that we would always have the poor with us. We should try to alleviate poverty, but realize that as long as we live in a fallen world, there will be terrible things like war, violence, crime, poverty, and power hungry leaders.

The other reason is that government was not given the responsibility to care for the poor. Government has the responsibility to govern—to make laws, enforce laws, and interact with other nations. When it does things beyond its scope of responsibility/authority from God, it will be unsuccessful.

The government that governs least, governs best. That's what our Founding Fathers like Washington, Jefferson, Adams, and Madison believed. They thought that freedom was the best environment to grow strong families, a strong economy, and a great nation.

Power corrupts and absolute power corrupts absolutely. The more power our government seizes or the more power we surrender to it, the more corrupt it will be. Power creates a hunger for more power. You cannot have the government provide for you without surrendering your freedom.

When we look to government as our provider, we sacrifice our freedom!

## Who Should Provide for Us?

The family is the first line of care, provision, and support, starting with the immediate family and moving out to the extended family.

The next in the line of care is the person's local church who can best help he/she to walk out whatever situation he/she finds himself in with love and wisdom.

Finally, private charities exist to help those whose needs cannot be met in the first two ways. The less people are taxed, the more money will be available to give to churches and other charitable organizations.

Ultimately, though, people and charities are not our providers and source of help either. God is our provider. He is our source of help.

Fasting and prayer is more effective than filling out forms to apply for welfare and food stamps. God promises to take care of us and provide all that we need.

## What God Promises to Provide!

"And my God will supply all your needs according to His riches in glory in Christ Jesus" (Philippians 4:19 NASB).

We all know that God promises to provide for us, to supply all our needs. But just what does that look like in our life? What needs is this verse talking about?

## What God Promises to Provide & The Concept of Profit

According to I Timothy 6:8, we are to be content with having food and clothing. Jesus also promises provision of food and clothing in Matthew 6:25-34 if we seek His Kingdom first. Food and clothing? We certainly need a lot more than that!

"What about housing, cars, cell phones, and vacations?" you ask.

That is extra blessing that is provided by surplus money, or what the Bible calls profit. God provides extras through your personal hard work. When it says that God supplies our needs, He is promising to provide food and clothing for us. Not that God is limited to only this provision. He also provides shelter, transportation, ways to communicate, and times of refreshing, but He is not limited by our definition of "what is best for us" or "what we really need." These things are most often the reward of hard work.

The only reason I bring this up is because I have seen God provide the need for shelter through hospitality. Family or friends open their home to a homeless family. Many times people have asked me why this happens, assuming that God promises that we will have our own home. I have not found that promise in Scripture, though I so often see God provide a home for His beloved people.

"In all labor there is profit, but mere talk leads only to poverty" (Proverbs 14:23 NASB).

God supplies our "extras" as payment for industriousness. This hard work is not only the work we do for a paycheck. God rewards elders financially for caring for God's flock, especially those who teach and preach (I Timothy 5:17). Running sound, ushering, teaching Sunday school, singing in the choir, and volunteering at a soup kitchen are all opportunities to work hard and receive a profit. Homemakers may not receive a paycheck, but they do receive a salary from the Lord, who rewards their labor!

Those who serve faithfully in their local church often receive "surprises" from the Lord such as gift cards, movie tickets, furniture, haircuts, used cars, or, even, vacations. God loves to bless us!

## Why Work is So Important

Many times when you see the people of God receiving miraculous provision, it is God's reward for their labor in His Kingdom. In fact, God values work as a means of provision, even for the basic necessities of life.

"For even when we were with you, we used to give you this order: 'If anyone is not willing to work, then he is not to eat" (II Thessalonians 3:10 NASB).

Why is hard work important to God? My grandfather always said, "Idle hands are the devil's workshop." Too much free time can lead to the pursuit of pleasure, harming our character. But working hard and receiving payment in the form of a check, or as a blessing from God, teaches us to value what we are given. We associate hard work with needs being met. There is no such thing as a free lunch. If we receive something for free, it is because someone somewhere worked hard and let their profit go to you.

I believe that God wants us to be grateful for everything we receive, understanding and appreciating the price that is paid. When we reward laziness with financial or material blessing, we harm the recipient of the gift. It would be better to imitate God, providing a job, however small or big.

## Provision for Kingdom Work

It has been my observation, over the years, that God provides all we need to faithfully fulfill all ministry obligations he has called us to. In our life, we have had supernatural provision so that we always have a home (our ministry involve large amounts of hospitality), bills paid, and a telephone (counseling is another big part!). A lady whose act of service is to drive people to church will see God miraculously provide for car repairs and gas. She may even receive free vehicles.

You see, God will provide for His work to be accomplished. He is very interested in seeing His agenda completed.

"Each one must do as he has purposed in his heart, not grudgingly or under compulsion, for God loves a cheerful giver. And God is able to make all grace abound to you, so that always having all sufficiency in everything, you may have an abundance for every good deed" (II Corinthians 9:7-8 NASB).

As we tithe, give, and work cheerfully to extend God's Kingdom, He will give us whatever is necessary to fulfill the ministry He has for us. Now, keep in mind, His plan may be different than our plan. Often we want to fulfill our own dreams, rather than take the path of service that He wants us to take.

God will supply our needs, and many times the "extras" too, especially whatever is necessary to fulfill ministry in His Kingdom.

# How God Provides

"And my God will supply all your needs according to His riches in glory in Christ Jesus" (Philippians 4:19 NASB).

We all know that God promises to provide for us, to meet all our needs. But just what does that look like in our life? How does He supply?

## God Provides through Paychecks

This is a "no-brain-er." The Lord allows us to have a job that pays us enough money to pay our bills. He also provides opportunities and ideas to bring in extra money through side jobs or starting our own business.

Remember that the Biblical work week is six days, sun-up to sun-down. Many times a second job is necessary to make ends meet, while still working less hours than the Scriptural work week!

## God Provides through Family

"Since we're here visiting, let me take you grocery shopping," my mom offered.

I swallowed back the tears that were springing to my eyes. We had little food left in the house and no money until the first of the month. My mom took me to Food Lion and filled the car with food, cleaning supplies, paper goods, toiletries, and special treats that we hadn't enjoyed since their last visit.

She also bought us clothing throughout Mike's seminary years. "I just couldn't resist," she would say with a grin. But we both knew the truth. Since when is a package of men's socks irresistible?

## God Provides through Birthday, Christmas, and other Celebrations

"There's not enough money to pay the rent, We're fifty dollars short," Tina moaned.

"I thought you just got a birthday check from your grandmother," I replied gently.

"But that's for me to spend on myself," Tina snapped.

"Tina, right now, that check is God's provision to pay your rent."

Why, in America do we get our priorities so out of order? It is not the time to buy frivolous things when we can't pay for necessities. If money is tight, use gift cards to buy groceries and toiletries. Ask for shampoo, body wash, and undergarments for birthday presents during difficult financial times.

## God Provides through Gifts

"A pretty lady with brown skin told me to give this to you," Katie Beth informed me, handing me an envelope that contained five one-hundred dollar bills. My toddler had been riding her tricycle outside while I was making dinner. It was a much needed and appreciated gift!

God provides through the generosity of His people to one another.

## God Provides through Divine Appointments

My niece, Kim, was staying with us, finances were lean, and it was her birthday. Our toddler, Katie Beth, Kim, and I prayed together that God would supernaturally provide for her birthday.

That day happened to be the Food Pantry day where we could buy one bag of food items for one dollar. Never before and never afterward did this occur. But, that day, I was able to pick up a cake mix and tub of frosting. Later that day, a friend arrived with a lawn trash bag filled with soft shell crab. Could they help us? They had just too many for their large family of seven to eat. Kim's favorite food? Soft shell crab. Is God amazing, or what?!

Bart suddenly found himself single and living in a studio apartment with his son. In an effort to win his wife's heart back, he gave her his paycheck and worked side jobs to pay his own rent. Where would they get furniture? Each day, another resident was getting rid of something (a couch, a dining room table, a bed, a dresser...). Did Bart want it? Yes, of course! Soon, his apartment was furnished—all because of divine appointments, just being in the right place at the right time.

## God Provides through Hospitality

When Mary and Steve needed a place to stay, another family in the church took them in for six months, giving them a spacious bedroom and attached bath while its occupant, their daughter, was on a missions trip to Israel.

This young couple and their two children would have been happier to have lived in their own apartment, but this was the way God chose to provide. It was a testimony to their family, confirming the Gospel message with love in action.

## God Provides through Miracles & Angels

Robert was needing to move his family out of the apartment where they were living, but he had nowhere to go. He was crying and for the first time in his life, he prayed. A few minutes later, he ran into a man in the parking lot who started a conversation with him. Learning that he needed a place to live, the man took him to an apartment complex nearby and provided first and last month's rent plus a security deposit. Robert signed the new lease in tears, dumbfounded.

"How are you going to move all your things over here?" the man asked, when they had returned to his family to tell them the good news.

Robert shrugged his shoulders sheepishly. He had no idea.

The stranger flagged a man in the parking lot with a truck, offering him money to move Roberts things to his new apartment.

A man Robert didn't know paid all the fees necessary to get Robert into a new apartment and paid to have his furniture moved. Robert never saw or heard from the stranger again.

I had the privilege, a year later, of leading this man to Christ. He is now part of our church family. Robert and I both wonder if the stranger was really an angel.

However God chooses to supply all your needs, He will lavishly provide with love. You are His beloved child. Just wait, and watch, and see the Lord bless you!

(Copyright Gospel Communications International, Inc - www.reverendfun.com )

ECONOMICS, FINANCES, & BUSINESS COURSE

# Is Government our Provider?

Who is our Provider?

What does God promise to Provide?

What does God Not Promise to Provide?

How does God Provide?

**The rest of the questions are from the "Social Justice vs. Personal Responsibility" section (pages 145-152)**

What is Gleaning?

How can it work in Modern Times?

Name different types of people who are considered unemployed.

Name people who do not work for a paycheck but are not considered unemployed.

What is Structural Unemployment?

Name some government programs that fight poverty and have a high success rate.

What is God's plan for taking care of the poor/unemployed?

Why is hard work so important in taking care of the poor?

# Economics in One Lesson Worksheet

## Chapter Twenty-one

What are functional prices?

What are functional wages?

What is wrong with the theory that the worker should receive enough to buy back the producti?

What is economic equilibrium?

## Chapter Twenty-two

In a free market economy, what role do profits play?

How are profits achieved?

How do profits reward, stimulate higher quality, and inspire innovation?

ECONOMICS, FINANCES, & BUSINESS COURSE

# 11 Summary Paragraphs

You will write eleven summary paragraphs based on the section on Family from *Principles Under Scrutiny* (also called *Using Your Money Wisely: Biblical Principles Under Scrutiny*) by Larry Burkett. These paragraphs are based on the eleven different areas of family finances that Mr. Burkett discusses in his book.

Just a reminder: your paragraph should have a topic sentence that is supported by the other sentences in the paragraph. Don't forget a concluding sentence.

**Husband-Wife Communication**

**What is the principle?**

**My Paragraph on Husband-Wife Communication:**

**Should Wives Work?**

**What is the principle?**

**My Paragraph on Should Wives Work?:**

**Financial Authority in the Home**

**What is the principle?**

**My Paragraph on Authority in the Home:**

ECONOMICS, FINANCES, & BUSINESS COURSE

**The Wife's Role in Business**

**What is the principle?**

**My Paragraph on Wife's Role in Business:**

**Disciplining Children**

**What is the principle?**

**My Paragraph on Disciplining Children:**

**Financial Discipline for Children**

What is the principle?

**My Paragraph on Financial Discipline for Children:**

**Symptoms of Financial Problems**

What is the principle?

**My Paragraph on Symptoms of Financial Problems:**

**Choosing the Right Vocation**

What is the principle?

**My Paragraph on Choosing the Right Vocation:**

**Keeping Christ in Christmas**

What is the principle?

**My Paragraph on Keeping Christ in Christmas:**

**Setting Goals**

**What is the principle?**

**My Paragraph on Setting Goals:**

**The Issue of Inheritance**

**What is the principle?**

**My Paragraph on The Issue of Inheritance:**

# November Week Two Class

☐ Go over Exam Answers

☐ Discuss Communist Manifesto

☐ Go over "Social Justice vs. Personal Responsibility" Worksheet

☐ Go Over "Is Government Our Provider?" Worksheet

Notes from Class

## November Week Two Home

☐ Read "Production, Retail, Credit, & Debt"

☐ Fill Out "Production, Retail, Credit, & Debt"

☐ Read *Economics in One Lesson* chapters 23-25

☐ Fill Out "*Economics in One Lesson* chapters 23-25 Worksheet"

☐ Optional: Read *Money Matters for Teens*

# Production, Retail, Credit, and Debt

When you hear about the economy, you usually hear about jobs and unemployment. Employment is an important economic factor. The ideal situation would be that everyone who wants a job has a job. Economists want to create favorable conditions so that the unemployment rate drops and those who want to work can work.

My dad used to tell this story about an American tourist visiting Communist Russia.

The tourist watched as two men worked together, making their way down the street. The first man dug a hole in the dirt and the second man shoveled all the dirt back into the hole.

Dumbfounded, the American tourist just had to ask in his best Russian, "What on earth are you doing?"

"We are planting trees," one man said.

"But the guy who sticks the tree in is sick today," the other added.

These men were working, but there was no production.

Economists like to look at production. Production is more important than employment. Production creates a need for employment.

## Production

Production is the process of growing, making, or packaging a service for distribution and sale.

Businesses get started because a man or woman decides to take a risk in the hope of making a profit. A man might start with an idea of a product or service that people will want to spend money on. He will organize his resources, gather money for start-up costs, and market his product or service. A successful company produces something that people want to purchase.

Farmers are business owners. They raise crops, animals, or animal products (like milk or wool) and sell them directly to consumers or to wholesale companies that sell them to consumers. A farmer might produce corn, wheat, milk, strawberries, or wool.

If a shepherd is raising sheep for their wool, then taking care of the sheep, shearing the sheep, spinning the wool, packaging the wool to sell to seamstresses or the public would all be part of production.

Some companies sell products that are produced in factories. Boxes of cereal, clothing, bars of soap, computers, televisions, cars, scrapbooks, wrapping paper, pens, and bottled water are all produced in factories, shipped to stores, and available for consumers to purchase. Cereal doesn't just climb into a box on its own. Boxes of cereal are produced.

It used to be that each automobile was made by one or two people working together on one vehicle at a time. Henry Ford wanted to produce a car in his factory that would be cheap enough for the average family to purchase. He built a factory and hired several workers. They made cars a new way! Mr. Ford created an assembly line that moved slowly past the workers. Each worker did their own unique job in putting the car together over and over. This allowed the process to go much faster. The Ford Model-T was made quickly and less expensively than other cars. Many families could purchase a car!

Henry had to buy a building and all the machines inside for his factory when he decided to start Ford Motor Company. He also had to hire workers. The workers, using the equipment, worked hard to put millions of car together.

Some companies offer a service. You might babysit neighbor children or mow lawns to earn extra money. A hair salon, gym, tutoring center, dentist, private school, and airline all offer a service from cutting hair to flying people to other countries. Just because they offer a service instead of a product doesn't mean they don't have start-up and production costs. A hair stylist will have to purchase a special chair, hair washing basin, scissors, hair dye, and other products necessary to take care of people's hair. An airline company will have to buy planes and hire pilots, flight attendants, ground crews, and ticket agents.

## Factors of Production

In order to produce goods and services that can be sold for revenue and profit, a company must purchase equipment and hire workers. This will cost the business money, but you have to spend money to make money.

Our shepherd will have to buy pastureland if he doesn't already own it and, of course, purchase the sheep. He will need to build a pen and buy equipment for shearing sheep. Of course, there is a lot more to raising sheep including vet bills, watering equipment, housing, and breed selection.

## Revenue

A company's revenue is how much money it brings in by selling their product or service. This amount of money does not include the cost of production.

Sally is a hair stylist. Sally's revenue for September was $5,000.00. She made that money on haircuts, shampoos, and coloring hair for clients.

## Cost of Production

The Total Cost of Production is all the costs incurred in the business of producing your product or service. This includes variable costs and fixed costs.

Fixed costs don't change much from month to month. This might be building rental, employee salaries, business insurance, and licensing fees.

Variable costs change each month. If you are mowing lawns with a gas mower, some months you will use more gasoline than other months.

Sally's cost of production was $2,000.00 for September. She paid $1,000.00 for rent and $500.00 for hair products. She also had to spend $500.00 on taxes, fees, and licenses.

## Profit

Profit is the money left over after production costs, but before taxes.

Sally's profit was $3,000.00. She still has to pay taxes.

## Wholesale

Some companies sell to other companies that sell products. A shepherd might sell his wool to a fabric company that would turn it into wool and sell it to a clothing manufacturer to make clothing out of the wool. The fabric company is a wholesale company. They sell to other companies.

## Retail

A retail company sells products to consumers, rather than other companies. They make their money selling products, often in a store. Lowes®, McDonald's®, Sears®, and WalMart® are all retail companies. They sell products in small quantities so they must sell a lot to make money.

## Capital to Start a Business

It takes money to start a company. Where does that money come from?

Mike and I started a lawn business when he was in seminary by using what was left in our savings account. It was scary, but we knew that investing our savings into lawn equipment would allow Mike to make a monthly income that would provide our needs.

Many business owners in the past worked hard to save money up to start their own businesses.

Scott wanted to start a business but needed more money. He asked some of his friends to purchase a part of his business (stocks) to to raise the needed capital for start-up costs. Four of his friends bought shares and became co-owners of Scott's business. They were taking a risk too. If Scott's business fails, they lose will their money too. If his business succeeds, they will share in the profits.

Many business owners allow investors to buy a portion of their company in the form of stocks.

Today it is popular to take out a loan to start a business. In fact the government offers loans to certain groups of people to help them start a business. It sounds like such a easy way to start a business, but let's not forget that God calls borrowing money foolish. That goes for businesses too.

## Credit

Credit is the ability of a person or company to receive goods or services before they are paid for, to borrow money. Many companies offer credit or use their credit line to borrow money.

## Debt

Debt is borrowing money. The Bible calls debt foolishness. Many companies operate with massive amounts of debt.

# Production, Retail, Credit, & Debt Worksheet

Which is more important: production or work?

What is the difference between wholesale and retail? Are some businesses both?

What is Credit?

What is Debt?

# Economics in One Lesson Worksheet

## Chapter Twenty-three

Why does money not equal real wealth?

What does increasing the quantity of money due to the purchasing power of each individual monetary unit?

How does an increase in the quantity of money raise prices?

Inflation may bring benefits for a short term to favored groups. What is wrong with that as an economic policy?

Why doesn't inflation affect everyone evenly?

How does inflation lead to debt?

## Chapter Twenty-four

Why is saving money in the best interest of an individual?

Why is saving money in the best interest of a nation?

Which brother has more fun: Alvin or Benjamin? Why?

Which brother has more money in the long run? Why?

What are some excuses people make for not saving?

Is there a fixed limit to the amount of new capital that can be absorbed? Explain.

# Chapter Twenty-five

Economics is a science of recognizing _____ consequences. It is also a science of seeing _____ consequences. It is the science of tracing the _____ of some proposed or existing policy not only on some _____ interest in the _____, but on the _____ interest in the _____.

Why is it important to look at long-range consequences when looking at economic policies?

Why do economic policies that work in a godly home work in a godly nation?

# Chapter Twenty-six

How many years later is this chapter written?

What examples does Henry Hazlitt give for the negative effects of disregarding his advice?

Can you think of any further examples in more recent times?

# Economic Biblical Principles Worksheet

List twenty Scriptures (write them out with address) relating to finances.

Define Contentment.

Locate and explain principle of contentment found in I Timothy chapter six.

Define Stewardship.

Locate four passages of Scripture (just give address) and explain principle of stewardship.

Give your personal theory of finances from a Christian perspective!

MEREDITH CURTIS

# *Money Matters for Teens* Review

by Larry Burkett with Marnie Wooding

According to this book, what does a steward look like?

How is money used in our world and why is it important?

What are some wrong attitudes we can have about money?

Why is financial planning important?

How is banking related to the Middle Ages order of knights called the Knights Templars?

How can you be wise in the way you spend your money?

How is diligence a "job keeper"?

Share one more thing you learned from reading this book.

# November Week Three Class

☐ Discuss "Production, Retail, Credit, & Debt" Worksheet

☐ Discuss "Economics in One Lesson chapters 21-25 Worksheet"

**Notes from Class**

# November Week Three Home

☐ Read Money Matters for Teens Workbook chapters 1 (Basics) & 2 (Banks)

☐ : Read *Myth of the Robber Barons*

☐ Fill Out "*Myth of the Robber Barons* Book Review"

ECONOMICS, FINANCES, & BUSINESS COURSE

# Myth of the Robber Barons Review

A short review on Myth of the Robber Barons by Forrest McDonald

**Vanderbilt**

Company founded?

Accomplishment?

Character?

Interesting tidbits?

**Hill**

Company founded?

Accomplishment?

Character?

Interesting tidbits?

**Scranton**

Company founded?

Accomplishment?

Character?

Interesting tidbits?

**Charles Schwab**

Company founded?

Accomplishment?

Character?

Interesting tidbits?

# ECONOMICS, FINANCES, & BUSINESS COURSE

**John D Rockefeller**

Company founded?

Accomplishment?

Character?

Interesting tidbits?

**Andrew Mellon**

Company founded?

Accomplishment?

Character?

Interesting tidbits?

## November Week Four Class

Happy Thanksgiving ☺

# November Week Four Home

☐ Read "Why Give a Speech on Ecnomics"

☐ Prepare Economic Speech

☐ Practice Economic Speech

☐ Complete "Monthly Consumer Price Index Project"

# Why Give a Speech on Economics

When I was a young woman, I was NOT interested in economics. It was confusing and boring to me. As I grew older, got married, had children, and started to mentor young women, I realized just what an important part money plays in our lives. The economy affects us. How we manage our family finances makes a big difference in our lives.

I learned something else too. Most of what you read in textbooks is confusing and hard to understand. There are very few good things to read to learn the basics about economics and personal finances. I discovered Larry Burkett's books and they helped me to understand more about what the Bible had to teach on finances and money. Reading the "Uncle Eric" books helped me to understand economic concepts that had been difficult for me to understand before.

My husband has had his own business for most of our married life. I had to learn about running a business because that's what our family does. We went through difficult times financially and we had to decide if we would apply for government money (we chose not to) or trust God to meet our needs. We have had many friends who have struggled financially and we have tried to help. Suddenly, Biblical principles are important because they involve my own budget, my close friends, or a neighbor across the street.

Now, I understand inflation, supply and demand, macroeconomics, socialism, capitalism, tithing, debt, accumulating wealth, investing wealth, giving to the poor, and government's role. When I share these things with others, they are so excited because many people find economics to be very confusing. It is much simpler than people realize. Many Christians don't even know that the Bible has A LOT to say about money!

It is the desire of my heart that you would be able to talk to people and help them to understand Biblical Economics. Giving a speech might feel awkward, but it will help you to communicate to others what you are learning. I hope that you will pass on to others what you learn in this course.

Think of all that we have talked about so far in this class. What topics interest you the most?

Which of those topics would you like to talk about?

Don't do a lot of research for this speech. Just go back over what you have already learned. What I want you to do is to share clearly and concisely on a topic that we have covered in this course so far.

Once you have your topic, ask yourself, "What do I want people to know about this topic? What is important for them to understand? Now, think about the audience who will be listening to your speech. What would they be interested in learning about the topic you have chosen?

What do they already know? Are there basic terms you will have to explain?

Remember when giving a speech or writing a paper, you do so with your audience in mind. You are serving your audience (or readers when you are writing). How can you serve your audience through this speech?

ECONOMICS, FINANCES, & BUSINESS COURSE

# My Economic Speech

**Title:**

Here is my Outline

**Introduction**

**First Point =**

**Second Point =**

**Third Point =**

**Fourth Point =** (you may not have a 4th point!)

**Conclusion**

# Monthly Consumer Price Index Project

This is an ongoing project for the duration of this class. You will have to go shopping once a month and record prices of each item. Once you choose an item, write it in on your monthly Consumer Price Index Project page. You will need to record the make, model, brand, and size—price the EXACT same item each month. You can go "shopping online." Go to the same store each month. This is a fun project and will provide interesting results at the end of the year.

## Durable Items

(These items are things that you purchase that have life spans of more than 1 year. Examples would be televisions, computers, refrigerators, radios, computers, calculators, washing machines, i-pods, shoes, clothing, chairs, beds, curtains, tables, blenders)

**Durable Item Shopping Bag for Month of** _____

| Durable Item | Store | Brand | Weight or Size | Color | Type/Model | Price |
|---|---|---|---|---|---|---|
| SLR Camera w Lens | Sam's | Nikon | 10 MP 3" LCK 3X Zoom SD/SDHC | | D3000 #23341 | $445.00 |
| | | | | | | |
| | | | | | | |
| | | | | | | |
| | | | | | | |
| | | | | | | |
| | | | | | | |
| | | | | | | |
| | | | | | | |
| | | | | | | |
| | | | | | | |

**Shopping Bag Cost for Durable Item =**

**Non-Durable Items for Month of** _____

(These items are things that you purchase that have life spans of less than 1 year. Examples would be toothpaste, aluminum foil, food, drinks, make-up, gasoline, oil, nail polish, after shave, napkins, fast food, mouthwash, deodorant, candy, vitamins, medicine, contact solution)

**Non-Durable Item Shopping Bag**

| Durable Item | Store | Brand | Weight or Size | Color | Type/Model | Price |
|---|---|---|---|---|---|---|
| Wheat Thins | Target | Nabisco | 10 oz. | | Low-fat Salted | $2.00 |
| | | | | | | |
| | | | | | | |
| | | | | | | |
| | | | | | | |
| | | | | | | |
| | | | | | | |
| | | | | | | |
| | | | | | | |
| | | | | | | |
| | | | | | | |

**Shopping Bag Cost for Non-Durable Item =**

### Service Items for Month of _____

(These are services your family purchases. Examples of services would be haircuts, oil changes, pedicures, lawn mowing, massage, car wash, doctor visit, dental visit, X-ray at hospital, ER visit, gym membership, lawyer consult, accountant consult, taxes, tutoring, college tuition)

Service Items Shopping Bag

| Durable Item | Store | Brand/Kind | Length of Time/Amount | Purpose | Type/Model | Price |
|---|---|---|---|---|---|---|
| Massage | Shear Bliss | | 1 hour | Relaxation | Deep Tissue | $85.00 |
| | | | | | | |
| | | | | | | |
| | | | | | | |
| | | | | | | |
| | | | | | | |
| | | | | | | |
| | | | | | | |
| | | | | | | |
| | | | | | | |
| | | | | | | |

**Shopping Bag Cost for Service Items =**

ECONOMICS, FINANCES, & BUSINESS COURSE

# December

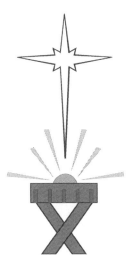

Buying Your First Home

Why It's Good To Pay Your Mortgage Off Early

A Banker's Confession Book Review

Essay: "Why It's Wise to Pay Your Mortgage Off Early"

Care Giving of Elderly, Funeral Arrangements, Making a Will

Care Giving, Funerals, Wills Worksheet

Book of Your Choice Review

Personal, Career, & Financial Security Review

Personal Consumer Price Index Project

# December Week One Class

☐ Discuss "Monthly Consumer Price Index Project"

☐ Give Economic Speech

☐ Discuss *The Myth of Robber Barons*

**Notes from Class**

# December Week One Home

☐ Read "Buying Your First Home" & "Why It's Good To pay Your Mortgage Off Early"

☐ Write Essay: "Why It's Wise to Pay Mortgage Off Early"

☐ Optional: Read *A Banker's Confession*

☐ Complete Money Matters for Teens Workbook chapters 3 (Checks) & 4 (Checking Accounts) & 5 (Budget I)

☐ Complete Money Matters for Teens Workbook chapters 3 (Checks) & 4 (Checking Accounts) & 5 (Budget I)

# Buying Your First Home

Buying a home can be a big step for anyone. Houses are very expensive and most people go into debt to buy a home. That debt is called a mortgage. Let's talk about that later. First, let's talk about finding and purchasing your first home.

## What Kind of Home Are You Looking for?

People purchase homes for a variety of reasons. Some want to own their own home as they raise a family. Others purchase a home as a financial investment and rent it out to others. Sometimes people buy a second home to use for vacations.

You will probably want to own your own home one day, so let's talk about searching for a home.

## What Is Out There?

With the internet, it is easy to sit back and house shop in your own family room. You can Google "Houses for sale" and add your zip code. Many homes for sale will probably pop up.

Now comes a reality check. You may find your dream home, but it is just too expensive. Be realistic about what you can afford.

Once you have looked around a bit and know what you are looking for, you might want to get a real estate agent. He will take you to visit all the homes you want to see and negotiate with the seller on your behalf. Most sellers will not consider your offer unless you are preapproved for a loan by a bank or can show evidence that you have the cash.

## Location, Location, Location

Location is the most important factor in pricing for homes. Certain neighborhoods will be more expensive while others with the same size homes will be cheaper. It is not just the idea of a "ritzy" neighborhood; you must also consider safety.

If you like a home, find out how safe the neighborhood is. You can call the police station and find out how many crimes are committed in the neighborhood you are looking at.

## Check Out the House Thoroughly

A bad water heater, a leaky roof, or a mold problem can turn your financial world upside down. Be careful about having the house checked out thoroughly. Hire an inspector and make sure that the seller fixes anything that needs to be fixed before you sign the paperwork.

## Look at All Expenses Before You Buy

Owning a home is not just about paying the mortgage each month. There are taxes and home insurance, as well as repairs and upkeep. Home owning is expensive. Make sure you are ready emotionally and financially for the responsibility.

## Purchasing a Home with Cash

Though it is very hard, some people save up money to buy a home with cash.

One way is to purchase the land first and to build the home on the land when you have enough money to build.

Some people use an inheritance to purchase a home debt-free.

## Mortgage

Most people go to the bank and get a loan. This loan, called a mortgage is often very long (15 or 30 years). The process of qualifying for a loan is intense.

If you are going to get a mortgage, I recommend putting at least 20% down when you purchase and paying your mortgage off early.

# Why It's Good to Pay Your Mortgage Off Early

Paying off your mortgage as quickly as possible is a wonderful idea. It is easy to do and the reward is years of interest payments wiped away and the joy of being debt-free.

## Joy

Having debt of any kind is a burden. People who have debt feel the pressure of it day after day. Being free of the debt is like being set free from a prison. There is joy in being debt-free.

## Security

Getting rid of your mortgage lowers your monthly expenses. If there is a financial disaster of any kind and you can't afford to make your payments, you won't lose your house.

## It Makes Financial Sense

The interest on a mortgage often doubles or triples the cost of the house for the buyer.

Often people hang on to their mortgages thinking that the tax breaks are worth the years of interest payments. Do the math. It doesn't add up. You save a lot more money by not paying years of interest than you do by getting small tax breaks. Once you finish paying off your mortgage, you have money in your hand that you can invest for the future.

Here's an example. If you have a $200,000 mortgage percent, you pay approximately 10% interest per years. If you make $70,000 a year, that $10,000 you are throwing away saves you only $2,500.00. You give four times the amount of money you save to the bank. And that is interest! Interest does not go toward the principle of your loan, or the real amount you owe.

Here is a mortgage calculator that will help you figure out how quickly you can pay off your mortgage. daveramsey.com/blog/mortgage-calculator/#/entry_form

# Economic Essay: "Why It's Wise to Pay a Mortgage off Early"

Here is my Outline

**Introduction**


**First Point =**


**Second Point =**


**Third Point =**


**Fourth Point =** (you may not have a 4th point!)


**Conclusion**

ECONOMICS, FINANCES, & BUSINESS COURSE

# December Week Two Class

☐ Discuss "Buying Your First Home"

☐ Discuss "Why It's Good To Pay Off Your Mortgage Early"

☐ Discuss *Money Matters for Teens* (chapters 3-5)

☐ Read "Why It's Wise to Pay Off Mortgage Early" Essays Aloud

**Notes from Class**

# December Week Two Home

☐ Read "Care of Elderly," "Funeral Arrangements," & "Making a Will"

☐ Fill Out "Care of Elderly, Funeral Arrangements, & Making a Will" Worksheet

☐ Read Money Matters for Teens Workbook chapters 6 (Budget) & 7 (Loans) & 8 (Credit Cards)

☐ Read Economics Book or Financial Management Book of Your Choice

☐ Complete "Book of Your Choice Book Review"

# Care Giving of Elderly

We will discuss care of elderly relatives, funeral arrangements, and making a will today. These next few topics can be unpleasant because death was not part of God's original plan—it is the result of sin. However, these issues are important and they affect us financially, as well as emotionally.

## Caring for the Elderly

We talked earlier about a family's responsibility to care for the needy within its own family first. When our parents and grandparents age, they need help with normal everyday activities that they used to do themselves. It is our privilege to serve them. In this way, we fulfill the law of Christ. It is not the government's responsibility to care for our family members, it is ours.

## Changes in the Elderly

As you grow older things change because the body is decaying. This happens because of what Adam and Eve did by sinning against God, bringing death into the world. Your body will decay too—yuck! But, we have heavenly bodies to look forward to that will never grow old! Isn't that great?

There are changes in the sensory system (sight, hearing, taste, touch, smell) and how they function in the elderly. Basically, the sensory receptors are less efficient and need higher levels of stimulation (louder voices, stronger light, more seasoning in food). The biggest problem with hearing and vision loss is that it can lead to a sense of isolation for these dear people.

Here are some of the visual changes that happen to the elderly.

- Acuity (sharpness)

- Farsightedness (need reading glasses)
- Color perception (greens, blues, and purples blur together)
- Decreased sensitivity to light (takes longer to adjust to a dark room or sudden bright light)
- Increased sensitivity to glare (shiny surfaces often produce glare for them)
- Possible Cataracts (lens gets cloudy and distorts vision—surgery will fix this!)
- Possible Glaucoma (high pressure on eye and optic nerve can lead to blindness—important for visits to eye doctor)
- Possible Macular Degeneration (cells in macula break down—lose central, but not peripheral vision)

Here are some ways to help older people with vision challenges.

- Use white paper with a dull finish and large black lettering
- Give them large print books
- Give them books on tape to listen to
- Use coding schemes (e.g. big colored dots at different places on the oven dial)
- Simplify visual field (remove clutter)
- Don't move anything in their world without telling them you have moved it
- Give pre-warnings when approaching
- Use touch to enhance communication
- When entering a new environment, explain people present and where they are located
- When walking, allow them to hold on to your arm just above the elbow and walk a half step ahead

Here are some of the changes the elderly experience in hearing.

- Sounds are more muffled
- High pitch sounds are distorted (harder to hear young children)
- Cannot make out words (words sound the same)

Here are some clues that an older person has difficulty hearing

- Accuses you of mumbling
- Talks very loudly or very softly
- Positions their head to hear better
- Asks speaker to repeat what has just been said
- Fails to respond
- Withdraws from social interaction
- Is distracted easily
- Is suspicious of others and what they are saying.

Here are some things that might help.

- Hearing aids
- Speak clearly in a moderate voice
- Get his/her attention before speaking
- Face person directly and at same level
- Use facial expressions, gestures, and objects to help you communicate
- Speak slowly and distinctly, but do not exaggerate with your lips
- Remove objects from your mouth when speaking (gum, food)
- Use longer pauses between sentences

- Decrease background noises
- Speak into their "good ear"
- Keep your voice at the same volume throughout a sentence
- My dad loved using "TV Ears" to watch television.

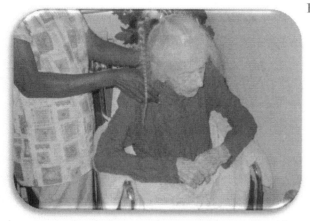

Elderly people also lose their sense of taste, smell, and touch. Realize that food won't taste or smell as good to them and it's not your cooking! Do everything you can to make food attractive and interesting. Find things that still taste and smell good; make them often.

Check up on them often, making sure they are not hurt…because they might cut or burn themselves and not realize it because of sensory loss.

Probably the hardest thing for older people to deal with is their loss of strength agility, and memory. Their minds and bodies simply won't do what they used to do. It is humiliating and frustrating. They can be grumpy, but it does not have anything to do with you.

## Helping Aging Parents

The best way to help aging parents (or other aging relatives) is to talk to them about aging before it happens. What are their wishes? Make plans, but realize that things change. We always thought Daddy would go first and Mom would come live with me because Daddy did NOT want to move back to Sanford. But Mom died first and Daddy moved back to Sanford. He did not want to live with us in our home, but, instead, chose an assisted living facility 2 minutes away. I was able to see him every day. Things turned out differently than we had planned.

One of the things that I regret was not staying in touch with my parents as much as I should have. I was busy raising five children, homeschooling, and being a pastor's wife. I would go months without talking to them. Before they died, I got into a habit of calling once a week. They looked forward to these calls and it was not hard to make it a habit.

Here are some things you can do to honor and be a blessing to your parents (and other aging relatives).

- Call once a week at the same time (older people love routine and this will be a highlight of their life!)
- Visit at least once or twice a year
- Write letters, notes, emails
- Foster a strong relationship between your parents and your children
- Focus on the good and forget the bad from the past—be thankful for your parents
- Remember them on birthdays, Mother's Day, Father's Day, St. Valentine's Day, Christmas
- Resolve any bitterness, ongoing quarrels, or battle of words

My parents needed my help just when my life was at its craziest and busiest. I had toddlers and teenagers, was homeschooling, and having medical problems of my own. It was hard to juggle everything, be faithful to my responsibilities at home, and honor my parents. I was honest with them when I couldn't do something and did my best to support them. I always tried to honor their decisions, even if I had a better plan. It was a privilege to care for them and I don't regret a single thing I did to help them at the end of their lives.

## What is Caregiving?

When older people need care, you move into a role of caregiver. The care needed can be simple or very complicated depending on health and mental faculties. Here are some of the tasks a caregiver might do.

- Making phone calls
- Shopping
- Managing financial and legal affairs
- Supervising medications
- Arranging for medical care
- Doctor visits
- Pharmacy visits
- Social outings
- Pushing/transporting wheelchairs/walkers/oxygen
- Listening, talking, providing emotional support
- Lifting/bathing/dressing/feeding
- Managing incontinence
- Supervision 24/7
- Supervise people who give direct care
- Traveling to and from his/her home
- Maintaining your home and his/her home

## When Caregiving is Stressful

Caregiving is stressful and causes some or all of the following:

- Emotional exhaustion and sadness
- Physical exhaustion
- Depression
- Marital problems
- Family problems
- Conflict between your life roles: spouse, parent, employee, caregiver
- Neglect of the older person

Here are some things to keep you sane.

- Pray and have people cover you in prayer
- Ask for and accept help from family and friends (be specific!)
- Set a realistic schedule and stick to it
- Take care of yourself physically (diet, exercise, sleep, down time)

## Caregiving from a Distance

This is so hard. I logged so many miles on my van driving back and forth from Lake Mary to Pembroke Pines. Then, when I moved Daddy to Sanford, my sister, Julie, was the long-distance caregiver. She handled all of Daddy's finances and I handled all of his physical and medical care. She flew down often and kept in touch with both Daddy and me.

Here are some tips for caregiving at a distance.

- Establish a network of people in your parent's world who will take care of them and keep in touch with you (relatives, church family, friends, neighbors, professionals)
- Lavish the local caregiver(s) with praise and thanks. You cannot appreciate them enough because the day-to-day is VERY hard! Bring gifts for them when you come to town
- Keep in touch with your parent as often as possible
- Be prepared to hop on a plane for emergencies (have your own world set up to do this)

## Coping with Death

I hate death! Jesus hates death too! In fact, Jesus hates death enough that He hung on a cross to conquer death. The Bible calls death our final enemy.

For the Christian, there is hope. Death for the Christian is falling asleep, only to wake up in the Presence of God. But, for those left behind, there is an ache and pain that we must live through. There are no shortcuts or pills that will make the pain go away.

When you lose someone you love, give yourself time to grieve. Do not be hard on yourself or put a time limit on your grief. Get plenty of rest, drink plenty of water, and surround yourself with people who are kind.

Pour your heart out to God who knows and understands our deepest emotions. Let Him carry you through this time.

## Comforting Those who Mourn

When you are in the place of comforting others, it can feel uncomfortable. You don't know what to say or how to make the person feel better. Relax. Everyone else feels the same way.

I will just share with you some simple ways to comfort those who are grieving.

Tell the person how much you love and care for him/her. Let them know that you are sad that they are hurting. Give affection and cry with him/her.

Offer to do something specific (Can I wash the dog? Can I clean the bathroom? Can I call the Funeral Home?)

Attend the funeral if you are invited. This means a lot to people who are grieving.

Bring food! Bring them dinner, snacks, frozen meals that can be used later on, and drinks. Arrange for meals to be brought over for 2 weeks, keeping in mind how many relatives will be there—provide enough for everyone.

Write a nice letter expressing your condolences and your appreciation of the person who died. Send a beautiful card. Send flowers, Worship CDs, Christian books, or other gifts.

# Funeral Arrangements

Most of the time, funeral arrangements are made right after someone we love has died. We are grieving, highly emotional, and have a difficult time making decisions. The most loving thing a person can do for their family is to make arrangements ahead of time or at least to have a plan. Whatever plans and arrangements are made, they need to be flexible. Here are the main things you need to decide for your own death.

- Deposition of your body (buried, vault, cremated and buried, cremated and ashes sprinkled, cremated and stay in urn with family
- Funeral and burial or Memorial service (any last wishes)
- Who will make the final arrangements (usually spouse or children)

Hopefully, your parents and grandparents have made arrangements, but, even if they have, there are always last minute things to do.

If you end up making the plans, be sure that you have emotional support—don't do this alone. A pastor, close friend, or mentor is a great person to have on hand for emotional support when you are making the arrangements. Realize that though the funeral director is being kind and solicitous, he is a salesman and might be trying to get you to spend more than you can afford. Taking someone stable along who will stop you from doing something foolish is a good idea.

## Special File Folder

Every person, married or single should keep a file folder that contains all information needed upon death. This should be easily found in case you die unexpectedly. Close friends and family members should know where it is. Your own folder should contain several items of personal information and legal information.

- Personal information: full name, address, length of residence, Social Security number, date and place of birth, father's name, mother's maiden name, marital status, full name of spouse, full name of each child (with addresses and phone numbers), schools attended with degrees received, honors received, career, employer, position held, favorite jobs, favorite hobbies, anything else that you think is important
- A letter of instruction about deposition of your body, funeral arrangements, and who will be in charge of making the arrangements
- Location of your will (most people keep their will in a safety deposit box)
- A copy of your will
- Names of friends and relatives you want informed of your death
- Location of important personal documents (birth certificate, baptismal certificate, Social Security card, marriage license, naturalization and citizenship papers, passport, discharge papers from armed services)
- Location of membership certificates in any lodges, fraternal organizations, or other societies
- Information about outstanding debts (including home mortgage)
- Location of Safe Deposit Box and keys to box
- List and location of life insurance policies—Include name of insured, policy number, amount, company, beneficiaries for each policy
- List of pension systems that may include death benefits (Social Security, Veterans Affairs, railroad)
- List and location of all bank accounts (checking and savings accounts), stocks, bonds, real estate, businesses, and other major property—you can make your accounts payable on death to your heirs so that they can receive that money without going through probate.

- List and names of various advisors in your life with addresses and phone numbers (Pastor, Lawyer, insurance agent, accountant, investment broker, financial consultant, banker, executor of the estate)
- Instructions concerned the running of your business
- An explanation of actions taken in your will, such as a disinheritance

## Planning a Funeral

Your loved one's body will be released to a funeral home who will await your instructions on what you wish done. Often they are attached to a cemetery where the body can be buried. There are four major expenses in the final good-bye.

- Funeral Home (professional staff, use of facilities, equipment, transportation of the body, casket or urn)
- Cemetery (or other method of disposition)
- Monuments and Markers
- Other (Honorarium for pastor, newspaper death notices, transportation, long-distance phone calls, telegrams, memorial folders, flowers)

The funeral director will often take care of applying for the death certificates—you will have to give him all the necessary information. You will need death certificates for many things after your loved one has died including filing for the life insurance benefit and closing out bank accounts.

Embalming is a process required if you are having an open-casket viewing, the body is crossing state lines to be buried, or death is due to a contagious disease.

Cosmetology is the use of make-up, arranging the hair, and dressing the body to look as presentable as possible. It is best to give the funeral home a picture of how your loved one looked in real life or you may end up with a loved one who looks completely different in the casket than you remember him/her.

Many times people will have a viewing and a funeral.

A viewing is an opportunity to see the body and pay your respects. Many times a viewing is private—just for the family. When my mother died so unexpectedly, I held a viewing because many of her family members and friends were in shock. It was an opportunity to say good-bye. When my father passed away, the viewing was a private one, just for the family.

The funeral is a religious service that can be held in the funeral home or at your church. Your loved one's pastor is the best one to conduct the service because he had a personal relationship with your loved one.

Many people leave plans for their funerals with songs they would like sung and Scriptures they would like read. My mother didn't leave me a list, but I remember things she had mentioned over the years. We sang her favorite songs and read her favorite Bible passages. We enjoy having a time for people to share funny or poignant things about the deceased. We also have a display of pictures and momentos to celebrate the life of our loved one.

It is nice to have a reception after the funeral for guests. Have good food, punch, and hot drinks. Greet people and thank them for coming.

## Planning a Cemetery Burial

Your loved one's body can be buried in the ground or in a vault. You would purchase a plot and a grave liner or a vault. You will also need a casket to bury the body in. A short graveside service (usually less than 20 minutes) is held at the grave site. This usually follows the funeral with a funeral procession going from the church to the cemetery (you may need to hire a police escort for this if there are lots of attendees). You also need to purchase a grave stone marker or memorial stone.

If your loved one is cremated, the ashes are put into an urn (which you purchase). The urn can be buried, just like a body is buried in a coffin, except with a smaller plot. Or, you can keep the urn in your home. Or, you can sprinkle the ashes at sea or at a place of your loved one's choosing.

## Planning a Memorial Service

Sometimes, no funeral or burial is planned because everything is handled privately by the family. In this case, you may consider a memorial service for the family and friends who were not able to participate but would like a chance to grieve and pay their respects.

A memorial service is just like a funeral but there is no body present. It can take place up to several months after a person has died, while a funeral takes place within a week or two.

## Financing a Funeral and Burial

My grandparents prepaid for their funeral, so there was little expense when they died. We had to pay for the reception after the funeral and an honorarium to the pastor who did the funeral and burial service. Funerals are very EXPENSIVE—be prepared for a shock. Here are the different ways to finance a funeral and burial

- Pre-paid
- Money set aside by deceased for funeral expenses
- Life insurance policy of deceased
- Money found in savings or checking account of deceased
- Family members and friends pitching in to cover costs

Do not go into debt for a funeral. It is tempting but don't do it. Pray, fast, and cry out to God for the money to bury a loved one.

# Wills & Trusts

## Why Should I Make a Will?

A will is a legal document that designates who your private property will go to after your death. If you have minor children, it will designate a legal guardian for your children. Most husbands and wives leave all their assets to one another and upon their spouses' death (or should they die together), all their assets go to their children.

If you die without a will, the state government where you live will decide who gets what. Often a married person with children's assets will be divided between the spouse and the children. A married person's assets might go to the spouse and the parents of the deceased. While a single person without children's assets could go to his/her parents and siblings. The government will take a cut too.

## Making a Will

Making a will is a very simple procedure. You can go to a lawyer who has done this many times and, for a nominal fee, he will take your information, write up a will, and have you sign it. Or, if your estate is fairly simple, you can write up your own will using a form from an office supply store or online. You simply fill in the blanks, sign it in front of a notary, and get it notarized. You now have a legal will.

Here are things to include in a will.

- Name your beneficiaries
- Name a guardian for your children
- Name an executor

Update your will as needed (new child, marriage, purchase of a home).

## Executing a Will

If you are named the executor of a will, your job is to carry out the terms and provisions of the will. You have many responsibilities and it is a lot of work. As executor of my father's will, I had a lawyer help me. Here are the responsibilities of an executor.

- Locate documents of deceased: wills, trusts, deeds
- Notify Social Security, Pension providers, annuity providers, and life insurance companies of death (will need death certificates)
- Initiate probate of the will
- Collect and inventory the assets of estate
- Collect debts owed to estate
- Pay off debts of estate
- Distribute assets to the beneficiaries of the will
- Close the estate

## What is a Trust ?

A trust is a special place where your property and assets go and are transformed into a brand new thing. This brand new thing (trust property) is not taxable, resists probate, and sits ready for your heirs to enjoy.

A trustee sets up the kind of trust that you need (there are many different kinds!) with a beneficiary and a trustee. The beneficiary will receive the trust property at a specified time, usually at your death. The trustee will manage your trust property. There are, of course, many legal rules regarding trusts. Please ask your lawyer to explain them.

The reason trusts exist to is protect inheritances for the next generation, though they can be used for other reasons.

# Care Giving, Funeral & Wills Worksheet

What are some changes as you age that are difficult for the elderly?

How can you respond with love to make life easier in spite of these challenges?

What do caregivers of the elderly do?

How can you help people who are grieving?

What are the 3 different services you could have for a deceased loved one?

What is embalming?

What is a will?

What is a trust?

What does an executor of a will do?

How is the cost of a funeral and burial paid for?

# Book of Your Choice Review

**Title:**

**Author:**

On a scale of 1 (low) to 10 (high), I rate this book a               .

This book is about….

Something new that I learned in this book is….

A great reminder in this book is…

Some things I can apply to my life from this book are…

One thing I don't agree with the author on is….

I would recommend this book to the following people:

Because…..

ECONOMICS, FINANCES, & BUSINESS COURSE

# December Week Three Class

☐ Discuss "Care Giving," "Funeral Arrangements," & "Making a Will"

☐ Share with Everyone about the Book of Your Choice

**Notes from Class**

# December Week Three & Four Home

- [ ] Read *Personal, Career, and Financial Security*

- [ ] Fill Out "*Personal, Career, and Financial Security* Book Review"

- [ ] Complete "Monthly Consumer Price Index Project"

# Personal, Career & Financial Security

A short review on Uncle Eric Talks about Personal, Career, and Financial Security by Richard J Maybury

What is Austrian Economics?

Why is having your own business a good idea?

What skills are necessary to be a successful business owner?

Where does our real personal, career and financial security come from?

What are some reasons that we have to trust the Lord rather than our abilities or the government? Use examples from the book!

# Monthly Consumer Price Index Project

This is an ongoing project for the duration of this class. You will have to go shopping once a month and record prices of each item. Once you choose an item, write it in on your monthly Consumer Price Index Project page. You will need to record the make, model, brand, and size—price the EXACT same item each month. You can go "shopping online." Go to the same store each month. This is a fun project and will provide interesting results at the end of the year.

## Durable Items

(These items are things that you purchase that have life spans of more than 1 year. Examples would be televisions, computers, refrigerators, radios, computers, calculators, washing machines, i-pods, shoes, clothing, chairs, beds, curtains, tables, blenders)

**Durable Item Shopping Bag for Month of** _____

| Durable Item | Store | Brand | Weight or Size | Color | Type/Model | Price |
|---|---|---|---|---|---|---|
| SLR Camera w Lens | Sam's | Nikon | 10 MP 3" LCK 3X Zoom SD/SDHC | | D3000 #23341 | $445.00 |
| | | | | | | |
| | | | | | | |
| | | | | | | |
| | | | | | | |
| | | | | | | |
| | | | | | | |
| | | | | | | |
| | | | | | | |
| | | | | | | |
| | | | | | | |

**Shopping Bag Cost for Durable Item =**


**Non-Durable Items for Month of** _____

# ECONOMICS, FINANCES, & BUSINESS COURSE

(These items are things that you purchase that have life spans of less than 1 year. Examples would be toothpaste, aluminum foil, food, drinks, make-up, gasoline, oil, nail polish, after shave, napkins, fast food, mouthwash, deodorant, candy, vitamins, medicine, contact solution)

**Non-Durable Item Shopping Bag**

| Durable Item | Store | Brand | Weight or Size | Color | Type/Model | Price |
|---|---|---|---|---|---|---|
| Wheat Thins | Target | Nabisco | 10 oz. | | Low-fat Salted | $2.00 |
| | | | | | | |
| | | | | | | |
| | | | | | | |
| | | | | | | |
| | | | | | | |
| | | | | | | |
| | | | | | | |
| | | | | | | |
| | | | | | | |
| | | | | | | |

**Shopping Bag Cost for Non-Durable Item =**

**Service Items for Month of** _____

(These are services your family purchases. Examples of services would be haircuts, oil changes, pedicures, lawn mowing, massage, car wash, doctor visit, dental visit, X-ray at hospital, ER visit, gym membership, lawyer consult, accountant consult, taxes, tutoring, college tuition)

Service Items Shopping Bag

| Durable Item | Store | Brand/Kind | Length of Time/Amount | Purpose | Type/Model | Price |
|---|---|---|---|---|---|---|
| Massage | Shear Bliss | | 1 hour | Relaxation | Deep Tissue | $85.00 |
| | | | | | | |
| | | | | | | |
| | | | | | | |
| | | | | | | |
| | | | | | | |
| | | | | | | |
| | | | | | | |
| | | | | | | |
| | | | | | | |
| | | | | | | |

**Shopping Bag Cost for Service Items =**

ECONOMICS, FINANCES, & BUSINESS COURSE

# January

Stocks, Bonds, & Mutual Funds

Insurance & Investing Worksheet

Investing $100,000.00

Insurance & Investing Worksheet

Advertising, Temptation, Being a Wise Consumer

Consumer Worksheet

Shopping with Mom's Grocery Money

Getting Your First Credit Card

Borrowing & Lending Worksheet

Renting Your First Apartment

*Rich Dad, Poor Dad* Review

Personalized Consumer Price Index Project

# January Week One Class

☐ Discuss *Personal, Career, & Financial Security*

☐ Discuss "Monthly Consumer Price Index Project"

☐ Discuss *Money Matters for Teens* chapters 6-8

Notes from Class

# January Week One Home

- [ ] Read "Stocks, Bonds & Mutual Funds"

- [ ] Invest $100,000 Dollars in Stock Market Game

- [ ] Read *Principles Under Scrutiny* section on "Insurance & Investing"

- [ ] Fill Out "Insurance & Investing Worksheet"

- [ ] Read *Money Matters for Teens* Workbook chapters 9 (Borrowing) & 10 (Giving) & 11 (Making Money with Money)

- [ ] Read *Rich Dad, Poor Dad*

# Stocks, Bonds, and Mutual Funds

Stocks, bonds and mutual funds made no sense to me until I was in my forties. I did own savings bonds and mutual funds but had no idea what they were. They were simply purchased by my parents or grandparents for me. When it came time to start investing for the future, I needed to understand these things a little better so that I could decide if these things were places that I want to invest my money.

To invest is to use your wealth to make more wealth. You can use cash (wealth) to purchase stocks, bonds, and mutual funds. Hopefully, they will go up in value. If they do go up in value, you will have made more wealth and a good investment!

## Stocks

Companies need capital to start up and expand. One way to raise capital is to sell shares of stock. When you purchase a share of stock, you own a part of that company. If a company does well, stock prices will go up and each share you own will be worth more money. Most companies also give their stock holders dividends. Instead of money, they give new shares of stocks. A 5% dividend would give stockholders one new share for every twenty shares they already own. Some companies are more generous than others. Coca-Cola (KO) has increased their dividends every year for fifty years.

A stockholder has a say in how the company is run. They can attend meetings and vote.

Historically, stocks have been a good investment, though they go through many ups and downs in their value. Of course, no stock is a safe bet. You can lose all your money if a company fails.

## Bonds

Buying a bond makes you a lender. Remember that borrowing is a curse and lending is a blessing in Deuteronomy 28. You can invest money by lending it to others who will pay you back with interest.

If you buy a government bond, you are lending money to the government, who will pay you back when the bond comes due (maturity date).

When you invest in bonds, the bond will have a face value (the amount of money being borrowed), a coupon rate or yield (the interest rate the borrower has to pay), and the maturity date (the deadline for paying the bond back).

Jenny Rose purchased a bond with a face value of $100.00, a yield of 10%, and a maturity date of 15 years. She will get an interest payment every six months for fifteen years and then get back the price she paid for it. So she will get her original money back plus all the interest payments she receives over 15 years.

Sounds great, right? Well, it can be great….if the purchaser pays the interest payments. Sometimes people default on their loan. If a bond has a good chance of not being paid back, it is called a **Junk Bond**.

## Mutual Funds

A mutual fund is a pool of money from many different investors that is invested together. Instead of buying stocks on your own, you get together with a bunch of people and purchase stocks together.

Professional money managers manage the mutual funds (for a fee) and, hopefully, make wise investment choices. Mutual funds are diversified so that you are investing in many different companies rather than just one. Mutual funds invest in stocks, bonds, money market funds, gold funds, real estate investments, and foreign stocks and bonds.

(Copyright Gospel Communications International, Inc - www.reverendfun.com )

# Invest $100,000.00 in Stock Market

This is very simple. You have $100,000.00 imaginary dollars (sorry, I'm not that rich!) that you are going to "invest." Choose your stocks. I want you to watch the stock market.

Go to E-trade to find out what costs are involved in purchasing stocks and bonds.

us.etrade.com/e/t/home

us.etrade.com/e/t/welcome/whychooseetrade/lowpricing

Choose what you will purchase (make sure you leave room for purchase price) and make a list of what you have purchased. Keep an eye on your stock. At the end of the year, we will find out if you lost money or made a profit.

Keep in mind that investing is done for the long haul, over decades, so don't be discouraged if you lose money!

I suggest doing this assignment online with virtual stock market games. You can play the Stock Market game online where you invest $100,000.00. It is fun and easy to use this website.

Our homeschool co-op loved this online stock game! It was easy to use and fun to play. My son loved the competition on state and national levels. It is just like playing the real stock market where you stock prices fluctuate according to the market. Of course, in this game, you are give $100,000.00 of play money to use. We played the game for three months.

Directions on the site are easy to understand and follow. Each student will need to make their own personal account.

Here is the website for the TD Bank WOW Zone Virtual Stock Market Game.

virtualstockmarket.tdbank.com/

# Insurance & Investing

A short review based on *Principles under Scrutiny* by Larry Burkett

What is a "Get Rich Quick" scheme? Give real life examples.

What areas in your heart do they appeal to?

Why should a Christian invest?

What are things a Christian husband/parent should invest for in the future?

What are things a Christian husband/parent should invest in?

Give two verses of Scripture to back up the idea of investing for the future.

Why is it so difficult to invest?

When would a Christian family NOT need insurance?

When would a Christian family NEED insurance?

ECONOMICS, FINANCES, & BUSINESS COURSE

# January Week Two Class

☐ Discuss Invested $100,000.00

☐ Discuss "Insurance & Investing"

☐ Discuss *Money Matters for Teen* chapters 7 & 8

**Notes from Class**

## January Week Two Home

☐ Read "Advertising, Temptation, & Being Wise Consumers"

☐ Fill Out "Consumer Worksheet"

☐ Shopping with Mom's Grocery Money Worksheet

☐ Read *Money Matters for Teens Workbook* chapters 12 (Spend) & 13 (Buy Car) & 14 (Pay for College)

☐ Read *Rich Dad, Poor Dad*

☐ Monitor Invested $100,000

# Advertising, Temptation, and Being Wise Consumers

One thing you see in a Free Market is advertising. In America, we are swamped with billboards, magazine ads, television commercials, and radio ads all trying to persuade us to buy a company's product.

## Marketing

To market a product or service, companies use advertising, name recognition, product placement, and customer satisfaction. To market is to present products or services to the consumers (people who buy stuff!) in a way that will make the consumers want to purchase the products or services.

If customers are happy with the product or service, they will tell other people, who will try it out too.

Name recognition is to paste the company name or logo all over the place so that the brand or company name is stuck in people's heads. When they see a Nike swoosh, the average American thinks, "Sports, victory, winners!" because Nike puts their logo everywhere (on billboards, workout suits, sports equipment).

A good example of product placement that I noticed was one year on the FOX television show, 24, Dell computers were everywhere. Anytime there was a scene with a computer, it was a Dell. Since 24 was a cool show, Dell must be a cool computer, right? That's the message anyway.

Advertizing can be seen, heard, or both on billboards, television, flyers, on the sides of buses, radio, magazines, newspapers, online, and through the mail.

## Methods of Advertizing

One way that companies try to get you to buy their product is to play up on your fears. You are afraid of growing old alone. Most single people are afraid of never finding their life mate. A toothpaste commercial will play on this fear by showing a man who cannot get women to notice him. But then, he uses Starglide toothpaste and instantly, women want to marry him.

Companies also appeal to your desires. You want to lose weight, get a promotion, fall in love, or live in a beautiful house. If you buy Carl's Cardboard Crackers, the commercial promises you will lose 20 pounds instantly—at least, that's what happens to Ethel on the commercial.

Association is a third method of getting you, the consumer, to buy a product. Do you notice that beautiful women are always hanging around cars and trucks in commercials? Hmmm....doesn't seem realistic to me. Of course, it's not. But men tend to be more interested in purchasing cars and trucks, so they plant beautiful women in ads. Now, a man seeing the ad will associate the beautiful woman with the truck he wants. It makes the truck a lot more appealing.

Outright deception is one more way businesses will use advertizing to get you to purchase what they are offering. "This diet pill will make you lose 20 pounds in 1 week," the ad promises. When you read the fine print, you see a different story. But most people will only read the bold headline, not the fine print.

## Temptation

Many times ads tempt us by appealing to our fleshly desires. Advertising can tempt us to sin by going in to debt or being unwise stewards of God's money (we purchase something God doesn't want us to buy). Or advertizing can tempt us to covet things we don't have or can't afford. It can also stir up greed in our hearts.

Lust of the flesh, lust of the eyes, and the pride of life, we are told in I John 2, are ways that we can be tempted to sin against God.

Lust of the flesh, or appetites, are things that we want to begin with. We are hungry or thirsty and we want something to eat or drink. We might want new clothes and see a sale flyer for Khol's. Suddenly, we are ready to go out and shop with our tithe money.

Lust of the eyes is a little different. We are tootling along in our life, content and happy in God when suddenly we see something (maybe in an advertisement) that catches our attention. When something appeals to us, we suddenly want it. I avoid going to the mall for this reason. When I go, I see things that I suddenly want or "need"—it is too tempting for me, so I just don't allow myself to be tempted. Please, don't think that it is wrong to go to the mall. For me, it is a place of temptation, so I avoid it.

The pride of life is anything that appeals to our vanity. We see something and think that it will make us impressive, better than others, smarter than others, or give us more power. We have to have it! Again, where is humility in that? God resists the proud, but gives grace to the humble. Who wants God resisting them? Not me!

Jesus overcame temptation with the Word of God. Read Matthew 3 and watch His showdown with the devil. Jesus won because He knew the Word of God and used it as a weapon. We may need to have our own set of "Advertizing Scriptures" that we memorize to combat temptation from ads. We don't need to give in to our flesh, but can be victorious in God no matter how many advertisements we come across!

## Education Disguised as Advertizing

I have a bachelor's degree in nursing, so I have taken many chemistry, biology, and anatomy courses. I have a good understanding of how the body works and how food and medication are digested chemically in our bodies. Many times I have listened to or read an "educational" piece on how an herb or food will affect your body. I sit back and listen amazed as people will share many "almost true, but not true facts" to sell a product. It will be disguised as a workshop, lecture, seminar, or infomercial, but the purpose is to sell a food item, medication, herb, exercise program, or book that will provide a "miracle."

Just because something is a class doesn't mean that its purpose is to educate—its purpose may be to sell.

At a homeschool convention, authors of books and curriculums will give workshops to teach how to use their curriculum or show why their curriculum is the best. What I appreciate is that they are very up front about it.

As a young homeschool mom, I had the privilege of being at one of Sue Dickson's first workshops introducing her wonderful Sing, Spell, Read, and Write phonics/reading program. She taught about teaching kids to read using phonics and showed how her program worked. I was sold! All my children learned to read using Sing, Spell, Read, and Write and I am a big fan. However, I realized as a wise consumer that the workshop I was attending was not purely educational—its purpose was to sell Sue's phonics program.

There is nothing wrong with doing a workshop to sell a book or product. But, you, as a consumer, need to realize what is happening. Don't assume the plan presented by the instructor is the only solution—God may have a different path for you to take. Be wise and wary.

## Wise Consumers

Wise consumers are not manipulated into purchasing things they do not need. Eskimos do not need air conditioning. You do not need the latest, the fastest, the newest, the best. Learn to be content. Spend time in prayer and thoughtful research before making purchases.

I drive my close friends crazy because I take so long to buy things, but the real reason is because I don't want to love stuff. I want to make sure that a purchase is God's will and not a fleshly desire. You can be a wise consumer too! Ask yourself the following questions when you are watching or looking at an ad, or attending a workshop.

- What product are they trying to get me to purchase?
- What method of selling are they using?
- Are they appealing to my flesh?
- How are they appealing to my flesh?
- What Scripture comes to mind?

Please collect some advertisements and discuss them with Mom (or in your homeschool co-op group). Analyze several ads until you are good at seeing through deception.

# Consumer Worksheet

What is the purpose of advertising?

What are methods a company will use in its advertizing to get you to buy its product?

How does a company try to disguise its advertising?

What ways can you use discernment in advertising?

When does it become unwise to go with the "bargain?"

Why should a Christian avoid debt?

How can a Christian avoid debt?

# Shopping with Mom's Grocery Money

It's one thing to talk about money and it's quite another thing to do it. If Mom is willing, make a grocery list with her and use her grocery money to shop. Try to find the best bargains you can. Does it save you money to use coupons or not? Be sure to check the sale papers and see what is on sale this week.

After you finish shopping with Mom's grocery money, answer the following questions.

What did you learn from this experience?

Were you able to find bargains?

What were these bargains?

What store did you shop in?

Did you notice anything about that store and their prices?

How is grocery shopping a challenge?

# January Week Three Class

☐ Discuss Invested $100,000.00

☐ Discuss "Advertizing," "Wise Consumer Choices," & "Shopping with Mom's Money"

☐ Discuss *Money Matters for Teens* chapter 12 & 13 & 14

☐ Analyze Commercials & Ads

Today you will analyze commercials and advertisements. Everyone should look on YouTube for commercials and in magazines and newspapers for ads and bring them to class time. Watch them and look at them together and try to discern the method used to lure customers to purchase the whatever is being sold. This is fun! Also be on the lookout for product placement in TV shows and movies.

**Notes from Class**

# January Week Three Home

- [ ] Read & Complete "Renting Your First Apartment Project"

- [ ] Read *Principles Under Scrutiny* section on "Borrowing & Lending"

- [ ] Fill Out "Borrowing & Lending Review"

- [ ] Read *Money Matters for Teens Workbook* chapters 15 (Get Job) & 16 (Keep Job) & 17 (World Changers)

- [ ] Read *Rich Dad, Poor Dad*

- [ ] Monitor Invested $100,000

# Renting Your First Apartment Project

Some teens can't wait to move out and rent their first apartment. You might end up renting an apartment if you go away to college. Are you hoping to rent an apartment one day?

## Benefits of a Godly Family

There are so many benefits of living with a godly family. You own family is the best idea. You can pay a little toward household expenses once you're working full-time and save up money for your own home. It's a lot easier to save money when you live at home.

A godly family helps to keep you grounded in the Lord and allows you to enjoy healthy relationships with people of all ages. Unfortunately, when you live in an apartment with other young people, there is often temptation to spend lots of time on entertainment and romance. These things, not evil things, can distract us from seeking God.

When my friend Seth was hired by Microsoft®, he moved across the country to start his job. Right away, he joined a church and built a friendship with a godly family. He rented a room from them, enjoying the benefits of living with a godly family and giving them some extra income.

Here are some skills you need to live on your own in an apartment. What skills do you possess right now (check them off) and what skills do you still need to acquire (circle them)?

- ☐ Live on a budget
- ☐ Save money for future expenses
- ☐ Write checks
- ☐ Balance a checkbook
- ☐ Do laundry
- ☐ Cook several different meals
- ☐ Pay bills promptly and in full
- ☐ Clean oven, refrigerator, and bathroom
- ☐ Clean sink drains
- ☐ Change lightbulbs
- ☐ Keep room clean
- ☐ Grocery shop/find bargains
- ☐ Shop for household needs
- ☐ Make doctor and dentist appointments
- ☐ Manage schedule
- ☐ Use a calendar

Now we are going to look in your area for an apartment to rent. Pretend you are moving out on your own, or with one roommate, to live in an apartment. Go driving with Mom, search online, or talk to friends to search for a place to live.

**Search online for an apartment complex.**

Name of Apartment Complex:

Address of Apartment Complex:

**Glue pictures of apartment here.**

Amenities at your Apartment Complex:

Closest Grocery Store:

How far from Church:

How far from your parents' home:

What is your floor plan like? Paste a copy here.

How much is rent each month? (Add to expenses chart at end of project) $ _____

How much is the security deposit? (Add to expenses chart at end of project) $ _____

What is the total down payment required? (Add to expenses chart at end of project) $ _____

Are there any other fees to get into the apartment? Pet deposits? Cable hook-up? Utilities hook-up? Water hook-up? (Add to expenses chart at end of project) $ _____

How much will it cost to get into your apartment? (Add to expenses chart at end of project) $ _____

Now, let's talk about phones, utilities and internet. You must pay for these things if you want them.

Will you have a home phone? If so, how much will that be a month, in addition to the hook-up fee? (Add to expenses chart at end of project) $ _____

Will you have a cell phone? What is the monthly cost of your plan? (Add to expenses chart at end of project) $ _____

How much will utilities run? (Add to expenses chart at end of project) $ _____

How much will water and sewage cost each month? (Add to expenses chart at end of project) $ _____

Will you have cable? How much will that cost each month? (Add to expenses chart at end of project) $ _____

Will you have internet? How much will that cost each month? (Add to expenses chart at end of project) $ _____

Will you drive your own car? How much will insurance cost each month? How much will that cost each month? (Add to expenses chart at end of project) $ _____

How much will gas cost? Or public transportation? How much will that cost each month? (Add to expenses chart at end of project) $ _____

Add up all these prices in your chart. How much will it cost you per month in bills? $ _____

**Now it's time to furnish the apartment**. Remember the apartment is empty. You will have to provide a bed, dresser, couch, chairs, TV, trash cans, and possibility a refrigerator. Go shopping and choose your furniture. Don't forget to write down how much everything costs.

Things I bought and how much they cost:

$ _____

$ _____

$ _____

$ _____

$ _____

$ _____

$ _____

$ _____ (total spent)

**Cut out pictures of your new furniture and glue here.**

Now, you will need to supply things for each room. Let's start with the **Living Room**. Here are some suggestions: bookshelf, mirror, coffee table, sofa, chairs, rugs, TV, throw pillows, trash can.

$ _____

$ _____

$ _____

$ _____

$ _____

$ _____

$ _____

$ _____

$ _____

$ _____

$ _____

$ _____

$ _____

$ _____ (total spent)

**Glue pictures of your living room purchases here.**

## ECONOMICS, FINANCES, & BUSINESS COURSE

Now, you will need to supply things for each room. Let's start with the **Patio**. Here are some suggestions: wicker furniture, plant stand, patio table and chairs, beach chairs.

$ _____

$ _____

$ _____

$ _____

$ _____

$ _____

$ _____

$ _____

$ _____

$ _____

$ _____

$ _____

$ _____

$ _____

$ _____ (total spent)

**Glue pictures of your patio purchases here.**

You will need to supply things for **Dining Room and Kitchen** too. Here are some suggestions: table, chairs, silverware, dishes, glasses, mugs pots, pans, placemats, tablecloths, napkins, blender, mixer, bread maker, coffee maker, teakettle, measuring cups, measuring spoons, food, cleaning supplies, paper goods, trashcan.

$ _____

$ _____

$ _____

$ _____

$ _____

$ _____

$ _____

$ _____

$ _____

$ _____

$ _____

$ _____

$ _____

$ _____ (total spent)

**Glue pictures of your dining room and kitchen purchases here.**

## ECONOMICS, FINANCES, & BUSINESS COURSE

It's time to purchase things for the **Bedroom**. Here are some suggestions: Bed, sheets, bedspread, pillows, dresser, full-length mirror, hangers, lamp, bookshelf, chair, trash can.

$ _____

$ _____

$ _____

$ _____

$ _____

$ _____

$ _____

$ _____

$ _____

$ _____

$ _____

$ _____

$ _____

$ _____

$ _____ (total spent)

**Glue pictures of your bedroom purchases here.**

Let's purchase things for the **Bathroom**. Here are some suggestions: brush, toothbrush, toothpaste, mouthwash, toilet paper, tissue, shower curtain, towels, washcloths, shampoo, conditioner, band-aides, first aid supplies, rugs, razors, soap, trashcan.

$ _____

$ _____

$ _____

$ _____

$ _____

$ _____

$ _____

$ _____

$ _____

$ _____

$ _____

$ _____

$ _____

$ _____

$ _____ (total spent)

**Glue pictures of your bathroom purchases here.**

Budget for Living in My Apartment

My Monthly Income is: _____

| Budget Category | Amount |
| --- | --- |
| Taxes | |
| Tithe | |
| Rent | |
| Utilities | |
| Water | |
| Phone/Cell Phone | |
| Internet/Cable | |
| Renter's Insurance | |
| Car Insurance | |
| Health Insurance | |
| Food | |
| Car Repair | |
| Saving for New Car | |
| Saving for House | |
| Books/Music/Gifts/Entertainment | |
| College Tuition? | |
| Other: | |

## Budget to Move into My Apartment

**Money Needed to Move Out:**

| Budget Category | Amount |
|---|---|
| First Month's Rent | |
| Last Month's Rent | |
| Security Deposit (& other fees) | |
| Packing Supplies | |
| Moving Truck Rental | |
| Pizza, Soda, & Donuts for Moving Helpers | |
| Pet Fee/Security | |
| Hook-up Fee for Cable/Internet | |
| Hook-up Fee for Electric | |
| Hook-up Fee for Water | |
| Hook-up Fee for Phone | |
| Purchase Furniture | |
| Purchase for LR | |
| Purchase for Patio | |
| Purchase for DR | |
| Purchase for BR | |
| Purchase for Bath | |
| Other: | |
| Total Expenses for Moving into my Apartment | |

ECONOMICS, FINANCES, & BUSINESS COURSE

# Borrowing & Lending Review

A short review based on *Principles under Scrutiny* by Larry Burkett

Should you ever co-sign a loan for someone near and dear to you, like Aunt Matilda or Brother Cody?

When is it WRONG to borrow money?

Is it ever okay, or necessary to borrow money?

What should be the mindset of paying off debt? Describe someone who is in the process of paying off debt? What would their lifestyle, spending habits be?

Should a Christian loan money to others? When? Give Scriptural reference.

Why is it better to give then to lend? What would be an alternative to both lending or giving to help someone out?

Give three Scriptures on borrowing and lending?

# January Week Four Class

☐ Discuss Invested $100,00.00

☐ Discuss "Getting Your First Credit Card"

☐ Discuss *Money Matters for Teens* chapters 15-17

☐ Analyze Commercials & Ads

Today you will analyze commercials and advertisements again this week. Everyone should look on YouTube for commercials and in magazines and newspapers for ads and bring them to class time. Watch them and look at them together and try to discern the method used to lure customers to purchase the whatever is being sold. This is fun! Talk about temptation this week. Do any of the ads tempt you? Why or why not?

**Notes from Class**

ECONOMICS, FINANCES, & BUSINESS COURSE

# January Week Four Home

☐ Read *Rich Dad, Poor Dad*

☐ Fill Out "*Rich Dad, Poor Dad* Book Review"

☐ Complete "Monthly Consumer Price Index Project"

# Rich Dad Poor Dad Book Review

A short review on *Rich Dad, Poor Dad* by Robert T. Kiyosaki

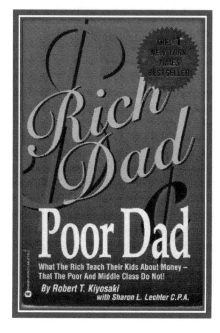

Who are Robert's "2 Dads"?

How are they so different from one another?

This book is not written from a Christian perspective. How can you tell?

What financial principles can you learn from this book?

What things would you like to do in your own life to apply these principles?

ECONOMICS, FINANCES, & BUSINESS COURSE

# Monthly Consumer Price Index Project

This is an ongoing project for the duration of this class. You will have to go shopping once a month and record prices of each item. Once you choose an item, write it in on your monthly Consumer Price Index Project page. You will need to record the make, model, brand, and size—price the EXACT same item each month. You can go "shopping online." Go to the same store each month. This is a fun project and will provide interesting results at the end of the year.

## Durable Items

(These items are things that you purchase that have life spans of more than 1 year. Examples would be televisions, computers, refrigerators, radios, computers, calculators, washing machines, i-pods, shoes, clothing, chairs, beds, curtains, tables, blenders)

**Durable Item Shopping Bag for Month of** _____

| Durable Item | Store | Brand | Weight or Size | Color | Type/Model | Price |
|---|---|---|---|---|---|---|
| SLR Camera w Lens | Sam's | Nikon | 10 MP 3" LCK 3X Zoom SD/SDHC | | D3000 #23341 | $445.00 |
| | | | | | | |
| | | | | | | |
| | | | | | | |
| | | | | | | |
| | | | | | | |
| | | | | | | |
| | | | | | | |
| | | | | | | |
| | | | | | | |
| | | | | | | |

**Shopping Bag Cost for Durable Item =**

**Non-Durable Items for Month of** _____

(These items are things that you purchase that have life spans of less than 1 year. Examples would be toothpaste, aluminum foil, food, drinks, make-up, gasoline, oil, nail polish, after shave, napkins, fast food, mouthwash, deodorant, candy, vitamins, medicine, contact solution)

**Non-Durable Item Shopping Bag**

| Durable Item | Store | Brand | Weight or Size | Color | Type/Model | Price |
|---|---|---|---|---|---|---|
| Wheat Thins | Target | Nabisco | 10 oz. | | Low-fat Salted | $2.00 |
| | | | | | | |
| | | | | | | |
| | | | | | | |
| | | | | | | |
| | | | | | | |
| | | | | | | |
| | | | | | | |
| | | | | | | |
| | | | | | | |
| | | | | | | |

**Shopping Bag Cost for Non-Durable Item =**

ECONOMICS, FINANCES, & BUSINESS COURSE

**Service Items for Month of** _____

(These are services your family purchases. Examples of services would be haircuts, oil changes, pedicures, lawn mowing, massage, car wash, doctor visit, dental visit, X-ray at hospital, ER visit, gym membership, lawyer consult, accountant consult, taxes, tutoring, college tuition)

Service Items Shopping Bag

| Durable Item | Store | Brand/Kind | Length of Time/Amount | Purpose | Type/Model | Price |
|---|---|---|---|---|---|---|
| Massage | Shear Bliss | | 1 hour | Relaxation | Deep Tissue | $85.00 |
| | | | | | | |
| | | | | | | |
| | | | | | | |
| | | | | | | |
| | | | | | | |
| | | | | | | |
| | | | | | | |
| | | | | | | |
| | | | | | | |
| | | | | | | |

**Shopping Bag Cost for Service Items =**

ECONOMICS, FINANCES, & BUSINESS COURSE

# February

Family Goals, Financial Records, Living Simply

Net Worth Worksheet

Saving Money

Living Within a Budget

Buying Your First Car

The Call On Your Life & How to Choose a Career

Apprenticeship, College, & Other Pathways to a Career

The College Question & How to Choose a Career

Career Exploration

College Majors & Careers

College Application Process & Going to College Debt-Free

Personal Mission Statement

Monthly Consumer Price Index Project

# February Week One Class

- [ ] Discuss Invested $100,000.00

- [ ] Discuss Monthly Consumer Price Index Project

- [ ] Discuss *Rich Dad, Poor Dad*

- [ ] Go Over Answers in *Money Matters for Teens Workbook*

- [ ] Share "Renting My First Apartment" Project

**Notes from Class**

# February Week One Home

- [ ] Read "Family Financial Goals" & "Family Financial Records & Files"

- [ ] Fill Out "Family Future Events" Worksheets

- [ ] Read "Your Net Worth" & "Living Simply" & "Living within a Budget"

- [ ] Fill Out "Our Net Worth" Worksheet

- [ ] Make a Financial Records File and a Net Worth File

- [ ] Make a List of Home Business Ideas

- [ ] Find and Read Blogs Online about Saving Money

- [ ] Complete "List of Ways to Save Money" Assignment

- [ ] Read "Buying Your First Car"

- [ ] Fill Out "Your First Car" Worksheet

# Family Financial Goals

We all have financial dreams. We might want to own a house or get a college education. We may imagine vacations in Europe or the Rocky Mountains. Everybody I know wants to be able to pay their bills on time and feed their families.

What is the difference between dreams and goals? Dreams are things that you want, but you don't really put any effort to making them happen. With goals, you think about what you want to accomplish and make a plan to make them happen.

Most Christians have financial dreams, but not financial goals, so they end up living paycheck to paycheck, in and out of debt, and full of frustration. Don't fall into that trap. Instead, be proactive!

# Goals

Financial goals come in three types: short-term, intermediate, and long-term. With short-term goals, you plan to attain them in one year. Taking a summer vacation could be a short-term goal. Intermediate goals are attained in two to five years. Saving for a new car might be an intermediate goal. Long-term goals are not attained for at least five years, but often longer. Saving for a comfortable retirement is a long-term goal, especially if you are only eighteen.

Before you start making family financial goals, you need to ask yourself the following questions.

- How does God want our family to live?
- How does God want our family to minister in His Kingdom?
- How does God want our family to minister in His local church?
- What career/calling does God have for each family member?
- What activities are important to us as a family?
- What do individual family members need?
- What do individual family members want?
- What financial resources are available to us?

Sit down with your family and discuss these things with the whole family. Ultimately, Dad will make final decisions with Mom's help, but it is good to get everyone's input.

Once you have an idea of God's will for your family, it is time to make goals and plans.

Here are some financial goals a typical family might have. (Talk with mom and dad. Circle all the dreams/goals that your family has on this list!)

- Tithe and give generously to the Lord
- Provide for daily living expenses, with a little left over to give to the needy and have fun
- Provide for the cost of having and raising children
- Establish a savings program
- Invest money and make a profit
- Set up an emergency fund (in case of job loss, injury, illness)
- Protect against financial risk
- Education
- Training for a career
- Purchase own home
- Plan for and make major purchases
- Budget for repairs
- Continuing education
- Save for kids to go to college
- Plan for and start family business

- Save for a comfortable retirement
- Invest and make a profit
- Avoid excessive taxation

Can you think of other family financial goals?

## Long-Range Goals

We always start with long-range goals because they can so easily become shoved aside ("When we have more money, we'll start saving for retirement"). We have to include these long-range goals in our planning, even though some are years away.

Most people should plan to save for retirement, purchasing a home, and education for self and children. These goals are expensive and take years of savings. Inheritances, tax refunds, and other one-time blessings of money should be put toward these goals, not spent on immediate desires such as computers, clothing, or vacations. Set money aside each month toward these goals and do NOT touch it, no matter what!

Long-range goals need plans to reach. These plans are incorporated into a budget.

Intermediate-Range Goals

These goals are usually things like trips, schooling, or replacing appliances and vehicles. They might be redecorating projects for your home, marriage, or adopting a child. You can open a separate savings account for short range goals or keep the money separated on paper, even though it is all in the account together.

Mike keeps a simple chart in our savings book that lists every category of savings we have (vacation, car repair, homeschooling curriculum, new car, appliance replacement, and more!). This way we keep track of our money in every category. It is easy to see if we can afford to take a vacation at a glance.

## Short-Range Goals

Short range goals can happen suddenly. Maybe the computer dies or the family is surprised to be expecting a baby. You have a window of nine months or less to save for the baby and as much time as your family can manage without a computer (not long in our house!). But short term goals can also be things like planting a large garden, buying homeschool curriculum for a new school year, or buying Christmas presents (expensive in our house because there are so many of us!).

## Can You Do It All?

Most of us will find that we cannot do it all. We need to pick and choose what is the most important to God and each of us. Our priorities will determine which financial goals come to pass.

Do not be discouraged by financial hard times. Keep plugging away at your goals. God has a way of coming through miraculously as long as we are diligent and persevere in our prayerfully made plans.

Meeting financial goals doesn't just happen by chance. It requires careful planning with budgeting and sticking to the budget you plan.

Turn your dreams into goals and budget those goals into reality!

# Future Events Requiring Planning & Money

List things that your family would like to do that will require money and planning. These are goals for your family—don't limit God!

40 Years


20 Years


10 Years


5 Years


3 Years


2 Years


1 Year


Now

ECONOMICS, FINANCES, & BUSINESS COURSE

# Future Events Requiring Planning & Money

List goals with the highest priority first and use more paper if you need to.

## Long Term Goals

| | Goals | Cost | Time | Action to take |
|---|---|---|---|---|
| 1. | Jimmy College | $50,000 | Fall 2016 | Job for Jim, Education IRAs |
| 2. | | | | |
| 3. | | | | |
| 4. | | | | |
| 5. | | | | |

## Intermediate Term Goals

| | Goals | Cost | Time | Action to take |
|---|---|---|---|---|
| 1. | New Washing Machine | $800 | June 2020 | Save $25 a month |
| 2. | | | | |
| 3. | | | | |
| 4. | | | | |
| 5. | | | | |

## Short Term Goals

| | Goals | Cost | Time | Action to take |
|---|---|---|---|---|
| 1. | Family Vacation | $1,200.00 | July 2018 | Save $, no fast food/movies |
| 2. | | | | |
| 3. | | | | |
| 4. | | | | |
| 5. | | | | |

# Family Financial Records

"Where is the title to the car?" Sally asked her husband.

"What? How should I know. It's your car," he answered gruffly.

"Well, you took it. Remember you were going to keep all our important papers together," she reminded him.

"Oh, yeah. What did I do with all that stuff…."


Financial and legal documents are important to be able to get to when you need them. How about bank account numbers, repair records of work done on your car, or birth certificates—do you know where they are?

My answer to everything administrative is to make a folder. I am a great believer in file folders. I keep manuscripts, passports, lesson plans, receipts, directions, and manuals in file folders. I have several file cabinets in my house and highly recommend a good filing system to keep track of important papers and records. Some things should be stored in a safety deposit box or home safe.

## Storage

Store your files in a file cabinet or tote. You can purchase a used filing cabinet at a thrift store or garage sale. Be on the lookout. The filing cabinet in my homeschool room is painted a pretty shade of blue. It was a garage sale find.

## Filing System

Group your folders in sections (temporary/annual, permanent, personal records, and dead storage). Each section will have its own folders.

No matter what kind of system you use, make sure that there is someone else besides yourself who understands it!

Dead storage folders can be packed away in a totes and put in the garage, basement, or attic. What would you save in dead storage? Well, tax returns should be saved for 7 years, but you only need the last year or two for help doing this year's taxes, unless you are audited. Tax returns and paperwork can go in dead storage. Anything else that you really don't need to get to, but feel uncomfortable to get rid of. We keep old business records in dead storage.

## Storing Permanent Records

Most permanent records should be stored in a home safe or safety deposit box at a bank. But that is your decision.

Permanent records are needed at various times in your life and at your death. Here are some of the records you should keep together in a folder, safe, or safety deposit box.

- Adoption papers
- Baptismal records
- Birth certificates

- Marriage license
- Divorce decree
- Citizenship papers
- Child custody/Support papers
- Copyright/Patents
- Military records
- Household inventories
- Passports
- Power-of-Attorney
- Records of inheritances received
- Wills/Living trusts

## Safety Deposit Box or Home Safe

If you store personal records and other valuables in a home safe or your safety deposit box at a bank, keep a folder (store with your permanent files) that lists everything in this box or safe.

Valuables are often kept in a safe or safety deposit box. Here a list of things that are considered valuable.

- Gold
- Silver
- Stock certificates
- Mutual fund certificates
- Bonds
- Family loans
- Heirloom jewelry
- Real estate titles/Deeds
- Vehicle titles
- Valuable coins
- Valuable collections (stamps, baseball cards)
- Registration numbers of valuable equipment (guns)

## Personal Permanent Files

These files are not used often, but need to be accessible. There are several categories of personal permanent files: medical, property, financial, employment/business, retirement, miscellaneous. I will just list some of the things you need to keep filed away where they can be accessible. Files folders are a great way to keep track of all of these things.

### Medical Files

- Family medical history
- Immunization record
- Prescription records
- Hospitalizations
- Allergies
- Names and addresses of doctors
- Names and addresses of dentists

- Dental records
- Health insurance policy booklet
- Pets

**Property: Home**

- Home Appraisal
- Homeowner's insurance policy
- Home improvements
- Well and septic tank location
- Mortgage papers
- Prior home owner's papers
- Lease agreement (if renting)

**Property: Each Vehicle**

- Service record
- Insurance policy
- Owner's manual and key codes
- Loans/Leases (hopefully NONE!)
- Service contract
- Warranties

**Property: Investments (earnings reports)**

- Annuities
- Bonds
- Stocks
- Mutual funds
- IRAs/Keogh
- Life Insurance Policies
- Savings Accounts
- Certificates of Deposit
- Real Estate

**Property: Household Goods (include receipts, use and care booklets and warranties)**

- Inventory of household goods for insurance
- Large kitchen appliances and equipment
- Small kitchen appliances
- Laundry equipment
- Personal care equipment
- Heating and air-conditioning
- Lighting and lamps
- Cookware/Dishes/Silver
- Furniture
- Cleaning equipment
- Entertainment/communication
- Accessories/Art

**Property: Other Equipment Headings**

- Outdoor/Gardening equipment
- Power tools
- Hand tools
- Firearms

**Employments, Retirement, and Military Records**

- Resumes/Dossiers
- Military/Veterans
- Salary/promotion
- Social Security earnings
- Pensions
- Retirement/Sick leave
- Transcripts/Diplomas
- Academic achievement/School records

**Financial Records**

- Net worth statement
- Checking account statements/balanced and unbalanced
- Credit card contracts
- Loan contracts
- Credit card numbers and notification requirements
- Miscellaneous
- Safety deposit box or home safe inventory
- Wallet inventory
- Copy of will/living trust
- Valuable papers inventory
- Burial agreements
- Letter of last instruction
- Genealogy records
- Copy of other people's wills

# Temporary or Annual Files

These files are used often. They are the files you use for records that accumulate or transactions that occur during the current year. At the end of the year, many of these files should be saved and added to your permanent files.

- Payroll check statements
- Wage/salary records
- Other income (Social Security, pensions, rental property, interest)
- Cancelled checks
- Bank statements and deposit slips
- Passbook Savings accounts
- Paid receipts
- Budget & expenditures

- Cars/Vehicles
- Tax information for current year
- Your Net Worth

We have learned how to set up and store our financial records. Now let's talk about cutting costs in running a household. How can we live frugally so that we have money left over to save and invest?

# Living Simply

## Living Below Your Mean

Is this an impossible dream or can people on less-than-desirable incomes live below their means? This is an important concept to address because it is one of the secrets to financial success, along with seeking the Kingdom first and delaying gratification.

If you are living beyond your means, you have accumulated debt because you are spending more than you earn. If you have debt, becoming debt free will necessitate you living below your means and using the extra money to pay off debt. It always costs more money to be in debt, so get rid of the debt and begin to live below your means.

"Well, we live within our means," you might say. "We have no debts, but we have a hard time saving any money." That is a good step toward the goal of living below your means, but it isn't good enough. You see, if you are living within your means, you have nothing saved up for your retirement and nothing left over to give away (I'm not talking about tithing--that should be done first!).

To live in financial freedom, we must learn to live below our income. The extra money we find can go to our savings account for future purchases and investments. The eventual goal for the Christian is to be dependent on no one, but to pull our own weight, financially and otherwise. We also want to be able to give to the poor.

"Bear one another's burdens, and thereby fulfill the law of Christ. If anyone thinks he is something when he is nothing, he deceives himself. But each one must examine his own work, and then he will have reason for boasting in regard to himself along, and not in regard to another. For each one will bear his own load" (Galatians 6:2-5 NASB).

Though we are to have compassion and help one another, it should be our goal to carry our own load, not rely on others, but trust God to provide for us as we work very hard. Hard work is God's plan to provide for our daily needs like food, clothing, and shelter. It may not be God's will for us to have a brand new car, the latest technological gadget, or a weekly pedicure (Gasp!). As we make the choice to live below our means, we need to put aside every excuse that is rising to our minds as we ponder living below our means.

Let's just be honest with ourselves. You and I do not have an income problem, we have a spending problem. If you are monitoring your spending, you are probably seeing that the little things we spend money on (like going through a drive-through or impulse items in the check-out lane) add up.

Make a list of all the things you spend your money on that are not absolute necessities. Don't worry, I'm not suggesting you stop all of that spending and live like a monk. What I am suggesting is that after you make that list, you lay your hands on it and pray. Ask God to show you what things you should stop spending money on so that you can live below your income. Pray for wisdom and self-control--wisdom to know what to cut out of your spending and the self-control to do it.

See saving money and spending less money as a challenge. It can be fun to cut back on spending and see a savings account grow. It might be good to cancel the Net Flix® account for a few months and dust off the old books. Maybe you could read them aloud together as a family while you munch on popcorn or chocolate chip cookies. This doesn't have to be permanent, but look for opportunities to sit back and observe. I can guarantee you that if you heart is to honor God with your finances and you take this challenge to live below your income seriously so that you can grow as a disciple of Jesus in the area of money management, then the Lord will do amazing things on your behalf. His heart is to bless you! Remember, in an earlier article, I mentioned that we spend on ourselves because we really don't believe that God wants to bless us because we are precious to Him?

Why not try this out for six months. Make whatever sacrifice you need to make so that you can live below your means. Keep God in the picture from beginning to end, praying and committing your way to Him. See if He doesn't surprise you with His goodness and the new self-discipline in your life.

I can't wait to hear your testimonies.

## Stop Spending Money on Yourself

There is one person in our life that we seem to spend lots of money on. Sometimes we don't even realize how much money we spend on her/him. We don't like to think of ourselves spending so much on that person, but we do. If you want to grow in godliness, stop spending so much money on yourself! There, I said it.

Without realizing it, we think about things we want and need, laying our plans to purchase these things now or later. We are bombarded with messages from advertising on television, at the movies, in the mall, in the newspaper, on billboards when we drive, and from the people we love who know exactly what we "need." Somehow our minds get wrapped around the idea that buying lots of stuff will make us happy, take away the pain in our lives, help us to become more organized, or help people to love us more. We know, of course, that stuff won't make us happy, but we are bombarded with the lie so often that we start to believe it.

We each have a secret stuff area. That is the area where we really believe that purchasing items of that kind will make us happy. My secret stuff area is shoes...it is just amazing how quickly a new pair of shoes can brighten up my day. Flowers, chocolate, clothes, music, CDs, DVDs, jewelry, electronic equipment, bling, designer purses, software, or accessories might be your secret stuff area. Maybe it is not so secret. Maybe it is more than one area...you just love to buy stuff for yourself.

We kid ourselves into thinking that the money we spend is all on others, but if you are honest and list everything you spend, you will find that you purchase all kinds of things for yourself. You might buy snacks, drinks, new clothes, comfort foods, music, books, or accessories on impulse when you are out shopping for the family or running errands. We don't think about it, but it adds up.

The money we spend on ourselves isn't the most important thing, but rather the preoccupation with making ourselves happy and feeding our appetites. Greed, the desire for more stuff, is an appetite. When we feed it with little snacks (a bag of Combos or a bestseller at the check-out line), we are feeding the appetite of greed.

What do we really need? How much do we really need? Can we wait to purchase this item later? How much more stuff does God really want us to have?

I'm not trying to sound harsh, but spending money on ourselves reveals the self-centered nature that is needing to be sanctified by the Holy Spirit. Another thing that reveals this selfish attitude is how unhappy we become when we cannot have what we want because our finances are tight. Is this really how a Christian should live and manage his/her money? How we spend our money reveals our heart and our priorities.

Examine this area of your life ruthlessly. Do you spend money on yourself? It may not be a lot of money, but is it often? Is there an aching need in your life that you are trying to meet with stuff? Is there pain in your life that you are trying to numb with shopping for things that you could live without?

"But godliness with contentment is great gain. For we brought nothing into the world, and we can take nothing out of it. But if we have food and clothing, we will be content with that," I Timothy 6:6-8 NIV.

Is contentment impossible in our culture? It just might be! There is such a pull on us to want stuff. But, if we are godly, we will be content with food and clothing alone. Wow! That doesn't even include shelter. Ouch, I feel convicted. I do want to be content and godly. What is it that wages war against contentment, so that we must indulge ourselves?

In trying to figure out why Christians spend so much money on themselves, I have become convinced that they honestly don't understand the love of God. When we know how much Jesus loves us and how He delights to bless us, we don't have to bless ourselves, we can wait and let God do it. There is such a hunger inside every man, woman, and child to be loved. We try every kind of substitute that exists, only to find they are all fakes. Only God's love completely satisfies. Only His good and perfect gifts come without strings attached that cause turmoil and heartache.

"Therefore, consider the members of your earthly body as dead to immorality, impurity, passion, evil desires and greed, which amounts to idolatry" (Colossians 3:5 NASB).

This verse teaches that greed is idolatry, not a big surprise, since it can be a substitute for experiencing God's love. This puts spending money on yourself in a more serious light, though. Consider carefully your ways and heart attitude in this area.

So, stop feeding the appetite of greed and start meditating on God's love for you. It will change your spending habits!

## Ways to Save Money

- Buy quality—it will last longer
- Barter/trade goods and services
- Use car less
- Fix simple nutritious meals
- Plant a garden
- Live without disposable items
- Mend clothing
- Recycle clothing
- Refinish basement or remodel garage for more living space
- Turn off lights when leaving the room
- Don't waste food
- Drink water instead of soda
- Shop as few times as possible

- Plan menu for a month
- Plan to use leftovers
- Take shorter showers
- Repair things when they break
- Make gifts

Can you think of any more ways to save money?

# Living within a Budget

You have filled out a budget in the teen workbook. It is one thing to fill out a budget and another thing to stay on that budget.

Mike and I have made many budgets for our family finances since 1984 when we got married. Some of our budgets just weren't practical. We can put down $100.00 for utilities, but if every month the bill is over $200.00, the budget is not practical.

The first step in making a budget is to figure out how much you spend right now.

## Put It on Paper

You probably find yourself spending money on drinks, food, clothing, cards, presents, movies, and downloads that you hadn't planned on spending. Even little things like drinks from a vending machine add up over time.

For two weeks, write down everything you spend. For a married couple, both husband and wife must do this. Write down everything.

Next, go over your bills for the last two years to find the average monthly amount. You will need to budget a little higher than this amount.

## Time to Pray

God cares about your finances. Lift up your list to Him and ask Him to both provide and prune. If you do not enough money coming in each month, ask for miraculous provision. Also seek Him to show you what you can do without or show you a realistic substitute.

If you pray for rain, you should get out your umbrella. If you pray for extra provision, you should be on the lookout for coupons, free items from friends, money gifts for birthdays, and all kinds of amazing ways that God provides. He is so good.

Ask God what the numbers on the budget should be. Sit down in a peaceful moment in a quiet room to work on your budget. If you are married, you will need to make your budget together.

Make Three Budgets

We always make three budgets: a bare bones budget, a realistic budget, and an ideal budget.

Our bare bones budget is for emergencies. We might lose a business account or get laid off. What do we just need to survive? You cannot last long on this budget. It is for emergencies. We might have to skip the entertainment, car repair, and clothing part of the budget on the bare bones. But, eventually the car will need an oil change or repair. In time, clothing will need to be replaced. This is in place for emergencies.

Our realistic budget includes everything we need for real living and is based on our income. We can only budget what we have money for. This budget needs to include tithe, taxes, bills, household expenses, insurance, food, clothing, gas, and entertainment. It must also include short-term savings for car repairs, appliance replacement, purchasing new cars, vacations, birthdays, and holidays, as well as long-term savings for retirement, purchasing a new home, and college tuition.

Often when we fill in our realistic budget, we realize that it falls short because we don't have enough income for some of the savings even after we have cut back on other things. We make an ideal budget and pray for the Lord to bring in extra money. Whenever extra money comes in, it goes to that budget. If we get an inheritance or large tax return, it goes toward the idealistic budget.

Many times God will increase our income as we pray over the idealistic budget.

## Get Rid of the Credit Card

Make up your mind to use cash only. When the cash is gone, you stop spending. If you have a credit card, I would cut it up. Or you can freeze it in the back of the freezer. To use it, you have to thaw it, so you will think twice about putting something on the credit card.

If you have credit card debt, pay it off. There is nothing that makes a budget bleed more than paying credit card debt each month.

## Pinch a Bit

Live as frugally as possible, avoiding the temptations of advertizing and keeping up with all the new gadgets friends have. A used car will get you where you need to go just as well as a fancy new car. Think in terms of what you really need and saving money wherever you can.

Wealthy people often are very frugal. They have been able to put money aside a little at a time and invest that money to make more money.

## Give It Away

God blesses generous givers. Don't be a hoarder or stingy. If you can't give money away, then give away stuff you don't need or use any more. You can bless someone else while positioning yourself for God's blessing. You can't out-give God!

## Evaluate Regularly

A budget should be evaluated regularly. Evaluate often when you are first getting used to living on a budget (once a week or once a month) and after you are faithful, take another look at your budget every year. Sometimes you can stay on the same budget and other times, you will have to tweak it.

Living on a budget is an adventure. It cultivates discipline in our lives. I challenge you to try living on a budget for a year and see the difference it can make in your finances.

# Bartering

Mary's parents bought her a new washing machine, even though the old one worked fine. What she really needed was shoes and clothing for her children. Betsy desperately needed a washing machine that was reliable and she had an abundance of clothing and shoes in good condition that would fit Mary's children. Mary traded her old washing machine for "gently-used" clothing and shoes for her children.

Sarah needed help with her taxes. Laura needed her hair cut, colored, and styled, but could not afford it. They decided to trade! Mike needed some work done on his car that he didn't have the time or ability to do. Tim needed help updating his resume because he was out of work and looking for a job. Mike's wife, Maggie, updated Tim's resume for him and Tim fixed Mike's car.

John and Karen needed some repair work done on the their house, but there was no money to pay someone to do it. Cole had a pile of clothing that needed mending and a daughter that needed a ride to work each day. Since his daughter worked near Karen, Karen gave her a ride and also did the mending. Cole was happy to do the repair work that John and Karen needed done.

## What is Bartering?

If you are like many Americans, your paycheck is getting smaller or maybe you find yourself without a job right now. Bartering might be one of the solutions to the problem of less money available to spend on your family's needs. Bartering is a way to get what you need without spending money, while at the same time sharing your talents and resources with others.

Bartering is a trade, or exchange, between two parties (individuals or families) of goods or services that does not involve money. The entire family can be involved in swapping resources and work.

The trickiest part of bartering is placing "value" on the good or service. Ultimately the two people, or families, involved in the bartering will determine the value of each item or task. Something is worth what another is willing to pay for it, or in this case, trade for it.

As a Christian, we want to give what is fair and then a little extra. At the same time, we don't need to let others take advantage of us either.

## What Can You Barter?

Any item that you don't want or need anymore can be traded. This includes appliances, clothing, bedding, furniture, food, musical instruments, books, textbooks, sports equipment, computers, DVDs, and anything else you can think of!

Here is a list of services that you can barter, but keep in mind that the possibilities are endless.

- Appliance repair
- Air conditioner or heater repair
- Oil change/tune ups/car maintenance
- Car wash/wax/detailing
- Baby sitting/elderly care
- Home health nursing
- Garden produce (fresh, canned, frozen)
- Weeding/pruning/hedge clipping/tree trimming

- Lawn mowing/edging/weed whacking/blowing
- Garden tilling
- Painting
- Insulation installation
- Plumbing
- Electrical work
- Minor fix-up
- Wall papering
- Furniture repair/refinishing
- Photography/videotaping
- Catering
- Baking & decorating cakes
- Meal planning/grocery shopping
- Cooking meals
- Massages
- Editing
- Hair cuts/trims/coloring/permanent/braiding
- Housekeeping
- Window washing
- Dish washing
- Laundry/ironing
- Sewing/alterations/mending
- Errands/rides
- Pet sitting/walking/feeding/grooming
- Moving furniture/households
- Flower arranging
- Painting/sculpting/macrame/knitting/embossing/card making/scrapbooking
- Music lessons/voice lessons
- Entertainment/singing/playing instruments/juggling/clowning/illusion shows
- Catering/party planning

# How to Barter Effectively

- Don't assume anything. Sit down and discuss ALL the details, exactly what will be done, who will do what, and who will pay for materials needed. In almost all cases, the person receiving the service pays for any materials
- Make sure that expectations are clear to everyone involved
- Don't spend someone's else's money without talking to them and having their permission to spend the money
- Communicate clearly and keep lines of communication open and humming
- Providing a Service when you Barter
- Be clear on the details of the service you are providing
- Be clear on what your friend is expecting. Say to him/her, "We have agreed that I will.... and you will...."
- Don't agree to something that is too difficult for you to do
- Keep your friend informed of your progress

- Let your friend know if there are delays or problems
- Receiving a Service when you Barter
- Carefully explain what you want done
- Supervise the work that is being done for you (but don't micro-manage)
- Be sure that your friend is qualified to do the task

## Bartering and the IRS

According to the IRS, the value of bartered services must be included in gross income. If you are bartering on a small scale, this will not be much of a concern. But, if you are bartering on a large scale, it will. An example of large scale bartering would be trading repair work on a house for free rent. Your monthly income from bartering would be the amount the landlord would be charging you for rent if you were paying him rent, rather than doing the repair work.

How about you? Do you have any success stories with bartering? I'd love to hear them. Until, next time, God bless and prosper each one of you!

MEREDITH CURTIS

# Net Worth Worksheet

(Total assets – total liabilities = Net worth)

| Asset or Liability | Number, Address or Description | Value of Asset | Value of Liability |
|---|---|---|---|
| Bank Savings Account | | | xxxxxxxxxxxx |
| Bank Checking Account | | | xxxxxxxxxxxx |
| Money Market Account | | | xxxxxxxxxxxx |
| Certificate of Deposits | | | xxxxxxxxxxxx |
| Husband IRA | | | xxxxxxxxxxxx |
| Wife IRA | | | xxxxxxxxxxxx |
| Stocks | | | xxxxxxxxxxxx |
| Bonds | | | xxxxxxxxxxxx |
| Mutual Funds | | | xxxxxxxxxxxx |
| Value of Home | | | xxxxxxxxxxxx |
| Values of Cars | | | xxxxxxxxxxxx |
| Value of Real Estate Investments | | | xxxxxxxxxxxx |
| Value of Jewelry, Fine Art, Electronics, Collectibles worth more than $500.00 | | | xxxxxxxxxxxx |
| Money Owed on Home | | xxxxxxxxxxxx | |
| Money Owed on Cars | | xxxxxxxxxxxx | |
| Other Debts | | xxxxxxxxxxxx | |
| Credit Card Debt | | xxxxxxxxxxxx | |
| Debts to Friends & Relatives | | xxxxxxxxxxxx | |
| Total Up Value of Assets & Liabilities | | | |
| Subtract Total Liabilities from Total Assets to get Net Worth | Our Net Worth = | | |

# Home Business Ideas

Think about everyone you know who has a business. Fill in this chart with names and what kind of business they have. I will give you 2 examples to get you going.

| Name | Business |
|---|---|
| Aunt Matilda | Does people's taxes |
| Uncle Ernie | Writes articles for magazines |
|  |  |
|  |  |
|  |  |
|  |  |
|  |  |
|  |  |
|  |  |
|  |  |
|  |  |
|  |  |
|  |  |
|  |  |
|  |  |
|  |  |
|  |  |

Now think of some ideas for yourself. What ideas do you have for starting a business? They don't have to be realistic. The important thing here is to brainstorm. You will be learning about how to start your own business and coming up with a business plan. Zack and Brian made their business plan about an airsoft park idea. It did not work out, but they applied everything they learned about starting their own business to a computer business that is keeping them very busy.

List your home business ideas in the chart below.

| My Home Business Ideas |
|---|
|  |
|  |
|  |
|  |
|  |
|  |
|  |
|  |
|  |
|  |
|  |
|  |
|  |
|  |
|  |
|  |

# Tips to Save Money

Find some blogs online about saving money. Here are some that I like, but you can use whatever blogs you want to use. Simply make a list of ideas on how YOU and your family can save money!

econobusters.com/

achristianhome.org/Homemaking/SimpleLiving.htm

miserlymoms.com/

Here are my ideas on how my family and I can save money!

| Ways My Family Can Save Money |
|---|
| |
| |
| |
| |
| |
| |
| |
| |
| |
| |
| |
| |
| |
| |
| |
| |

# Buying Your First Car

Teens, especially guys, often dream of owning and driving a cool car. They might gaze longingly at photographs and videos of their dream car. To many, owning a car can symbolize freedom and maturity.

Songs have been written about cars. "Little Deuce Coupe", "Little Honda", "Fun, Fun, Fun", and "409" are all songs about cars. Surprised?

Here is a reality check. Owning a car doesn't make you mature and jumping into a car purchase might reveal immaturity in your character. It doesn't take maturity to buy a car, but it does take maturity to delay gratification and save money for college instead. It takes a mature man to save longer to get a better car than to rush out and buy what is affordable in the short-term.

## Alternatives

What if you need to save your money for college, but you have your driver's license and are itching to drive? Can you drive the family car? If you drive the family car, be sure to put gas in the car and help maintain the car with oil changes.

Can you carpool with others and chip in for gas?

Can you walk or ride your bike?

What kind of public transportation is available? Here in Florida we have buses and the Sun Rail. In big cities, many people take the subway or train and never even get a driver's license. Living in Florida, that is hard for me to imagine.

Julianna and Jenny Rose carpooled to college together, splitting the gas. It was a win-win situation.

## Upkeep Costs

Owning a car is expensive. Once you purchase a car, it will be harder to save money for college. You will need to budget for these costs.

These costs will be more manageable.

- Gas
- Oil
- Anti-Freeze
- Brake Fluid
- Windshield Wiper Fluid

Here are the big expenses.

- Car Repairs
- Tune-Ups

- Car Insurance
- Car Club Membership (e.g. AAA®)

## Benefits of Delayed Gratification in the Car World

Don't rush into purchasing a car as soon as you have a few thousand dollars. There is a big difference in quality when you have $2,000.00 vs. $10,000.00. Be careful, pray, and wait for the right car.

Before you spend money, pray and ask God for a car. I have seen God provide cars for people many times in answer to prayer. My father gave Julianna his car when he could no longer drive. It was in great condition.

I will not even discuss going into debt for a car except to say: DON'T DO IT!

Car loans are a drain on anyone's budget and should be avoided. If God doesn't provide the car or cash, it is not His will for you to buy a car yet. Wait on Him.

## Where to Find a Car to Purchase

Now that you have waited and prayed, where should you look for a car?

Friends or relatives might have a car they will sell. Members of your local church might also have a vehicle they can sell. Get the word out that you are looking for a car.

Do a little research. Talk to people who have purchased previously owned cars and have had good experiences. Where did they buy their cars?

Car lots or dealerships are good places to look for previously owned cars. We often browse on the internet which saves a lot of looking in person. We can narrow our search down to a few vehicles to see in person. Be careful of individuals selling on the internet—sometimes they are sketchy so bring someone with you when you go check the car out (father or uncle would be good).

We often get our cars at car auctions. We know a man who looks for cars at the auction and he gets a commission on our purchase like a car salesman at a dealership. Looking at a car auction can be overwhelming because there are thousands of vehicles. Be careful of auctions too because you don't know the car's history or problems.

## The Car Salesman

It's off to the car lot. In his book, *Buying Your First Car*, Larry Burkett mentions different sales techniques that car salesmen use to trick you into purchasing a car at a higher price that you want to pay. They size up customers and deal with them accordingly. Here are some of their tricks.

### Laydown

This customer accepts every price at face value and lets the salesman walk all over them.

### Pounders

This is a Laydown who will accept face value price and extra fees piled on top.

Here are some car salesman tricks to get to you to spend more than you should.

## The Bump

Once a price is agreed on, the salesman tacks on additional fees to bump up the price.

### Wearing You Down

Salesman sometimes hand a customer off from one salesman to another with the purpose of wearing the customer down so they will agree to any price. They finally are with the top salesman who is good at making a sale.

### Being Flipped

The process of being sent from one salesman to another is called being flipped.

### Bait and Switch

The bait is an ad with the perfect car you want and can afford. When you get to the lot, the switch takes place. That car is unavailable and the salesman tries to sell you a more expensive car.

### Low Balls

After hours of haggling, the salesman tells you that you can have the car at a amazingly cheap price if you come in tomorrow. When you arrive the next day, the price is not honored and it's back to haggling.

## Dealing with Car Salesman

Here are some tips to help you deal with car salesmen.

- Don't trust them
- Check out the car completely on your own
- Do not believe that any sales or coupons will actually give you a better deal
- Take a test drive
- Decide on what you are willing to pay for a car and do not budge over it

## The Wise Car Purchaser

Here are some tips to help you make a wise purchase. You want to bargain with the salesman. Make a bid that is much lower than their offering price and much lower than you are willing to pay. Car dealers will refuse at least the first three bids, so be willing to start low and slowly work up to what you are willing to pay.

Do your research beforehand so you know the Blue Book value of the car. Use this in your negotiations.

Notice defects that are unimportant to you, but can be used to lower the price. Bring these to the salesman's attention in your negotiations.

## Car Purchase Checklist

Here is a check list to help you sniff out a lemon and avoid a bad choice.

- Rust anywhere?
- Odometer mileage?

- Gas mileage?
- How many previous owners?
- How driven (highway or around town)?
- Repairs made?
- Condition of Tires?
- Condition of Brakes?
- Windows work?
- Doors work?
- Broken Glass?
- Oil leakage?
- Fluid levels?

Test drive the car to check how it drives, how the brakes work, how it turns, and to discover any unusual engine noises.

Bring a car mechanic with you to do a thorough check of the car.

## Cost of a Car Purchase

You have agreed on a price and it is time to make the purchase. Give the owner $100.00 deposit and go to your bank to get a cashier's check for the rest. You don't want to carry around large amounts of cash. Make sure you get a bill of sale.

The bill of sale should include the date, your name, the seller's name, the VIN number, and the price. You should also get a transfer of ownership form signed by the owner.

Take both forms to the Department of Motor Vehicles (DMV) to register the car. There will be a registration fee, as well as a transfer fee, and taxes on the sale. You will also have to purchase car insurance before you drive the car.

The cost of buying a car is more than the price of the car. Make sure to budget for these extra expenses.

# Your First Car Worksheet

Do you want a car?

What is your dream car? Find a picture of your dream car and glue it to this page?

What are some alternatives to owning your own car?

What is the upkeep cost of a car?

What are the benefits of waiting to purchase a car?

Where can you find a car to purchase?

Describe the way car salesmen size customers up so they can push them into a sale and their sales tricks.

Pounders

The Bump

ECONOMICS, FINANCES, & BUSINESS COURSE

Wearing You Down

Being Flipped

Bait and Switch

Low Balls

What are some tips for being a wise car purchaser?

List ten things on the "Car Purchaser Checklist"

What are the costs of purchasing a car?

## Car Ad Info

Find a car you like in the classifieds in the newspaper or online. Pretend you are going to buy that car. Based on the information provided, answer the following questions.

I need $_____ to buy the car outright!

I will not borrow money—borrowing is stupid!!!!!

I have $_____ saved up.

I am saving $_____ a month extra.

I'd like a car, God willing, by ____/____/____ (within _____ months).

By then, I'll have $_____ and will need $_____ more.

I'll earn the extra by _____

I'll take on extra jobs such as _____ making $_____

Any used car might have surprises you will have to deal with as the new car owner. List problems that might arise with the car include:

## February Week Two Class

- [ ] Discuss Invested $100,000.00

- [ ] Discuss "Net Worth" & "Long-Range Savings" & "Making Wise Financial Decisions"

- [ ] Discuss "Living within a Budget" & "Tips to Save Money for a Household"

- [ ] Watch Youtube Videos about Buying a Car

- [ ] Discuss "Buying Your First Car" Worksheet

**Notes from Class**

## February Week Two Home

☐ Read "The Call on Your Life" & "How to Choose a Career" & "Your Ministry"

☐ Complete "God's Call for Career & Ministry" Worksheet

☐ Listen to and Complete "FW Radio Interviews" Assignment

☐ Read "Apprenticeship, College, & Other Paths to a Career"

☐ Read "The College Question" & "How to Choose a College"

☐ Start Reading *The Clipper Ship Strategy*

# The Call on Your Life

Every year on my birthday, I read Psalm 139. I call it My Birthday Psalm. It reminds me that I was knit together in my mother's womb and I am loved. God is with me and He has a plan for my life.

You have a call on your life. Jesus said, "You did not choose me, but I chose you and appointed you to bear fruit" (John 15:16 ESV).

For those who have been rescued from darkness and belong to Jesus, "We are His workmanship, created in Christ Jesus for good works, which God prepared beforehand so that we can walk in them" (Ephesians 2:10 NASB).

We can walk in the call of God or choose to ignore it. We have free will. I want to challenge you to seek God and discover His will for your life. He has a plan for your career and your ministry. It is not a terrible, boring plan. God has an exciting adventure planned for you to extend His Kingdom to the ends of the earth.

So how do you discover the will of God for your life?

"Therefore I urge you, brethren, by the mercies of God, to present your bodies a living and holy sacrifice, acceptable to God, which is your spiritual service of worship. Do not be conformed to this world, but be transformed by the renewing of your mind, so that you may prove what the will of God is, that which is good and acceptable and perfect. For through the grace given to me I say to everyone among you not to think more highly of himself than he ought to think; but to think so as to have sound judgment" (Romans 12:1-3 NASB).

To discover God's plan for your career and ministry, follow these steps: surrender, renew, and appraise.

## Surrender

Start by surrendering your life to the Lord and living for Him each day. Daily commit your life to Him in prayer, as well as feeding your mind on the Word of God. As you walk in obedience to the Scriptures, you will be transformed.

## Renew

Renew your mind in the area of career and ministry. Your career isn't about making lots of money, though men will need to make enough money to support a family. Ministry isn't about having a platform to show off your talents. Your calling is all about the glory of God. You exist to bring honor and praise to Jesus and to extend His Kingdom to the ends of the earth.

The question shouldn't be "How can the Lord bless me in my choices?" but rather "What is God doing in the earth and how does He want me to fit into His plan."

## Appraise

Assess yourself soberly. What are your strengths and weaknesses? What experiences have you had that you enjoy? How do you serve others and see the most fruit? This will show you where you can be the most effective.

## Fasting and Prayer

If you are serious about seeking God and His will for your life, I encourage you to fast and pray. Set aside one to three days and spend extra time in the Word and prayer, asking Jesus to reveal His plan for your life. Drink plenty of water and juices to stay hydrated. You might want to skip one meal a day and use the time you would normally eat to pray.

Talk to your parents first about fasting before you take the plunge.

## Be a World Changer

Jesus said, "Seek first His Kingdom and His righteousness, and all these things will be added to you" (Matthew 6:33 NASB). Jesus had just been talking about food and clothing. If we seek Jesus and His Kingdom first when choosing a career and our ministry, He will provide our daily needs. He loves us and cares for us. You cannot out-give God!

Look around you. What needs are there? How can you meet those needs? What can you bring to the world that will benefit the people you will impact? The answers to these questions will help you choose a career.

# How to Choose a Career

God cares about how you spend your time and what career path you take. For the believer who obeys the Word of God, some careers are immediately out of the question such as being a bank robber or a hijacker. If you don't feel a peace about your career, then do not pursue it. Matt was a bartender when he got saved. He found another job because he felt uncomfortable about helping people get drunk.

If you are a man, I encourage you to think about providing for a family in the future. You might like poetry, but poets have a hard time making ends meet. Maybe you could fix cars and write poetry on the side.

If you are a young woman, consider the years ahead when you stay home to raise children. It is nice to choose a career that can bring in a little extra money when you are a homemaker. Julianna majored in accounting. Right now she works for Verizon®, but when she is a homemaker, she might do taxes for people to bring in extra money if she needs to. Sarah worked full-time as a hair stylist until she got married. Now she cuts hair occasionally to earn a little extra money for the family.

## Talk to God

We have already talked about seeking God for His direction about your career path. Don't forget to pray and ask Him to lead you the right career. Don't pray about this once. Continue to pray each day for wisdom and direction. Pray that the Lord would open the right doors and shut the wrong ones.

God can direct us on our career path through provision, or lack of provision. He can provide divine appointments where we meet the right people at the right moment to give us wisdom or help us in our quest.

## Talk to Your Parents

Talk to your parents about your future. Ask them to pray with you about your future. Get their opinion on what kind of careers they can see you doing. Our parents know us so well. You would be surprised how many things they notice about your skills, aptitude, and gifting.

## Assessments

We will take several personality, interest, and values assessments to help you pinpoint your interests. Ask God to give you an interest in and an excitement about the career He has called you to.

## Interview People in Various Careers

Most people are happy to talk about their jobs, unless, of course, their jobs are classified. Ask people questions and write down their answers.

- What is your job title?
- What does your job entail?
- What is a typical work day or shift like?
- What do you love about your job?
- What is the most challenging about your job?
- How are you able to witness and minister in your position?
- What skills are needed in your job?

- What schooling or training is required for your job?
- What things have you learned on the job?
- What is the salary range for an entry level position?
- What is the market like for your job?

## Spend a Day in Different Work Environments

A great way to explore different careers is to go to work with different people and experience a typical day at the office, in the hospital, at the crime lab, or wherever they work.

Meg went to work with her aunt. They took the train into Philadelphia from the suburbs. She walked from the train station to a tall skyscraper and spent the day in her aunt's executive office. Her favorite part of the day was a marketing strategy meeting in the afternoon. Meg's opinion of working in an office changed. She hadn't realized how exciting it was to be in the marketing department of a big company.

On the other hand, Tim went to work with his father, a doctor in the emergency room of a nearby hospital. Tim realized that the sight of blood and gaping wounds made him sick. He put his plans of being a surgeon on the shelf.

## How Can You Minister in a Career?

As much as careers are important, ministry is more important. Is there opportunity to share the Gospel and minister to people in the career you are considering? Remember that working hard, especially going the extra mile, makes the Gospel attractive to unbelievers.

As a nurse, I was able to pray with many of my patients before and after surgery. The opportunities to share the Gospel were fewer, but I did lead two of my patients to Christ. Ministry doesn't just happen at work.

# Your Ministry

Every believer is called to be plugged into a local church. Each member has a job to do. What needs to be done in your local church? Start there. Serve where you are needed. Sometimes career and ministry overlap. Pastor Dan earns his living by working for a church and its congregation. Jose is a Bible study leader and impacts many lives too, but he has a full-time job as a policeman.

In our church, almost everyone helps out by teaching Sunday school or working in the nursery one hour a month. Not all of these people are excited about their week to serve, but they want to meet a need. Some of them are extremely gifted at ministering to children and they become the lead teacher and oversee the other helpers.

You will find that you become skilled at certain ministries and really enjoy them. This is how God planned it. Josh started helping his dad lug sound equipment to church when he was eight years old. When he was twelve, he joined the sound team. At nineteen, he often serves as stage manager or sound technician, as well as leading the PowerPoint team. You see, Josh was faithful in the little (helping his dad carry equipment carefully and with a cheerful heart). As he grew, he got more and more responsibility. He was faithful in each new step. When we are faithful in our ministries, God will give us more responsibility.

# ECONOMICS, FINANCES, & BUSINESS COURSE

Here are some ways young adults serve at our church.

| Children's Ministry | Teaching/Mentoring | Worship/Sound Team | Other |
|---|---|---|---|
| Lead Teacher | Mentor | Sound Helper | Greeter |
| Assistant Teacher | Teach Homeschool Co-op Class | Stage Manager | Usher |
| Nursery Worker | Give Music Lessons | Sound Technician | Plan Teen Events |
| | Tutor | PowerPoint Slides | Plan Church-wide Events |
| | | Musician | Witnessing |
| | | Singer | Share Testimony |
| | | Lead Worship at LIFE Group | |

## Your Life Verse

My husband's life verse is Romans 8:28: "And we know that God causes all things to work together for those who love God, to those who are called according to His purpose" (NASB). This verse came alive to him as a teenager when a damaged knee prevented him from going to state finals for wrestling. He had prayed beforehand that the Lord would take away anything that would keep him from growing closer to Jesus. He loved wrestling so Mike had to press into God and trust Him. For the rest of his life, this verse has ministered to him.

You might have a verse like that that comes to your mind over and over. There might be a passage of Scripture that you cling to when you are afraid or discouraged. I don't have just one, there are several passages that are precious to me.

If you have a life verse, write it out here:

_____
_____
_____
_____

## Your Mission Statement

Our company mission statement is "Being world changers; raising world changers." That is our family mission statement too because we want to impact the world for the glory of God. If you have a purpose, a dream, a vision, then try to put it into a short phrase. Sheryl's mission statement is "Love God; love His people; reach the lost." It reminds her of her purpose here on this earth. Your mission will influence the job you choose.

**Here are some personal mission statements.**

"To live my life with integrity so that my example motivates others to raise their standards."

"Using my musical creativity, I will make people laugh and inspire them to trust God."

"I will be a safe place where people can pour their hearts out and receive healing."

"Love God. Love my Neighbor. Change my neighborhood for God's glory!"

"Researching the past for accuracy, I will teach others HIS story from creation until He returns."

"Teaching to change lives."

"With my eyes on Jesus and my arms around people, I will help others discover their purpose in life."

"I will teach biblical principles with my life and words."

To create your own mission statement, identify success in the past, what you value most, and who/what you want to impact.

Steve has had success in reaching out to children through basketball. He values leading people to Christ and growing stronger in his relationship with the Lord. Children living in inner-city poverty stir up his heart.

Mary has an amazing ability to create artwork for church events on posters. She even painted Bible scenes on the nursery wall. She has a passion to see teens walk in purity and has high standards of modesty and wholesome talk in her own life.

Jordan plays the guitar and writes songs that people love to sing along with. He loves the holiness and grace of God and is often found studying the Bible when not playing his guitar. Jordan is always challenging other teens to study the Bible more and focus on Christ.

**Write a Mission Statement for Steve, Mary, and Jordan.**

Steve's Mission Statement:_____
_____
_____
_____

Mary's Mission Statement:_____
_____
_____
_____

Jordan's Mission Statement:_____
_____
_____
_____

Now it's time to think about your own mission statement. First, list your past successes in work, volunteer work, or ministry._____
_____
_____
_____

List things that you value. What is important to you? _____
_____
_____
_____

Finally, list the people you want to impact. Where do you want to make a difference?_____
_____
_____
_____

Write your own personal mission statement._____
_____
_____
_____

# God's Call for Career & Ministry

What are the steps to discovering God's Will for your career?

How does prayer help you choose a career?

How does talking to your parents help you choose a career?

Let's interview five of your family members, acquaintances, and friends about their careers. Try to choose a wide variety of careers.

| Name | |
|---|---|
| Job Title & Description | |
| What is a typical work day or shift like? | |
| What do you love about your job? | |
| What is the most challenging about your job? | |
| How are you able to witness and minister in your position? | |
| What skills are needed in your job? | |
| What schooling or training is required for your job? | |
| What things have you learned on the job? | |
| What is the salary range for an entry level position? | |
| What is the market like for your job? | |

| Name | |
|---|---|
| Job Title & Description | |
| What is a typical work day or shift like? | |
| What do you love about your job? | |
| What is the most challenging about your job? | |
| How are you able to witness and minister in your position? | |
| What skills are needed in your job? | |
| What schooling or training is required for your job? | |
| What things have you learned on the job? | |
| What is the salary range for an entry level position? | |
| What is the market like for your job? | |

| Name | |
|---|---|
| Job Title & Description | |
| What is a typical work day or shift like? | |
| What do you love about your job? | |
| What is the most challenging about your job? | |
| How are you able to witness and minister in your position? | |
| What skills are needed in your job? | |
| What schooling or training is required for your job? | |
| What things have you learned on the job? | |
| What is the salary range for an entry level position? | |
| What is the market like for your job? | |

| Name | |
|---|---|
| Job Title & Description | |
| What is a typical work day or shift like? | |
| What do you love about your job? | |
| What is the most challenging about your job? | |
| How are you able to witness and minister in your position? | |
| What skills are needed in your job? | |
| What schooling or training is required for your job? | |
| What things have you learned on the job? | |
| What is the salary range for an entry level position? | |
| What is the market like for your job? | |

| Name | |
|---|---|
| Job Title & Description | |
| What is a typical work day or shift like? | |
| What do you love about your job? | |
| What is the most challenging about your job? | |
| How are you able to witness and minister in your position? | |
| What skills are needed in your job? | |
| What schooling or training is required for your job? | |
| What things have you learned on the job? | |
| What is the salary range for an entry level position? | |
| What is the market like for your job? | |

# FW Radio Interviews on Careers

I have interviewed several people on FW Radio about their careers. You can listen to the show on the Ultimate Radio Network page or on I-tunes. Listen to both shows and answer the questions below.

## Exploring Careers in Real Estate and The Pool Industry

You will meet Leanne Benjamin, owner of her own real estate company and Donald Nolette, manager at a pool company. Leanne started out as a teacher, but decided to switch to real estate, first as an agent, and eventually starting her own company. Donald started cleaning pools as a teen, working his way up in the pool business to management. You will learn about the responsibilities, benefits, education, and future possibilities in these fields.

ultimateradioshow.com/fw-radio-exploring-careers-in-real-estate-the-pool-industry/

As you listen to these interviews, please answer the following questions.

Before Leanne became a real estate agent, she was a teacher. What made her leave teaching to go into real estate?

What skills are required for Leanne's job? What did she learn in real estate school and what did she learn on the job?

What does Leanne enjoy the most about her job?

What salary and benefits come with her job? Why is there such a wide salary range?

What is the most challenging for Leanne in being a real estate broker?

Donald is a manager at a pool company. After high school graduation, he did not go to college. How did he get started in the pool industry and what made him stay in the pool industry?

What is Donald's favorite part of the job?

What is the most challenging part of the job?

How important are people skills in Donald's management job?

What advice would Donald give someone who wants to work in the pool industry?

What advice would Leanne give someone who wants to become a real estate agent?

## Exploring Careers in Business and Rescue

You will meet two homeschool grads first who have careers in the business world. Zack is an Account Executive for AAA® and Julianna works for Verizon® as a Technical Analyst. (They went through this economics course too!). You will also meet a homeschool dad. Sam is a fire fighter for Orange County, Florida. Zack, Julianna, and Sam will talk about their jobs and what a typical work week looks like. You will learn about their responsibilities, benefits, education, and future career possibilities.

ultimateradioshow.com/fw-radio-exploring-careers-business-rescue/

As you listen to these interviews, please answer the following questions.

What did Julianna do to get her first job? How did others help her?

What was that first interview like?

Describe Julianna's job description. How did she show integrity in changing jobs?

What skills did Julianna learn in school?

What skills did Julianna learn on the job?

What does Julianna enjoy most about her job? (It might surprise you!)

What does Julianna suggest asking in a job interview?

What are future possibilities for Julianna in her career?

Julianna has a bachelor's degree in accounting. What are some other possibilities that Julianna could have pursued?

How has Julianna ministered to others at her job?

Zack got a business degree with a focus on marketing. He got his job in an unique way. How did Zack get his job?

What is one tip for a phone interview that seems kind of weird? Why does it help?

Why were AAA®'s values important because of Zack's job in marketing?

Describe Zack's experience as an intern?

What is marketing? How is it more than advertizing?

What skills did Zack learn in school and what skills did he learn on the job?

What does Zack enjoy most about her job?

What is the most challenging thing about Zack's job?

What future possibilities exist for Zack in the future because of his degree and chosen field?

Sam is a firefighter. What is the best part of his job?

## ECONOMICS, FINANCES, & BUSINESS COURSE

What skills did Sam learn in school and what did he learn on the job?

Why do Sam's co-workers love it when Sam calls in sick?

What is the entry-level salary for a firefighter? How is it determined? What does a fire chief make a year?

What is the most challenging thing about being a firefighter?

What are the benefits of being a firefighter?

How did God lead Sam to become a firefighter?

# Apprenticeship, College, & Other Pathways to a Career

There is not a one-way-fits-all career path. Once you have chosen your career or field of study, here are some options for training.

## Apprenticeship

Apprenticeship is a great way to prepare for a career. There are also technical schools where young adults can be trained to repair engines, lay circuitry, fix computers, and work in a lab. Whether you go to college or not, you might consider learning to start and run your own business because learning a trade often lends itself to running your own business.

You can apprentice with a plumber, carpenter, or seamstress. It is a long-term commitment where you work for a small salary and in return you receive on-the-job training in the field. When you finish an apprenticeship, you are ready to go out on your own.

## Internships

Many college students find internships that last from three to six months with a company in the field of their choice. Some internships are paid, but many are not. You simply volunteer your time in return for the experience.

Brian spent a summer in Texas between his freshman and sophomore year with a paid internship from NASA. This looked great on his resume when he graduated and he got helpful hands-on experience in an exciting field.

## Volunteer Work

Seth volunteered in his mega-church office once a week all through high school. He learned to update the website, man the phone lines, and give administrative assistance to the pastors and support staff. Eventually he was designing the website which opened the door for a job with a large company as a webmaster.

## Ministry

Jimmy served at his church on the sound team. When things broke, he learned to fix them. He found a love of learning how things work electronically. This opened the door to an interest in electrical engineering.

## Vocational School

Tom is going to go to vocational school for a short time to become a car mechanic, earning a certificate. Esther is attending beauty school to become a hair stylist. Vocational schools take less time to finish than traditional college and prepare people for trades.

## College

To go to college or not is a big question for you to answer. Not all great jobs require a college education. However, there are many fields that do require a college degree. We will talk about college next.

# The College Question

In this course, we have been talking about managing family finances and saving money for household expenses. For some of you, that will be a few years ahead. However, most of you will decide if you are going to college or not within a few years. Maybe you are applying for colleges right now.

Let's talk a little bit about college.

## Why Do People Go to College?

College is a big investment of time and money. In fact, many people go into debt to get a college education. We will talk about going to college debt-free today. But first, let's talk about why people go to college.

For some families, college is a rite of passage. Every child will graduate from high school and then go to college before getting married and having children.

Many young adults go to college to get trained for their future careers. Ted wants to be an engineer. Ted gets a degree in engineering and then gets a job as an engineer. Sandra wants to be a nurse. She can get a bachelor's degree in nursing or get an associate's degree in nursing (two years shorter). Phillip wants to be a pediatrician. He will get a bachelor's degree in biology (or another science degree) and then go on to four years of med school followed by two years of residency. College is a necessary step for Phillip's to pursue his dream of medicine.

Before the Industrial Revolution, people went to college because the loved to learn. A college degree was simply for the purpose of pursuing an education. As a Christian, we are disciples of Jesus. The word disciple means "student". Learning and continuing our education for a lifetime is a good thing. We don't need to go to college to be educated, but many having a degree can open doors for work and ministry in the future.

Do you know anyone in college right now?

Shine is in college and she is always reading books or writing on her laptop. College requires a lot of time studying for exams and writing papers. Classes move through material quickly. Students must work hard to keep up. Some people love the pressure and others get stressed out.

While my daughter, Shine, doesn't like the stress of due dates and exams, she loves being surrounded by so many young people who are interested in her faith in Jesus. There are so many opportunities to share the Gospel in a college setting.

## Difference between College, University, and Grad School

A college is a school that offers a degree in a specialized field of study. You could have a College of Education that offers degrees in special education, elementary education, and secondary education. A Bible College offers awards degrees in Bible, theology, and counseling. A community college offers two-year degrees (associate's degree) in general education so that graduates can go on to a university or four-year college to get a bachelor's degree.

A university has several colleges together in on institution. At Stetson University where my daughters graduated, there is a Business College, School of Music, College of Arts and Sciences, and College of Law.

A Graduate School offers master's degrees and doctorate degrees to students who have completed their bachelor's degrees with high grade point averages and quality for the admittance requirements. Master's degrees generally take two extra years of college and doctorate degrees take four. Grad schools are often part of universities. Seminaries are free-standing grad schools that offer degrees for those with a bachelor's degree that want to be pastors.

## What is College Like?

Every college is different. Some Christian colleges are very conservative with students who love the Lord and live upright lives. Some college students indulge in a party lifestyle that involves drugs, alcohol, and sex outside marriage. I am also sorry to tell you that most secular colleges and universities are very anti-Christian. Professors mock Christianity and work hard to undermine the faith of Jesus' followers.

Keep in mind that for over a century, most colleges have been bastions of secular humanism and Marxism. With the rise of post-moderism's hopeless philosophy, professors hammer home their belief that there are no absolutes. Most of today's colleges are anti-Christian, ridiculing students' faith in Christ, conservative political beliefs, and moral values. Pornography is shown in classrooms, though some professors will warn before showing it so that "prudish students can walk out first if they need to" or close their eyes. Often Christian students don't want to appear "immature."

My children have all gone to secular colleges with professors and policies that deny Christ and His way of life. Yet, my children have held firm to their faith and defended that faith inside and outside the classroom. God can use Christian young people to stand firm in their faith and lead others to Christ. I would prepare for a secular university by learning more about worldviews and defending your faith. A great book on worldviews is Understanding the Times by David Noebel. Josh McDowell has some helpful books on defending your faith including More than a Carpenter and Evidence that Demands a Verdict. Also make sure to stay plugged into your local church while you are in school. If you go away to college, find Christian fellowship and a church to plug into right away.

## Should I Go to College?

The college question is something that everyone has to answer for himself. The best thing to do is to pray and ask God if you should go or not. Talk to your parents and get their input.

Certain careers will require that you get a college degree. I have a bachelor's degree in nursing and my husband has a bachelor's in psychology and a master's of divinity. I worked a few years as an RN before becoming a full-time mommy. Medicine, physical therapy, respiratory therapy, architecture, engineering, law, teaching, and accounting all require college degrees at various levels. In recent years, many careers are requiring bachelor's degrees that did not require them in the past.

On the other hand, my daughter has a master's degree in English and taught at a university. A young man graduated from high school at the same time and apprenticed with a plumber. He is making three times more money than my daughter made as a college professor. So, don't assume that a college education is always a pathway to a higher income or standard of living.

College isn't for everyone, but God can use you to share the Gospel and train you to test everything you hear, holding on to the good. I am still in touch, thirty years later, with friends I led to Christ in college. Young people are looking for answers and you have the answer: Jesus!

## What are Colleges Looking For?

Colleges want the best and brightest students they can find. For homeschoolers, colleges tend to focus on SAT or ACT scores, as well as leadership experience. If you are a public school, Christian school, or umbrella school student, colleges will look at your grades too.

For everyone applying to college, the transcript is important because it reveals the types of courses you have taken in high school. Make sure you have four years of each of the core subjects: English, Math, Social Studies, and Science. Also consider taking extra electives in one or more of the core subject.

# How to Choose College

We talked what colleges look for in students, but what should you look for in a college? How should you pick out the university that's right for you?

It is never too early to think about college. Start thinking about college right now. Ask yourself the following questions:

- Do I want to go to a Christian college or a non-Christian college?
- What is the worldview of the colleges I am interested in?
- Will I live on campus or commute?
- What careers am I interested in?
- What majors are required for those careers?
- What majors am I interested in?
- Do the colleges and universities I like offer those majors?

## Research Colleges

Start looking into various colleges and universities. Each college has its own atmosphere. It is made up of the professors, classes, administration, and students who attend. You want to have a feel for the college. Talk to students, faculty, and administrators if possible. Don't just talk to the people who are recruiting you. That is their job. The recruiters want you to choose their college. Talk to young adults who have just graduated or are attending college. Ask about the school. I recommend visiting the colleges and universities you are considering during the four years of high school.

Read course descriptions in catalogs. Find out what majors and minors are offered. Here are some questions to ask.

- What is the worldview of the college?
- What are the professors like?
- How big or small are the classes?
- What is the availability of professors & deans to the students?
- What is the availability of professors & deans to the parents?
- What majors do they offer?
- What are the graduation requirements?

## If You are Going to a Community College First

Community or state colleges are a great way to get the first two years in, especially if finances are an issue or SAT scores are low. However, if you have a major and university in mind for the last two years, make sure the community college credits will be accepted. I have known young people who finish up two years at a community college and transfer to a state university only to find that some of their credits don't transfer.

Here is my advice: if you are going to start at a community college, visit the university you will finish at and get their counsel on which classes to take.

## Consider a Christian College

The best college experience would be one that teaches every class from a biblical perspective. When choosing a Christian college, make sure that every discipline, every class is taught from the standard that the Bible is the inspired and infallible Word of God.

Realize that even if you find a conservative, Bible-believing school, many students who attend the college may be unbelievers or Christians who are behaving badly. There may also be professors that do not conform to the high standards of the school. Dr. Gary Parker spoke at our Finish Well conference in 2013 and shared that he taught evolution in a Christian college. So, be careful.

Here are some websites to find Christian colleges.

Christian College Guide christiancollegeguide.net/

Free Christian College Resource Center christianconnector.com/

## Online Opportunities

My friend Bruno lives right here in Lake Mary, Florida. He is working and getting his business degree from Liberty University. Yes, that is Liberty University in Lynchburg, Virginia! He is going to school online. What a great way to continue homeschooling right through college!

The great thing about studying online is that you can go to class in your pajamas. However, some students prefer meeting their professor in person and being in a classroom setting. I know many students who do some classes online while they do others on campus.

Liberty University Online onlineatliberty.com

## How Much Does it Cost to Go to College?

College is not cheap. Choose a nearby college and find out how much it costs to go to that college. Fill in the chart with the information you discover.

| **School Fees** | Application Fee | $ |
| --- | --- | --- |
| | Tuition per Credit Hour | $ |
| | | Total for Semester: $ |
| | Lab Fees | $ |
| | Registration Fees | $ |
| | Student Association Fees | $ |
| | Books | $ |
| | School Supplies | $ |
| **Living Expenses if Living On Campus** | Rent or Board | $ |
| | Utilities | $ |
| | Internet | $ |
| | Phone | $ |
| | Furniture & Supplies | $ |
| | Meal Plan | $ |
| | Groceries | $ |

# High School Years Check List by Grade

Here is a check-off list to help you stay on track for choosing a college and applying to the college.

## In 9th & 10th Grade

- ☐ Take interest and skills assessments to help you explore careers that interest you
- ☐ Talk with Mom and Dad about career options and education required for those careers
- ☐ Talk about paying for college
- ☐ Participate in extracurricular activities
- ☐ Volunteer in the community
- ☐ Review your high school class plan. Take the most difficult classes you can handle
- ☐ Join Scholarship websites. Make a list of potential scholarships and deadlines (some scholarships must be applied for junior year)
- ☐ Summer: study for PSAT

## In 11th Grade

- ☐ Take the PSAT in the fall to prepare for the SAT, and to identify areas where you need improvement
- ☐ Request materials from schools that interest you, and visit their websites
- ☐ Arrange campus visits to those schools that interest you
- ☐ Go visit colleges of interest (if far away, may need to wait for the summer)
- ☐ Participate in extracurricular activities
- ☐ Volunteer in the community
- ☐ Request admissions and financial aid forms
- ☐ Sign up for classes now that will earn you college credit during your senior year of high school (dual enrollment)
- ☐ Take the ACT and/or SAT in the spring
- ☐ Research your private scholarship options.

## In 12th Grade

- ☐ Participate in extracurricular activities.
- ☐ Volunteer in the community.

## September - November

- ☐ Arrange campus visits to those schools that interest you. It's okay to go more than once
- ☐ Take or retake the ACT and/or SAT
- ☐ Select the schools to which you will apply
- ☐ Make a list of deadlines for each school
- ☐ Ask for recommendations (if required) from teachers, counselors, pastors and others who can comment on your character, abilities and talents
- ☐ Sign up for spring classes that will earn you college credit (dual enrollment)

## December - February

- ☐ Apply to four or more colleges that interest you. Some may have earlier or later deadlines.
- ☐ Make copies of each application.
- ☐ Apply for scholarships offered by the colleges to which you have applied
- ☐ Apply for financial aid by completing the Free
- ☐ Application for Federal Student Aid at fafsa.gov as soon as possible after January 1. You and your parents will need the previous year's income tax information to complete it
- ☐ Review your Student Aid Report (SAR) for accuracy (result of FAFSA)

## March - May

- ☐ Have your final high school transcript sent to the colleges to which you've applied
- ☐ Carefully review and compare the financial aid packages offered by each college to which you applied Each college is different and may offer you different amounts of different types of aid
- ☐ Choose a college and notify in writing those you don't plan to attend
- ☐ Send in any required forms or deposits

## Summer

- ☐ Get a job to earn money for college or volunteer
- ☐ Review orientation materials from the college you selected
- ☐ If living on campus, check with the college for a list of what's provided by the school and what the school expects the student to provide
- ☐ Contact your roommate

# February Week Three Class

☐ Discuss Invested $100,000.00

☐ Career Panel

## How to Host a Career Panel

Today you will invite several different people to your class who are willing to share about your careers. Try to get as wide a variety as possible.

Suggestions: medical profession (doctor, dentist, nurse, physical therapist, respiratory therapist), vocation (plumber, mechanic, chef, hair stylist), business (executive, accountant, marketing, stock broker, banker), rescue (police, firefighter, paramedic), full-time ministry (pastor, counselor, missionary), homemaker, teacher/helping (librarian, counselor, teacher, professor, probation officer, fitness trainer), and law (defense attorney, prosecuting attorney, paralegal, judge).

Serve a nice lunch and have your guests sit in a row at a table in comfortable chairs. Make sure they have a bottle of water. Your teen, or teens, should be prepared to ask questions about education, job description, challenges, salary range, and favorite part of the job.

| Name | Career & Job Description | Education Required/Job Training | Best Part of Job | Most Challenging Part of Job | Typical Work Day/Week | Opportunities to Minister at Job |
|------|--------------------------|--------------------------------|------------------|------------------------------|-----------------------|----------------------------------|
|      |                          |                                |                  |                              |                       |                                  |
|      |                          |                                |                  |                              |                       |                                  |
|      |                          |                                |                  |                              |                       |                                  |
|      |                          |                                |                  |                              |                       |                                  |

# ECONOMICS, FINANCES, & BUSINESS COURSE

| Name | Career & Job Description | Education Required/Job Training | Best Part of Job | Most Challenging Part of Job | Typical Work Day/Week | Opportunities to Minister at Job |
|---|---|---|---|---|---|---|
|  |  |  |  |  |  |  |
|  |  |  |  |  |  |  |
|  |  |  |  |  |  |  |
|  |  |  |  |  |  |  |
|  |  |  |  |  |  |  |

## February Week Three Home

- [ ] Read & Complete "Career Exploration: Personality Assessment"

- [ ] Read & Complete "Career Exploration: Skills, Interests, & Values Assessment"

- [ ] Read "College Majors and Careers"

- [ ] Complete "Match Interests & Careers to Majors" & "Potential College Majors and Careers"

- [ ] Read & Complete "Career Exploration: Careers You Like"

- [ ] "The College Application Process" & "Going to College Debt-Free"

- [ ] Fill Out "Preparing for College" Worksheet

- [ ] Discuss College Years with Mom & Dad

- [ ] Read *The Clipper Ship Strategy*

# Career Exploration: Personality Assessment

We are going to explore careers by taking several tests that will offer you career suggestions. Remember this is a just a manmade test and does not replace your need to seek God for His will for your life.

We will look at personality first. God created you uniquely you. You have your own sets of strengths and weaknesses. Sometimes our personality can make us well-suited for specific jobs.

The website truity.com/ offers personality tests for free, as well as some tests that cost money. The 300-Question Personality Test, the Personal Strengths Inventory, and the DISC Behavior Inventory are all free. We will take the 300 Question Personality Test and the DISC Behavior Inventory, recording our scores.

# ECONOMICS, FINANCES, & BUSINESS COURSE

**Take the Personality Test and list your styles.**

My Cognitive Style (Decision-Making) is _____

(Creative/Pragmatic/Practical)

My Organizational Style (How Hard You Work) is _____

(Driven/Balanced/Slacker)

My Energy Style (Do People Energize or Drain You?) is _____

(Extravert/Introvert)

My Stress-Management Style (How You Handle Stress) is _____

(Laid-Back/Balanced/Reactive)

My Interpersonal Style (Working with Others) is _____

(Independent/Balanced/Cooperative)


List some other personality traits that you discovered taking this test.

_____
_____
_____
_____
_____
_____

Now take the DISC Behavior Inventory. What Personality Type are you?

| | | |
|---|---|---|
| INFP: The Healer | ENTP: The Visionary | ISFP: The Composer |
| INFJ: The Counselor | ENTP: The Visionary | ESTJ: The Supervisor |
| ENFJ: The Teacher | INTP: The Architect | ESTP: The Dynamo |
| ENFP: The Champion | ESFJ: The Provider | ISTJ: The Inspector |
| INTJ: The Mastermind | ESFP: The Performer | ISTP: The Craftsman |
| ENTJ: The Commander | ISFJ: The Protector | |

Personality type _____

Look at the career suggestions below based on your personality type and list some of your favorites below.
truity.com/view/types

Career Suggestions can be found for each personality type. I will just list a few below. Look up your personality profile and list the ones that you like the best (at least twenty-five).

_____
_____
_____
_____
_____
_____
_____
_____
_____
_____
_____
_____
_____
_____
_____
_____

### INFP: The Healer

Artist, Fashion Designer, Graphic Designer, Counselor, Librarian, Museum Curator, College Professor, Preschool Teacher, Chiropractor, Nutritionist, Midwife, Massage Therapist, Physical Therapist, Veterinarian, Archaeologist, Historian, Writer, Editor, Photographer, Interpreter.

For more see truity.com/personality-type/INFP/careers

### INFJ: The Counselor

Family Doctor, Psychiatrist, Massage Therapist, Counselor, Pastor, Special Education Teacher, Elementary Teacher, Librarian, Museum Curator, Editor, Writer, Artist, Musician, Interior Designer.

For more see truity.com/personality-type/INFJ/careers

### ENFJ: The Teacher

Marriage Counselor, Reporter, Author, High School Teacher, Middle School Teacher, Elementary School Teacher, College Professor, Principal, Actor, Producer, Director, Floral Designer, Interior Designer, Fitness Trainer, Flight Attendant, Real Estate Broker, Lawyer, Physical Therapist, Receptionist, Sales Manager.

For more see truity.com/personality-type/ENFJ/careers

### ENFP: The Champion

Actor, Dancer, Music Director, Composer, Singer, Musician, Producer, Director, Fashion Designer, Interior Designer, Sales Agent, Real Estate Agent, Travel Agent, Animal Trainer, Hair Stylist, Fitness Trainer, Waiter, Reporter, Writer, Editor, Psychologist, Teacher (all ages), Chiropractor, Fundraiser, Manager, Buyer, Midwife, Physical Therapist, Veterinarian, Convention Planner.

For more see truity.com/personality-type/ENFP/careers

### INTJ: The Mastermind

Accountant, Auditor, Financial Analyst, Loan Officer, Mathematician, Statistician, Aerospace Engineer, Architect, Chemical Engineer, Civil Engineer, Electrical Engineer, Nuclear Engineer, Surveyor, Chemist, Biochemist, Microbiologist, Editor, Translator, Photographer, Optometrist, Pharmacist, Physician, Surgeon, Podiatrist, Professor, Software Developer, Systems Analyst, Web Developer, Building Inspector.

For more see truity.com/personality-type/INTJ/careers

### ENTJ: The Commander

Accountant, Loan Officer, Top Executive, Insurance Sales Agent, Real Estate Broker, Sales Manager, Aerospace Engineer, Architect, Chemical Engineer, Drafter, Civil Engineer, Nuclear Engineer, Scientist, Chef, Dentist, Optometrist, Pharmacist, Systems Analyst, Software Developer, Building Inspector, Judge, Lawyer.

For more see truity.com/personality-type/ENTJ/careers

### ENTP: The Visionary

Executive, Entrepreneur, HR Recruiter, Corporate Trainer, Venture Capitalist, Financial Planner, Stockbroker, Real Estate Agent, Reporter, Producer, Director, Journalist, Actor, Photographer, Chiropractor, Lawyer.

For more see truity.com/personality-type/ENTP/careers

### INTP: The Architect

Computer Programmer, Systems Analyst, Software Developer, Aerospace Engineer, Chemical Engineer, Civil Engineer, Mechanical Engineer, Electrical Engineer, Nuclear Engineer, Historian, Economist, Chemist, Microbiologist, Psychologist, Physician, Accountant, Auditor, Lawyer, Musician, Composer, Graphic Designer, Photographer, Technical Writer, College Professor.

For more see truity.com/personality-type/INTP/careers

### ESFJ: The Provider

Elementary Teacher, Counselor, Police Officer, Hotel Manager, Cosmetologist, Hair Stylist, Family Physician, Dentist, Optometrist, Nurse, Surgeon, Physical Therapist, Fitness Trainer, Pediatrician, Pastor, Corporate Trainer, Fundraiser, Real Estate Agent, Funeral Director, Receptionist, Customer Service.

For more see truity.com/personality-type/ESFJ/careers

### ESFP: The Performer

Police Officer, Animal Trainer, Elementary Teacher, Nurse, Physical Therapist, Massage Therapist, Dietician, Child Care Provider, Cosmetologist, Hair Stylist, Corporate Trainer, Receptionist, Flight Attendant, Rancher, Farmer, Fashion Designer, Interior Designer, Jeweler, Chef, Florist, Musician, Artist, Photographer, Firefighter.

For more see truity.com/personality-type/ESFP/careers

**ISFJ: The Protector**

Dentist, Nurse, Physical Therapist, Family Physician, Optometrist, Preschool Teacher, Funeral Director, Paralegal, Probation Officer, Farmer, Rancher, Jeweler, Interior Designer, Biologist, Librarian, Curator, Real Estate Agent, Hotel Manager, Bookkeeper.

For more see truity.com/personality-type/ISFJ/careers

**ISFP: The Composer**

Chef, Tailor, Carpenter, Gardener, Florist, Fashion Designer, Interior Designer, Jeweler, Graphic Designer, Nurse, Fitness Trainer, ER Physician, Pharmacist, Paralegal, Office Manager, Insurance Appraiser, Botanist, Translator, Air Traffic Controller, Firefighter, Police Officer, Animal Trainer.

For more see truity.com/personality-type/ISFP/careers

**ESTJ: The Supervisor**

Stockbroker, Insurance Agent, Hotel Manager, Police Officer, Pilot, Farmer, Rancher, Chef, Lawyer, Judge, Auditor, Principal, Dentist, Physician, Pharmacist, Athletic Trainer, Coach, Civil Engineer, Mechanical Engineer, Real Estate Agent, General Contractor, Funeral Director.

For more see truity.com/personality-type/ESTJ/careers

**ESTP: The Dynamo**

General Contractor, Mechanic, Surveyor, Forester, Landscape Architect, Farmer, Rancher, Biologist, Chiropractor, Fitness Instruction, Respiratory Therapist, Real Estate Broker, Stock Broker, Sales Manager, Insurance Agent, Financial Planner, Vocational Teacher, Air-Traffic Controller, Parmedic, Flight Attendant, Pilot, Firefighter, Civil Engineer, Mechanical Engineer, Photographer.

For more see truity.com/personality-type/ESTP/careers

**ISTJ: The Inspector**

Auditor, Actuary, Accountant, Office Manager, Estate Planner, Property Manager, Bank Teller, Economist, Pilot, Mechanic, Civil Engineer, Power Plant Operator, Geologist, Farmer, Rancher, School Administrator, Police Officer, Surgeon, Optometrist, Judge, Librarian.

For more see truity.com/personality-type/ISTJ/careers

**ISTP: The Craftsman**

Carpenter, Surveyor, Mechanic, Systems Analyst, Database Administrator, Paralegal, Athletic Trainer, Photographer, Jeweler, Police Officer, Firefighter, Pilot, Civil Engineer, Electrical Engineer, Air Traffic Controller, Machinist, Chef.

For more see truity.com/personality-type/ISTP/careers

ECONOMICS, FINANCES, & BUSINESS COURSE

# Career Exploration: Skills, Interests, & Values Assessments

Rutgers University offers online career planning to help perspectives students choose a major. You don't have to be a student to take advantage of these resources. There are three different tests, or assessments: interests, skills, and values. You can find the tests here: careers.rutgers.edu/page.cfm?section_ID=8&page_id=350 .

Here is a quote from their website that explains the theory behind the assessments they offer. "The interests assessment and skills assessment are based on John Holland's 'Theory of Vocational Development.' Briefly, this theory maintains that based on your preference and personal style you can be loosely classified into six different categories: realistic, investigative, artistic, social, enterprising, and conventional. College majors and career can also be organized into these same six categories. If you choose a college major and career from one of these six categories that is consistent with your preferences and personal style, you are more likely to be satisfied with your choice." (careers.rutgers.edu/page.cfm?section_ID=8&page_id=350 ).

**Take Interest Assessment. List scores.** careers.rutgers.edu/page.cfm?section_ID=8&page_id=337

**Interest Scores**

Realistic _____

Investigative _____

Artistic _____

Social _____

Enterprising _____

Conventional _____

**Take the Skills Assessment. List scores.** careers.rutgers.edu/page.cfm?section_ID=8&page_id=338

**Skills Assessment Scores**

Realistic _____

Investigative _____

Artistic _____

Social _____

Enterprising _____

Conventional _____

**Take the Values Assessment. List scores.** careers.rutgers.edu/page.cfm?section_ID=8&page_id=339

**Values Assessment Scores**

Achievement _____

Challenge _____

Independence _____

Money _____

Power _____

Recognition _____

Service to Others _____

Variety _____

## Now it's Time to Generate Career Options!

On this page, careers.rutgers.edu/page.cfm?section_ID=8&page_id=351 , you can link to the pages of the categories you scored highest on based on your interests, skills, and values assessments.

**Generate Options**

You will find lots of options. Write down the collage majors and careers that appeal to you.

**College Major Suggestions**

_____
_____
_____
_____
_____
_____
_____

**Career Suggestions**

_____
_____
_____
_____
_____
_____
_____

# College Majors and Careers

If you decide to go to college, you will need to pick a major. We have talked about your personality and you have received career suggestions based on your personality, interests, and skills. Now its time to put everything together and consider college majors. First let's take a look at how many college majors are out there.

My Majors mymajors.com/

Here is a website that lists 1,800 college majors mymajors.com/list-of-college-majors.cfml

Just to check it out, I took their college major quiz. The degrees they recommended for me (at age fifty) were Religious Studies, Communication, History, Journalism, and a major related to public speaking. What do I do right now? Lead worship, lead the women's ministry at our church, write, and speak to homeschooling families about biblical homeschooling. My favorite subject to teach at home and in co-ops: history! The quiz was right on the money for me. ☺

## College Majors & Connected Careers

Today, we will look at different majors and potential careers that are connected to those majors. We will visit Florida State University's Career Center Match Major Sheets. career.fsu.edu/Resources/Match-Major-Sheets

Choose any 15 college majors. Follow the link to discover related careers and work settings. You will fill in the chart below with the chose major in the first column, connected careers in the second column, and potential work settings in the third column. The first one is done for you.

| College Majors | Connected Careers | Potential Work Settings |
|---|---|---|
| Communication | Advertizing Copy Editor<br>Event Planner<br>Graphic Designer<br>Social Media Manager<br>Writer/Author | Corporate Setting<br>Consulting Firm<br>Digital Media Companies<br>Magazines<br>Publishing Companies |
| | | |
| | | |
| | | |
| | | |
| | | |
| | | |
| | | |

| College Majors | Connected Careers | Potential Work Settings |
|---|---|---|
|  |  |  |
|  |  |  |
|  |  |  |
|  |  |  |
|  |  |  |

## Match Interests & Careers to Majors

Now we're off to the College Board website where we will look up careers based on your interests. Go to the website and choose a field of interest. bigfuture.collegeboard.org/majors-careers

If you are interested in Health and Medicine, there are three categories under that heading: Health Care Support, Health Diagnosis and Treatment, and Health Technology. Under each heading are a large number of careers to choose from.

| Interest Area | Connected Career | Education Needed |
|---|---|---|
| Health and Medicine: Health Care Support | Physical Therapist Assistant | 2 Year Associate Degree from accredited program |
|  |  |  |
|  |  |  |
|  |  |  |
|  |  |  |

## ECONOMICS, FINANCES, & BUSINESS COURSE

| Interest Area | Connected Career | Education Needed |
|---|---|---|
| | | |
| | | |
| | | |
| | | |
| | | |
| | | |
| | | |
| | | |
| | | |
| | | |

# Potential College Major and Careers

Choose three college majors that you are interested in. List ten possible careers for each one. Be prepared to discuss chart!

| Example of BA/BS in BA in Music | BA/BS in _____ | BA/BS in _____ | BA/BS in _____ |
|---|---|---|---|
| Concert Pianist | | | |
| Vocal Instructor | | | |
| Worship Leader | | | |
| Homemaker/ Homeschool Mom | | | |
| High School Band Teacher | | | |
| Elementary Music Teacher | | | |
| Songwriter | | | |
| Studio Musician | | | |
| College Music Professor | | | |

ECONOMICS, FINANCES, & BUSINESS COURSE

# Career Exploration: Careers You Like

By now you should have a list of at least twenty different careers you are interested in as a result of praying, talking to your parents, interviewing different people about their occupations, and take so many assessments. Make a list of twenty careers that you would like to learn more about.

_____
_____
_____
_____
_____
_____
_____
_____
_____
_____
_____
_____
_____
_____
_____
_____
_____
_____
_____
_____

## Let's Find Out About Your Careers

Now we will use the Occupational Outlook Handbook. This online compilation of information on every career imaginable is put out by the federal government each year. You will look up twenty different careers, recording the information I request in your chart. All the information is in the online handbook.

You will find the Occupational Outlook Handbook here: bls.gov/ooh/

You will need to fill in the following information: Job, Job Description, Workplace, Entry-Level Education, Work Experience in a Related Occupation, Median Pay, Job Outlook, and Number of Jobs. This will give you a bird's eye view of what they do, where they work, and what the pay is like. It will also tell you if the career is growing or declining. This makes a huge difference when looking for jobs. In some jobs, previous related work experience can open the door.

Please look through the very long list of jobs first. It is a amazing how many jobs people do in our nation. When you choose twenty different jobs, please choose jobs you are truly interested in so that this assignment is a productive use of your time.

I will do a few careers for you in the chart.

| Job | Job Description What They Do | Workplace | Entry-Level Education | Work Experience in a Related Occupation | Median Pay | Job Outlook | Number of Jobs 2014 |
|---|---|---|---|---|---|---|---|
| Accountant Auditor | Prepare, examine, and audit financial records | Office or home. Full-time | Bachelors degree in accounting | None | $65,940 $31.70/hr. | 11% growth | 1,332,700 |
| Air Traffic Controllers | Coordinate movement of air traffic to ensure safety | Airport control towers, approach facilities or route centers. Full-time Shift work | Associate's degree & Long-term on-the-job training | None | $122, 340 $58.82/hr. | 9% decline | 24,500 |
| | | | | | | | |
| | | | | | | | |
| | | | | | | | |
| | | | | | | | |
| | | | | | | | |
| | | | | | | | |
| | | | | | | | |

## ECONOMICS, FINANCES, & BUSINESS COURSE

| Job | Job Description What They Do | Workplace | Entry-Level Education | Work Experience in a Related Occupation | Median Pay | Job Outlook | Number of Jobs 2014 |
|---|---|---|---|---|---|---|---|
| Civil Engineers | Build, supervise, operate, & maintain construction projects: roads, buildings, airports, tunnels, dams, bridges, & water systems | Variety of locations, including outside. Full-time | Bachelors degree in civil engineering | None | $82,050 $39.45/hr. | 8% growth | 281,400 |
| | | | | | | | |
| | | | | | | | |
| | | | | | | | |
| | | | | | | | |
| | | | | | | | |
| | | | | | | | |
| | | | | | | | |

| Job | Job Description What They Do | Workplace | Entry-Level Education | Work Experience in a Related Occupation | Median Pay | Job Outlook | Number of Jobs 2014 |
|---|---|---|---|---|---|---|---|
| Editor | Plan, review, & revise content for publication | Office or home | Bachelor's degree in English, Journalism, or Communications | Less than five years | $54,890 $26.39/hr. | 5% Decline | 117,200 |
|  |  |  |  |  |  |  |  |
|  |  |  |  |  |  |  |  |
|  |  |  |  |  |  |  |  |
|  |  |  |  |  |  |  |  |
|  |  |  |  |  |  |  |  |
|  |  |  |  |  |  |  |  |

# The College Application Process & Going to College Debt-Free

Julianna and I often share information on applying at colleges and going to college debt-free to homeschooling familes. Julianna is amazing! She did the college application process and scholarship hunt herself, sifting through the wealth of information and help online. Then three years later, she helped Jenny Rose do the same thing.

You've chosen a college and now it's time to apply. Just like Julianna, you can do this!

## The College Application

The application is easy to fill out. Each college has its own application, but they all ask similar questions related to your high school and extra-curricular activities. Sports, volunteering, leadership positions, GPA, SAT scores, awards, and honors will give the college admissions people an idea of whether you are a student they want to attend their college. It is also an indicator to them about whether or not you will be a successful student. Many college freshmen drop out and never finish their degree. The application usually contains an essay and is turned in with transcripts and class descriptions.

## The Essay

This is an awkward assignment for Christians who want to be humble because you have to "sell yourself" to the college.

Some colleges just have you turn in a high school essay that has already been graded. That's what Stetson University had Julianna do. She submitted one that she wrote for Grandpa's Shakespeare Class.

When you are writing the essay and filling out the application, be sure to talk about why you want to attend the college and how you will be an asset to the campus life and academic world of the campus. Think about leadership positions you have held and volunteer activities that allowed you to learn a new skill. You could share how sports and music commitment taught you discipline and perseverance. Mentioning how wonderful the college is couldn't hurt either!

## Combine Your SAT Scores

You can combine the highest math score with the highest reading score for your overall score. You can take the SAT as many times as you need too.

## Application Fees

Application fees typically run between fifty and a hundred dollars, so put those fees into your budget.

## The Problem with Student Loans

While we are on the subject of application fees, let's talk about college loans. Many of my friends are still paying off their students loans and we are in our fifties. I do not know anyone who is paying student loans that is glad he or she borrowed money.

Over 60% of college graduates will have loans to pay off as soon as they start working. Yes, payment is deferred while the student is at school, but the interest begins accruing right away. The average amount a student will over is over $25,000.00 and the average amount a parent will owe is over $30,000.00. Yikes! That is way too much money to owe when going to college debt-free is possible and not as hard as you think.

When my husband went to seminary we lived on a bare-bone budget with very little for food and no money for recreation. The first two years of our marriage, we both worked, but lived on one income. We saved the second income to pay for tuition. I stayed home with our two children and made crafts to sell in nearby stores. It was the late 1980's and Victorian hair bows were all the rage. I made and sold hundreds of them. Still, times were tough, but we were faithful to tithe and stick to our meager budget. Mike graduated and the lessons of self-control during those years have served us well. We have only borrowed money once for a house. That loan is almost paid off. Best of all, we have never had the pressure of debt in our lives. Most of the marriage counseling we do involves conflict over money, often debt. We are so thankful for that time of financial struggle and hard work. We saw God provide in amazing ways! Amazingly, we learned that life without debt is possible.

I want to challenge you to start adulthood and live life debt-free!

## Freedom From Student Loans

You and your parents will be bombarded with offers of student loans. In fact, if you refuse to get a student loan, some college administrators will act like you are crazy. Make it clear that student loans are not an option for you or your parents.

So, if we avoid debt, how will we pay for college? We have already talked about the biblical work week, but let's review.

## Biblical Work Week

I hear people complain all the time because they worked fifty or sixty hours one week. I smile. God gave us a work week of six days from sun-up to sun-down. That is roughly a 72 hour work week. Now, part of that work week is the time that goes into household chores, training children, ministering at church, and serving in the community. But that work week does not include television watching, video game playing, or meandering through the mall.

We live in a time where the Marxist rejection of hard work is evident everywhere. In Europe they only work 35 hours a week. While I am not advocating 60 hour work weeks, I do think that young adults (and older ones) spend way too much time recreating instead of working hard.

## Hard Work

Hard work is commended by God in Scripture. He tells us that all hard work brings a profit in Proverbs 14:23. That hard work includes chores, housework, ministry, and our jobs. You can work hard. You can work hard at your schoolwork, volunteer at the local dog pound, and cut lawns to earn money to save for college. You can get part-time jobs or start their own businesses. When my son was thirteen, he started a lawn business and budgeted his earnings carefully. Some of that money went into savings for college.

## Use Earliest Deadlines

When you are applying for college, there are several deadlines for turning applications in. Always use the earliest deadline. The early bird gets the worm is definitely true when it comes to getting into colleges and getting scholarship money.

Keep track of all your deadlines in one place so you don't miss anything.

## Research Scholarships

Research college scholarships and private scholarships, as well as grants, or government scholarships. Each university has its own scholarships, as well as access to information about government grants and other scholarships. fastweb.com is a search engine for all kinds of scholarships.

There are basically three kinds of scholarship money you can receive: grant money from the state or federal government, scholarships from the college itself, and private scholarships.

Each university has its own scholarships, as well as access to information about government grants and other scholarships. But, don't stop at the college. Look beyond to other scholarships.

## Grants Need/Merit

Grant money from the federal government is often need-based, but not always. The income cut-off may be higher than you think because they do take into account how big the family is and how many children are attending college.

Some grants are merit-based. This means that even if you don't qualify for aid financially, you ocan get grants for academic or civic merit.

For more information about federal and state grants, check out these websites. You can google information on your state.

## The FAFSA

What on earth is the FASFA? Oh, you will become very familiar with it! The Free Application for Federal Student Financial Aid is filled out every year by college students and prospective college students to determine if a student is eligible for federal grants, work study, or student loans. I do NOT recommend taking out student loans, but you do have to fill this out to get grant money, as well as many scholarships.

To fill this out, you will need to get a lot of information from your parents.

## Apply to at Least Six Colleges

Apply to at least six colleges because all colleges offer different packages. This way you have back-ups if things don't work out the way you hope unless you are positive about where you want to go or money is no object. In our house, my daughters wanted to stay home and commute so we were limited in our options.

## Don't Accept the First Offer

Don't get me wrong. I am not suggesting that you refuse the first offer a college gives you. Simply say, "Thank you so much for your package. I am still waiting to hear back from other colleges so I will get back to you." Sometimes when a university hears you are getting offers from other universities they will offer you a better deal.

## Colleges Don't Negotiate, However....

Colleges always say that they don't negotiate. It is a taboo word for them, but they do have an appeals process and you can ask them about it.

## Start Own Business

Brian and Zack started a computer repair business that morphed into a web-design business. Katie Beth and Jenny Rose have both done tutoring for pay. From a lawn business to a tax preparation service, you have many talents that could be used to make money.

## Slower Pace to Work

There is nothing that says you have to finish college in four years. A slower pace of working and going to school is a great way to avoid debt. Sarah took her time in getting her two year degree so that she could work full time as a hair dresser.

## Work During School/Summer Job

Julianna and Zack both enjoyed working in the dean's office while Rose worked in a coffee shop for her work study. Many restaurants, fast-food joints, retail stores, and other businesses are willing to work around a school schedule. The opportunities are endless for finding a part-time job.

## Community College/State College

Community and state colleges are a wonderful way to begin college education. Classes are usually much cheaper and the entrance requirements are easier. There are remedial classes available for those who struggle with math, writing, or reading. In our state, no one can be turned away from community college if he/she passes the entrance exam. If a student does well at a community college, scholarships are often available for the next leg of college. Just remember to make sure all your classes will transfer into your chosen major. You don't want to repeat classes.

## How They Did It

Let me introduce you to just a few of the godly young people I know who have gone to college debt-free. I know each of them personally and I am so proud of these men and women. All of these young adults stayed plugged into a local church during college and were involved in ministry. They defended their faith in the classroom and at social events. God used each of them to share the Gospel with professors and fellow students.

## How Sarah Did It

Sarah was a twenty-two year old hair dresser when she decided to go back to school. She started at a community college, taking a course or two each semester while continuing to work full time at a hair salon. She studied on her lunch hours and after work. She joined student government and the honors program.

Her excellence soon caught the eye of the professors and administration. She was awarded an amazing JKC scholarship because she was the first in her family to go to college. Sarah got a fantastic free ride for the last two years with a stipend for living expenses, books, and a laptop. The summer between junior and senior year, Sarah got a paid internship that was great experience. Throughout the years, Sarah stayed involved with her church leading LIFE groups and mentoring young women.

All in all, it took her five years, including summers, to finish her bachelor's degree. Today, Sarah is happily married and home taking care of her children.

## How Zack Did It

Zack works harder than any other young person I know. He was awarded scholarships and income-based grants, but those did not cover his full tuition and school expenses. So, Zack got a job at UPS® and started a computer business with his friend, Brian. He worked in the dean's office for work study his junior year followed by a summer with a paying internships at AAA®. UPS has tuition reimbursement provision that covers a small part of his private college tuition. Hard work on Zack's part? Yes! But, he also managed to work with the teen ministry at his church and play drums on the worship team.

## How Julianna Did It

Julianna earned several college credits her senior year of high school which enabled her to take a lighter load and do work-study. She also had great scholarships at a private university and the Florida Bright Futures so there was little out-of-pocket expense for her parents. She worked in the dean's office of the Business and Finance College where she majored in accounting. She was very active in campus life received several awards and honors that helped to pay for tuition. Today, she has a great job with Verizon®.

## How Brian Did It

Brian chose a community college where he started with some remedial classes. The first years of college he started and ran his own computer repair business. However, his good grades and excellent work caught the attention of his professors. He was awarded a full scholarship as well as need-based grants that enabled him to cut his work hours and take a full course load. He was also awarded an internship with NASA one summer. Brain transfered to a state university where he completed his engineering degree. It took Brian a total of six years to complete his degree.

## A Final Word about Colleges

When I walk around the campus of a university that has been dedicated to the Lordship of Christ and is working so hard to turn Christian students away from their faith, I am filled with sorrow. Please remember that most universities are not neutral when it comes to Christianity, they are aggressively against it, making students feel foolish for believing in moral absolutes, creation, or the truth of Scriptures. Make sure you are grounded in

Scripture, apologetics, and worldview training so that you are quick to recognize the lies of the enemy and refute them with the truth.

My friend, Mary, who lost her faith in college, but has come back to Jesus as an older adult, has often told me that she wishes other Christians would have stood up for the Lord and the Bible in her classes. No one did. You can be the one who stands strong for the Lord Jesus Christ on your college campus.

# Discuss College Years with Mom & Dad

Your parents know and love you more than anyone else in the whole world. Whether or not to go to college is an important decision to make with your parents. If you choose to go to college, there are more decisions to make such as which college to go to and what your major will be.

Sit down with your parents and discuss their college years and your own college years. I would make this a serious and special time. Go out for coffee or ice cream so you have uninterrupted quiet time.

Here are some questions to guide your discussion. You might want to take notes.

## Their Educational Experience

Did they go to college?

What was their college experience like?

How has it impacted their life and career?

Did they have another pathway to their career?

What was that experience like?

How did it help or hinder them in their life?

What things would they do differently if they could do it all over again?

## What Advice They Have about Your Career and Educational Pathway

What strengths, gifting, and abilities do they see in your life?

Do they see you going to college? Why or why not?

What career could they see you succeeding in?

What areas of character do they think you need to grow in to be successful?

What skills do they suggest you acquire?

## Hopes & Dreams They Have for You

Are there any hopes and dreams they have for you?

Do they feel that God has shown them anything that is significant about you or your future?

# Preparing for College Worksheet

Answering these questions will require a little bit of research, as well as reviewing the readings and assessments we have finished. I would suggest going on college websites and exploring. Visit at least one college and talk to some college students who are receiving scholarships and grants. Above all, talk to your parents. Let them help you answer these questions and make decisions about preparing for college if college is in your future.

My Personal Mission Statement:

Areas I need to grow in for future life/career/ministry:

Careers I am interested in pursuing:

Majors I'm considering:

Courses and grades that I need for majors I'm considering:

# ECONOMICS, FINANCES, & BUSINESS COURSE

Schools I'm considering and their tuition:

Financial plan for college:

Is it Biblical to borrow money for college?    Support with Scripture.

What does borrowing money do?

What does paying your own way do?

Scholarship options for me:

Federal and private grants available to me:

_____
_____
_____
_____
_____

God's will for my life about college:

_____
_____
_____
_____
_____

ECONOMICS, FINANCES, & BUSINESS COURSE

# February Week Four Class

☐ Discuss Invested $100,000.00

☐ Share Personal Mission Statements & Pray for One Another

☐ Discuss Results of All Assessments

☐ Discuss "Career Possibilities," "College," & "College Majors"

☐ Discuss Ways to Go to College Debt-Free

**Notes from Class**

# February Week Four Home

☐  Read *The Clipper Ship* Strategy

☐  Complete Monthly Consumer Price Index Project

☐  Study for Second Exam on Financial Management

ECONOMICS, FINANCES, & BUSINESS COURSE

# Monthly Consumer Price Index Project

This is an ongoing project for the duration of this class. You will have to go shopping once a month and record prices of each item. Once you choose an item, write it in on your monthly Consumer Price Index Project page. You will need to record the make, model, brand, and size—price the EXACT same item each month. You can go "shopping online." Go to the same store each month. This is a fun project and will provide interesting results at the end of the year.

## Durable Items

(These items are things that you purchase that have life spans of more than 1 year. Examples would be televisions, computers, refrigerators, radios, computers, calculators, washing machines, i-pods, shoes, clothing, chairs, beds, curtains, tables, blenders)

**Durable Item Shopping Bag for Month of** _____

| Durable Item | Store | Brand | Weight or Size | Color | Type/Model | Price |
|---|---|---|---|---|---|---|
| SLR Camera w Lens | Sam's | Nikon | 10 MP 3" LCK 3X Zoom SD/SDHC | | D3000 #23341 | $445.00 |
| | | | | | | |
| | | | | | | |
| | | | | | | |
| | | | | | | |
| | | | | | | |
| | | | | | | |
| | | | | | | |
| | | | | | | |
| | | | | | | |
| | | | | | | |

**Shopping Bag Cost for Durable Item =**

**Non-Durable Items for Month of** _____

(These items are things that you purchase that have life spans of less than 1 year. Examples would be toothpaste, aluminum foil, food, drinks, make-up, gasoline, oil, nail polish, after shave, napkins, fast food, mouthwash, deodorant, candy, vitamins, medicine, contact solution)

**Non-Durable Item Shopping Bag**

| Durable Item | Store | Brand | Weight or Size | Color | Type/Model | Price |
|---|---|---|---|---|---|---|
| Wheat Thins | Target | Nabisco | 10 oz. | | Low-fat Salted | $2.00 |
| | | | | | | |
| | | | | | | |
| | | | | | | |
| | | | | | | |
| | | | | | | |
| | | | | | | |
| | | | | | | |
| | | | | | | |
| | | | | | | |
| | | | | | | |

**Shopping Bag Cost for Non-Durable Item =**

ECONOMICS, FINANCES, & BUSINESS COURSE

**Service Items for Month of** _____

(These are services your family purchases. Examples of services would be haircuts, oil changes, pedicures, lawn mowing, massage, car wash, doctor visit, dental visit, X-ray at hospital, ER visit, gym membership, lawyer consult, accountant consult, taxes, tutoring, college tuition)

Service Items Shopping Bag

| Durable Item | Store | Brand/Kind | Length of Time/Amount | Purpose | Type/Model | Price |
|---|---|---|---|---|---|---|
| Massage | Shear Bliss | | 1 hour | Relaxation | Deep Tissue | $85.00 |
| | | | | | | |
| | | | | | | |
| | | | | | | |
| | | | | | | |
| | | | | | | |
| | | | | | | |
| | | | | | | |
| | | | | | | |
| | | | | | | |
| | | | | | | |

**Shopping Bag Cost for Service Items =**

ECONOMICS, FINANCES, & BUSINESS COURSE

# March

Starting a Business to Glorify God & Serve People

Taking Initiative & Meeting Customer's Needs

Hard Work has Its Specialization & Meeting Customer's Needs

Write Your Own Children's Story

Profit, Perseverance, & Perfecting

Business Planning & Marketing Your Business

Slogans & Logos

*Clipper Ship Strategy* Review

Scheduling

My Schedule Worksheet

Personalized Consumer Price Index Project

## March Week One Class

☐ Discuss Invested $100,000.00

☐ Discuss Monthly Consumer Price Index Project

☐ Take Second Exam on Financial Management

**Notes from Class**

ECONOMICS, FINANCES, & BUSINESS COURSE

# March Week One Home

- [ ] Read "Starting a Business to Glorify God & Serve People" & "Taking Initiative & Meeting Customer's Needs"

- [ ] Complete "Starting a Business Worksheet" & "Taking Initiative & Meeting Customers' Needs" Worksheet

- [ ] Read "Hard Work Has It's Reward" & "Specialization" & Complete "Hard Work & Specialization Worksheet"

- [ ] Complete *Consumer Mathematics Lifepac 8: Business Services*, Section 1 Financial Records: Balance Sheet & Cash Budget

- [ ] Read *The Little Engine that Could* by Watty Piper

- [ ] Write Your Own Children's Story Illustrating the Economic Principle in *The Little Engine that Could*

# Starting a Business to Glorify God & Serve People

We start a business to honor the Lord and serve people. It is not about us or our selfish desires to acquire wealth. We have a need to provide for our family or a desire to sow more money into the Kingdom of God. Along with the need for finances should be a genuine desire to serve people.

We only go around once in this life so we should be careful in how we live. Starting a business is a great idea. Often we start with thinking about what we are good at or what would make us feel fulfilled, but that is not how Christians operate. We put others' needs before our own. How about asking, "What needs are out there that I can fill?"

## How to Start Your Own Business

With the economy shaky, many businesses are downsizing. Our children's soccer coach lost his job a year ago and is starting his own personal training for children business. He is now leading our homeschool coop's P.E.

class. One of my musicians (I am a worship leader) injured his back and is starting a T-Shirt company. His designs are amazing and I look forward to wearing his products. After months of job searching to no avail, my niece is beginning to sell Avon. Our pilot friend lost his job in flight instruction and has started a home improvement and repair company.

My husband and I have had a family business since the early nineties, enjoying the joys and challenges of self-employment. Several years ago, we incorporated our business, making it an umbrella for several businesses, including my new publishing company, Powerline Productions, that my friend, Laura, and I are getting off the ground.

It seems that I am surrounded by people who have, or are starting, their own businesses!

## Reasons for Starting Your Own Business

Reasons abound for starting your own business. What a blessing it would be to be your own boss and have a flexible schedule. You could plan your work hours around the children's school hours and family needs. There is potential to make more money, thus sowing more into the Kingdom of God. You also have the opportunity to cultivate your own leadership skills and impact employees and customers. There is so much to make starting your own business attractive, why doesn't everyone start their own business?

Here is a little reality check. If you are used to working nine to five, or some other forty hour a week job, starting a business will be a shock. Most business owners put in at least 70 to 80 hours a week, especially when they are getting their business off the ground. Many times, there is no profit (and thus, no paycheck) for two to three years. There are, of course, exceptions to this, but, for the most part, starting your own business is a huge undertaking, best begun with lots of prayer and clear direction from God.

"There is no wisdom, no insight, no plan that can succeed against the LORD" (Proverbs 21:30 NIV ©1979).

The most important reason to start your own business is that God has called you to start a business. His heart and plan is for you to be blessed so that you can be a blessing to those around you. If God's plan and destiny for your life includes starting your own business, it will impact the people around you for His glory. That doesn't mean that it has to be a ministry, but that you minister through it to your employees and customers. Don't even try to start a business that isn't God's will or plan for your life. If a business doesn't honor the Lord, it is not God's will.

"Plans fail for lack of counsel, but with many advisors they succeed" (Proverbs 15:22 NIV ©1979).

Get counsel from trusted friends and family members before beginning your own business. What do they think? Write down their counsel and prayerfully consider it! It is good to talk to mature Christians, other business owners, and people who know the real you to get a broad range of counsel and insight.

## Pitfalls to Owning Your Own Business

Before we talk about the character traits necessary to owning your own business, let's talk about three very big character flaws that cause problems for business owners. If you see yourself in these pitfalls, don't despair. The Lord can change and mature you in Him. Work on these areas and get them straightened out before you start your own business. I have seen these three things cause businesses to fail.

### Self-Government

"Like a city whose walls are broken down is a man who lacks self-control" (Proverbs 25:28 NIV ©1979).

A business owner without self-control will not be able to run her business effectively. Self-government is simply the ability to run your own life well, control your emotions, manage your time, manage your money, maintain healthy relationships, and follow through with personal plans and goals. Without the ability to manage yourself, you will not be able to manage a business.

## Scheduling

"Teach us to number our days aright, that we may gain a heart of wisdom" (Psalm 90:12 NIV ©1979).

Hard work is required to get a business off the ground. Hours and hours of work must be scheduled into your life without taking away from the priorities of family, church, and time with the Lord. If you cannot prioritize and schedule your life, when you start your business, you may let important things in your life fall through the cracks.

## Administrative Abilities

"Let love and faithfulness never leave you; bind them around your neck, write them on the tablet of your heart. Then you will win favor and a good name in the sight of God and man" (Proverbs 3:3-4 NIV ©1979).

Bookkeeping, accounting, record keeping, and other administrative tasks have always bored me, but I realize their importance if a business is to succeed. You not only risk trouble with the IRS and other government agencies, but you can find yourself in trouble with customers, employees, and vendors if you are not careful. Cross every "t" and dot every "I" in your business! It is a matter of integrity. People should be able to trust you completely, down to every last administrative detail.

# Character Qualities Business Owners Need

## Upbeat/Positive Attitude

Starting a business requires faith in God. It is hard, if not impossible to start a business if you are not trusting God, knowing you can trust Him no matter what.

My friend, Bruce, lost his job and, a month later, got into a car accident. Both times, he kept his eyes on the Lord, proclaiming to all who would listen, "God allowed this to happen. So He will bring good out of these situations." His faith encouraged others, but more importantly his faith sustained him through the trials. He believed that God keeps His promises even when bad things happen.

If you start a business, bad things will happen sometimes. Customers won't pay, orders will be lost, mistakes will be made, sales might slow down—will you keep your eyes on Jesus when these things happen or give in to worry?

## Integrity

My husband, Mike Curtis is the godliest man that I have ever met. He has never told a lie, cheated on someone, taken revenge, or done a dishonest thing in his business. As a result, customers trust him to keep his word and do good work. They know that they get what they pay for because he is trustworthy. Can people trust you? Are you a man or woman of integrity? Are you tempted to cheat, steal, or lie? Do you give in to temptation in these areas?

Walk uprightly with the Lord and God will bless you in all your ways, including your business. Have a reputation that is above reproach. God will take care of your business if you honor His Name. A good reputation will not only be good for your business, but will bring glory to God!

## Hard Work

"What are you doing tomorrow afternoon?" I asked my friend, Zack, a young man of nineteen.

"We're going over to my grandparents' house to do some lawn work for them," he answered with a big smile.

"That is so sweet of you!" I commended him. I silently made note that his attitude at serving and working hard was different than other young men his age and I told him so. I was impressed.

"Oh, I enjoy hard work," he grinned.

Wow! Someone who enjoys hard work is miles ahead of the game. Learn to love working hard. Profitable businesses are built by hard work. If you are considering starting your own business, plan to work very hard!

## Going the Extra Mile!

I met Coach Chris when he coached my son's basketball team. The next season, I wanted to put my youngest son, Jimmy on the older age team with his sister. To my surprise, Coach offered to meet Jimmy and I at the YMCA and work with him on a few areas so that he would be able to play with the older children. Jimmy caught on quickly and held his own with the older kids' team.

Later, when Coach Chris started a business, he offered to do a free class for our church homeschool coop. Coach Chris goes the extra mile. A good businessman/businesswoman is willing to go the extra mile, to do a little extra, so that his/her customers and employees feel valued. This can be as simple as remembering people's names, praying for customers, or serving free fresh hot coffee in your store. Look for ways to serve, going the extra mile for God's glory!

ECONOMICS, FINANCES, & BUSINESS COURSE

# Starting a Business Worksheet

What are some good reasons to start your own business?

How can a business glorify God and serve people?

What are some pitfalls to avoid?

How do these pitfalls harm your business?

Give real life examples that you have seen of pitfalls that harm a businessman or businesswoman.

What are godly character qualities that will help a man or woman to be successful in a business adventure?

Give real life examples that you have seen of godly character qualities that profit a businessman or businesswoman.

How would you need to change to be an effective and successful business owner?

# Taking Initiative & Meeting Customer's Needs

When you start a business you want to take initiative and meet customer's needs. A satisfied customer will not only come back, but will tell others about your business.

Make it your ambition to have integrity and honor in all your business dealings. Refuse to compromise. God honors integrity and servanthood.

## Choosing a Business to Start

What business should you start? Let me tell you about two different business experiences where I was led by the Lord.

The first happened when my husband was attending seminary. He was working part-time and going to school. I was home with babies, watching an extra child to bring in extra money, and making crafts that I sold at craft shows or in local country stores. I also made lots of hair bows for my daughters and myself. (It was the late eighties when hair bows were in.) While I was praying for wisdom, people began asking for me to make hair bows for their girls too and soon I was making hair bows for all my friends. It was very quick to make them. I made a ruffle on the sewing machine, attached it with fishing wire to a hair clip. The materials were inexpensive. Suddenly, I realized that I had a cost-effective craft that could be made quickly. I made thousands of hair bows, selling them along with my crafts. They outsold everything else!

A few years later, I was reading the food section of the newspaper. They were having a cookie recipe contest. I sensed that the Lord was telling me to enter the contest. So, I did and won! The next urging from the Lord was to write an article for Teaching Home magazine. Though I love to write, I felt nervous, but I had confidence because I had won the contest. I submitted my first article and it was accepted. This led to writing many articles for magazines. The Lord built my confidence first with the recipe contest! Ask Him to build your confidence too!

What business should you start? The possibilities are endless. Here are some things to pray and think about in choosing a business to start. Why not come up with a list of every possible business idea that you might try and then use the following things to narrow your list down to some real possibilities.

- Personal skills/acquired skills
- Passions
- Assess need in market (Research, target, look at a wide range of services)
- Start-up costs and risk involved

## What Will Make Your Business Different?

The big question, once you have chosen a business is this: What will make your business different from its competitors? (Price? Service? Innovation?)

Once you have chosen a business to start, research other businesses that will be your competitors. Look into the prices they charge, the services they offer, and anything that makes customers choose to use them.

Now, what can you do that's different? Can you offer a better price? Can you offer a free service or a free warranty? Can you offer a twist to the product or service that others are offering? What can you do that is innovative and creative?

## Serve your Customer

Serve your customers and potential customers. If you are starting a massage business (you can practice on me ☺), then offer free massages. Or, when you give your massages, make it your ambition to encourage your customers in the Lord and help them to leave refreshed in spirit as well as body.

Take a personal interest in your customers. Remember their name and greet them when you see them. Pray for them, and with them, if the opportunity arises. Try to be a blessing. Don't sell them something they don't need. If you can't offer them what they need, then send them to a place where they can get what they need.

Ask the Lord for creative ideas and ways to serve your customers and He will do it!

With my business, I offer free or inexpensive seminars to encourage and equip homeschooling families to be successful in their homeschooling adventures. On my Facebook page, I share anything that I think would be helpful to them, including other publishers, seminars, freebies, and words of encouragement. They are important to me as people. If they buy my books, that is great, but if they don't, I still want to build them up in the Lord.

## Take Initiative

Do not be passive. Be proactive and take initiative to build your business. When Zack and Brian started their computer business, they did several things to get their business off the ground. Here are some of the ways they got things moving when they started their computer repair business.

- Fasted and prayed
- Asked friends to fast and pray for them
- Received godly counsel
- Followed godly counsel
- Filled out all the government forms and requirements to start their own business
- Made business cards
- Set up a table at Stetson University
- Visited businesses with their flyers (dressed up in shirts and ties)
- Offered new customer discounts
- Made a website
- Made a Facebook fan page
- Fixed people's computers for free
- Asked people to write testimonial letters for their website

I could go on, but you get my point. They were aggressive in starting their business. They took initiative to get things up and running. Their initiative, followed by hard work and meeting their customers' needs has paid off!

## Make a Mission Statement

Make a Mission Statement for your business. This will sum up your business's purpose for existing. It should clearly communicate your business's reason for existence.

Show your mission statement to your grandmother or younger sibling. If they don't understand it, it's too complicated! Start over.

Here are some business mission statements. Can you guess who they belong to?

- To give ordinary folk the chance to buy the same things as rich people
- To preserve and improve human life
- We exist to refresh and benefit everyone we touch
- A Natural Habitat Refuge where elephants can once again walk the earth in peace and dignity
- Plugging into the Source and changing the world with God's power
- Solve complex network computing problems for government, enterprises, and service providers

You will share your mission statements with your parents and siblings (or your coop class) and they will help you to tweak it.

## Record Keeping and Diligence

There are many legal aspects of starting and running a business. You will learn about these things in Business by the Book and as you do research to make your own business plan.

The important thing to remember is to set up a record keeping system and be faithful to keep it up to date on a daily basis. There is so much to do.

It is also important to stay on a schedule so that you put lots of hours into your business. There is lots to do. If you need help with scheduling and time management, talk to your parents and ask for their help and input.

## Alpha Omega Consumer Math Lifepac 8: Business Services

You will start Alpha Omega's *Consumer Math Lifepac 8: Business Services* this week. You will do the first section on keeping financial records. You will learn about making a balance sheet and a cash budget. This lifepac will teach you to do some business record keeping. Have fun!

ECONOMICS, FINANCES, & BUSINESS COURSE

# Taking Initiative & Meeting Needs

Use the business you are going to start or make up a business that you might start for this exercise.

Name of business:


What this business sells (product or service and what specifically):


Who will your customers be (teenage baseball players, forty-something homemakers, homeschool dads, college students)?


How will you make this business better than the competition?


How will you serve your customers & meet their needs?


How will you take initiative to get this business started?


With all of this in mind, what is your mission statement going to be?

# Hard Work Has Its Rewards & Specialization

A business takes lots of hard work. The "Puritan work ethic" is a recipe for success. A business owner puts in many more hours than an employee. Another important aspect of success is specialization. Let your company do something that it is particularly good at. Don't try to do or make a million things to sell. Instead, specialize. Focus on one or two things that will be the best of the best.

My friend, Roxane is a great example of hard work. She is the owner of a clothing and jewelry boutique, Walk on Water. She has also specialized in clothing and jewelry. Let me introduce you to Roxane. She is a great example of a good Christian running a business to glorify the Lord and serve people.

## Walk on Water I

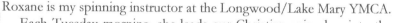

Roxane is my spinning instructor at the Longwood/Lake Mary YMCA. Each Tuesday morning, she leads our Christian spin class into the Presence of God with Christian music, prayer, and carefully chosen Scripture passages. Roxane is also a godly wife, doting mother, and owner of Walk on Water, an upscale clothing boutique, offering fashionable clothing, handbags, shoes, and jewelry. Roxane carries a selection of Brighton, Vera Bradley, Pandora & Yellow Box Shoes at her lovely store. She generously gives to charity and proclaims Christ throughout her life, including in her business.

I wish you could meet Roxane in person. You would love her! I'd like to introduce you to her right now. Let's learn from our dear sister in Christ. Roxane has wisdom for those wishing to start their own business and carefully balance the demands of family, home, and business.

**Meredith:** Roxane, why did you start Walk on Water??

**Roxane:** Through a long journey God directed us to this amazing opportunity to open a store that would glorify Him and help those in need. After 17 years working with a family retail business, we were able to agree to sell that business to a national chain. I realized I was working for a paycheck and not for God's purposes. When Jesus came into my heart, I understood the priority of putting Him first, my husband second.

Through God's blessing, we were able to have our precious son after 12 years of marriage. I was able to take many Bible studies and grow in God's Word through this time. When my son entered the first grade, God started moving my heart to take a business affinity course that would teach me how to run a business using godly principles.

The location at Lake Mary Colonial Town Park was just undergoing construction and my husband and I prayed about the possibility of opening a business that would make a difference in our community and follow biblical principles. I knew I would not follow the world's principles of working all the time and would need a great assistant who would share my responsibilities. My previous assistant was available and interested in helping me. She had 2 children as well. We decided we could work and open a store without missing out on being there for our families. My husband made the final decision as I was concerned about the business being a success, starting a new concept, being able to keep my priorities in order, and how it would affect our family. We sought God's counsel through our pastors, a Christian counselor, and friends who were mentors to us. God clearly opened every door to open Walk on Water.

**Meredith:** Why did you choose the name, Walk on Water?

**Roxane:** I knew when God first put the thought of Walk on Water on my heart that this was the name for the store. I also knew that we would be challenged because of the bathing suit store, Walk on Water and the thought in the consumer's mind that this was a bathing suit store. However, God directed me, so there was no doubt this was the name.

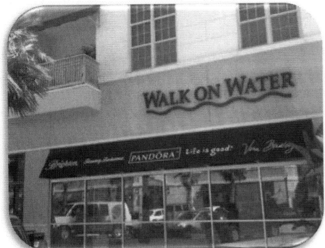

"During the fourth watch of the night, Jesus came to them walking on the water...'Lord, if it's you,' Peter replied, 'Tell me to come to you on the water'" (Matthew 14:25,28 NIV ©1979).

When we take our eyes off Jesus, like Peter did, and focus on the difficult circumstances, it causes us to get under our problems. But when we cry out to Jesus, He catches us by the hand and raises us above the seemingly impossible surroundings.

Peter started out with good intentions, but his faith faltered. When Peter, in fear, cried out to the Lord, the only one who could help him, the Lord pulled Peter out. It is such a lesson for all of us in every circumstance.

**Meredith:** What things are you careful to do in your business to honor the Lord?

**Roxane:** Walk on Water is dedicated to the Lord. There are Scriptures under the tile and carpet, a compass representing the Bible over the center of the store, and a dove on the East marker representing Christ's return. We have John 3:16 on the bottom of our receipt.

Our mission statement is "We are a Christian business focused on glorifying God through the store and helping those in need."

When someone asks me who owns the store, I always respond, "God owns the store, but He lets me run it."

We pray over the store and ask God's guidance with our outreach projects for the community and those in need.

**Meredith:** Tell me about your employees?

**Roxane:** My associates are amazing. They are blessings. I am so blessed to have such a wonderful team. My average associate works 20 hours and is hired because she has a kind heart, loves the Lord, loves serving, and are working for much more than a paycheck.

I have 25 of the most amazing ladies who work with me. I am so blessed as they represent what the store is about and serve our customers and build relationships. They understand the mission of the store and are focused on making a difference in the lives of those in our community.

**Meredith:** I love that you call your employees, associates. This title conveys respect and appreciation. What can you recommend to other business owners about getting along with their associates?

**Roxane:** We follow the Golden Rule and treat our associates with great respect. They represent Walk on Water, being the front line of who the customer sees. I love my team! I have them to my home for a huge Christmas party every year where they are honored, given gifts, and acknowledged in front of each other for the wonderful gifts and talents they have. They bring their husbands. We have a wonderful time of dinner and fellowship together. My advice is to treat your employees with respect and love. Remember, your roles could be reversed one day, so treat them the way you would want to be treated.

**Meredith:** Your store is generous in donating to charities. Why do you do what you do? What fruit have you seen from this?

**Roxane:** We know that the store is the Lord's store and everything in it is His. We are to be good stewards of what He has given us.

There are 2,300 verses in the Bible about money. After taking the Crown Ministries and the Business Affinity course, I am well versed on the fact that everything we have is the Lord's and we are here to glorify Him, serve Him, tell the world about Jesus, and make disciples. He has blessed us greatly, giving us amazing opportunities to help many organizations.

When the earthquake hit Haiti, we immediately prayed about giving the Lord a percentage of our January earnings. We had a record January. I can tell you story after story of similar cases.

The Lord directs our path with the various needs in the community and He blesses our efforts. We started an annual run in August for Safehouse of Seminole. Our first year we had over 200 participants. This year we will have the same run on August 7. I know the Lord will bring over 300 participants. All the money goes to help those women and children in the most difficult of circumstances. To be given the opportunity to have a business that is the Lord's and to do these types of events is what drives our business.

**Meredith:** You were able to expand from one store to two stores. How did this come about? What were the challenges?

**Roxane:** We prayed about expanding the business and God opened up the Winter Park opportunity. My husband made the decision after intense prayer and godly counsel.

We decided to keep the store small and sell only women's items. This would help us with our buying power, customer requests, and, most importantly, bringing our vision to another community.

The challenges are great because I can't be in two locations at once. I have my priorities of God first, husband second, child third, church fourth, and, then, work. I follow these principles. Because I can't spend as much time in Winter Park, I have additional challenges, yet God continues to bless us and we work through these challenges.

Having a second location, though, does split all our expenses in half to help us be more profitable. So, we have more to give to the Kingdom.

**Meredith:** How do you manage two stores, take care of your family, teach classes at the YMCA, stay involved in your church, and do everything else you do?

**Roxane:** "Only one life will soon be past; only what's done for Christ will last!" The Lord has brought me out of the pit and turned my life around! I owe Him everything!

He has given me gifts that are to glorify Him. I have a wonderful husband, a wonderful team at Walk on Water, and wonderful people in my life who support me so I can use the gifts God has given me. As long as I keep my priorities in check, God gives me the energy and ability to serve Him in all these ways.

He created me with a lot of energy as I have always been involved in many things. I pray to use this energy to glorify Him in all parts of my life and am so grateful for what He has done for me on the cross that I want to use every waking moment that I can to do what He has for me to do.

I plan for time away and breaks to refresh and be still--this also energizes me. My Bible study and fellowship with sisters in Christ is such a refresher and energizer as well. My husband and son are with me, travel with me to shows, and help me at the stores. Even though my husband works full time as a financial planner, he also handles all our business finances and finds time to coach my son in his sports endeavors. I could never do this without the Lord, my precious family, my church family and friends, and my amazing team at the store.

**Meredith:** Roxane, what final wisdom can you leave us with?

**Roxane:** Follow what God's plan and purpose is for your life using the gifts and talents He has given you. Never let the world tell you that you can't do something the Lord puts on your heart. Knowing His Word and having a personal relationship with Him is the most important thing in our lives. Give Him first place and it is amazing what He can do through you. The highest calling we have is being God's children, wives, and moms. There is no higher call or privilege!

**Meredith:** Thank you, so much. May God bless you, your family, and your business in every way! Thank you for being such an inspiration to me!

# Hard Work and Specialization Worksheet

What kind of business did Roxane start?

Had she ever had her own business before Walk on Water?

What place does God play in her business?

How is Roxane a blessing to people?

How does she glorify the Lord?

What role does her husband play in her business?

How does she put the Lord first in her business?

What is her mission statement?

How does she treat her employees?

How did she specialize in her Winter Park store?

How has the Lord blessed Roxane and her family?

# March Week Two Class

☐ Read Stories Aloud in Class

☐ Discuss "Starting a Business", "Taking Initiative and Meeting Customer's Needs", "Hard Work has Its Rewards", & "Specialization"

☐ Discuss Business Finances

**Notes from Class**

## March Week Two Home

☐ Read "Profit, Perseverance, & Perfecting"

☐ Complete "Profit, Perseverance, & Perfecting Worksheet"

☐ Read "Business Planning" & "Marketing Your Business"

☐ Complete "Business Planning Worksheet"

☐ Read *Principles Under Scrutiny* Section on "Business" and Create 14 Slogans with Logos for each Principle of Business

☐ Read *The Little Engine that Could* by Watty Piper and Write Story that Illustrates this Economic Prinicple

☐ Complete *Consumer Mathematics Lifepac 8: Business Services* Section II Financial Records

☐ Read *The Clipper Ship Strategy*

# Profit, Perseverance, & Perfecting

The purpose of a business is to make a profit. The purpose of a business is not to provide jobs—that is a by-product. You are in business to make a profit. Out of that profit comes income for your family, profit to expand, and extra money to sow into the Kingdom of God.

## Profit

Profit is the money that is left after you subtract all expenses. Remember, we said earlier that businesses require capital to start up. Some businesses require a lot of capital and some a small amount of capital.

Most businesses will not make a profit for a couple of years because of the start-up costs and the money required to keep the business growing.

A non-profit organization (like a church) does not exist to make a profit, but they have to operate within their financial means. They cannot spend more than they take in. A business must spend even less than they take in to make a profit.

There are many expenses that are subtracted from the sale of your service or product before you can make a profit. Here are some of them

- Licenses
- Insurance
- Employee Salaries (plus health insurance, workmen's compensation, unemployment insurance, Social Security taxes, vacation days, training, other benefits)
- Raw materials to make product
- Machines, building, other overhead
- Office supplies, computers
- Advertizing, business cards
- Taxes
- Social Security
- And more….

There are many expenses involved in a business. Here is a profit/loss statement to help you see how profit is determined.

## Perseverance

Remember I told you that we invested the last of our money in a lawn business when Mike was in seminary. Well, he got several residential lawns to cut after going door to door and distributing flyers. This was not enough, though, to give us the income we needed.

He was really discouraged. I was sad too. Had we thrown our money away? Hadn't we prayed and fasted? Had God forgotten us? What a bad time it was for us—those weeks and months in the beginning.

Finally, we were desperate and Mike said to the Lord, "I guess you don't want me in seminary. So, I will look for a job and give up this dream. I thought I was obeying You, but I guess somewhere I missed Your voice."

Mike sensed in his heart that God wanted Mike to give Him one more week.

So, we held on.

A week later, the manager of the grounds at Mike's seminary saw Mike on his way to class and asked how his business was going. He also asked Mike if he would like to put in a bid to mow the student housing lawn. Mike agreed to put in a bid.

What would we do? Mike tried to get counsel, but no one knew what to tell him to do. So, he prayed and came up with a figure. It was the exact figure that the other company gave too. And, since, Mike was a student at the University, they gave the account to him.

What a joyous time! I am so glad we persevered.

It is easy to give up when you are starting a business, but don't give up! Hang in there! You will reap what you sow!

"Let us not become weary in doing good, for at the proper time we will reap a harvest if we do not give up" (Galatians 6:9 NIV ©1979)

## Perfecting

Continual improvement is your goal as a business owner. You want to get better and better at what you do. Always strive to be better at what you do in your business. Do not become complacent. Instead, work hard and get better at what you do!

"Do you see a man skilled in his work? He will serve before kings; he will not serve before obscure men" (Proverbs 22:29 NIV©1979).

ECONOMICS, FINANCES, & BUSINESS COURSE

# Profit, Perseverance, & Perfecting Worksheet

What is the purpose of a business?

What is profit?

What expenses must be subtracted from the price of your product/service?

Why would someone have to persevere when they are starting a business?

What are your plans to grow and improve your product/service?

# Business Planning

There is so much involved in getting a business off the ground. It can feel overwhelming. But, take everything step by step and you will get there!

## Get Ready

Learn all you can learn about starting a business before you take the plunge, but realize you will have to learn many things as you go! Write a business plan, gather finances, and trust the Lord to help you in this new adventure.

## Write a Business Plan

A business plan has several components that help you to begin your business with wisdom and confidence. Here are the parts of a business plan.

- Mission Statement
- Description of business
- Market Analysis (Identify target market and learn about them, how will you reach your customer base)
- Company Description
- Organization & Management (Roles, type of cooperation—sole proprietor, partnership, S or C cooperation)
- Marketing Strategy
- Service or Product line (what you are selling)
- Finances (Projected income, projected expenses, start-up costs)

## Find a Mentor

Look for someone in your life that is a successful business owner and a godly Christian. He or she doesn't have to have the same kind of business you have, just be willing to give you advice, answer questions, and walk you through some of the confusion of starting a business.

## Gather Finances for Start-up

There are many ways to gather finances. You can use savings, an inheritance, or a large financial gift to get started. Zack worked at UPS and saved as much money as he could from his paycheck, while Brian sold musical equipment to help with the start-up costs. Don't borrow money!

## Name your Business

This is the fun part! Get ideas by talking to friends and family members, looking online, and looking at advertisements.

## Choose a Structure

Your business can be a sole proprietorship (one owner), a partnership (co-owners), or a corporation (the business is a separate entity). Often when you start out with a small business, you are a sole proprietorship and then as you grow and add employees, you incorporate.

## Get Licenses and Permits

Every state has different laws and fees so check with your state government office to find out what you need to do to be legal in your state.

## Market and Price

Study the market for your product or service. What would a fair market price be where the customer will be happy and you can still make a profit?

## Market and Sell

Produce or offer a service that your target market will want to buy. Then let them know that it is available. That is the essence of marketing. Use name recognition, advertizing, and customer satisfaction to market your product.

## Use the Golden Rule

Jesus told us to treat others as we want to be treated ourselves (Roxane mentioned this too in her interview!). Be honest and kind in all your dealings. Believe the best about your customers and suppliers. Treat your employees the way you would like to be treated.

## Pay your Taxes

Yes, the government wants its share. It is a good idea to have an accountant help you with setting up your taxes and payment schedule.

## Get Insurance

Mike has to have general liability insurance and workmen's compensation. Depending on your industry, you will need to have different kinds of insurance.

## Financial Growth

Put some of your profit into growing the business. The temptation might be to take it all as salary, but make a financial commitment to growing the business and improving your product and service.

Grow in your abilities/Improve your Product or Service

Grow in your relationship with Jesus. Grow in your relationships with your family and friends. And, grow as a businessman or businesswoman. Attend workshops, read books, read blogs, talk to other business owners, network, and do all you can to be the very best you can be. Look for ways to improve your product or serve and meet the needs of the customer.

(Copyright Gospel Communications International, Inc - www.reverendfun.com )

## Alpha Omega Consumer Math Lifepac 8: Business Services

You will continue with *Alpha Omega's Consumer Math Lifepac 8: Business Services* this week. You will do the second section on keeping financial records. You will learn about reconciling a bank statement and recording payroll deductions. This Lifepac will teach you to do some business record keeping. Have fun!

# Business Planning

What are ingredients of a business plan?

How long will it take to get ready to start a business (this is what you think!) and why?

What are some of the things that need to be done to keep a business going?

What are some different ways to structure a business?

What are the different roles in your business? Who will fill each role?

# 14 Slogans and Logos

Read *Biblical Principles Under Scrutiny's* Section on "Business" There are fourteen different principles. Make a logo and slogan to go with each principle. A logo is a design that can be easily recognized as belonging to an organization or business. Nike's logo is a swoosh. Powerline's logo is a cross with a plug at the end. A slogan is a short catchy phrase that people will have no trouble remembering. There are 14 principles—make a logo with a slogan for each one. Thank you so much!

Principle # 1 is

Principle # 2 is

Principle # 3 is

Principle # 4 is

Principle # 5 is

Principle # 6 is

Principle # 7 is

Principle # 8 is

Principle # 9 is

Principle # 10 is

Principle # 11 is

Principle # 12 is

ECONOMICS, FINANCES, & BUSINESS COURSE

Principle # 13 is                    Principle # 14 is

Okay, how about a logo and slogan for your company!

# The Clipper Ship Strategy Review

A short book review based on *The Clipper Ship Strategy* by Richard J Maybury

Answer the following questions using complete sentences!

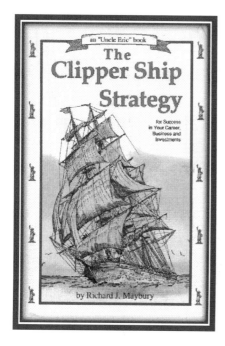

What is the Clipper Ship story?

What is the Clipper Ship strategy?

Explain "cones" and "hot spots".

How can you take advantage of "cones" and "hot spots"?

What are some different types of "cones"?

Share a real life investment idea based on the clipper ship strategy.

# March Week Three Class

☐ Read Stories Aloud in Class

☐ Discuss "Profit, Perseverance, & Perfecting", "Business Planning", & Slogans & Logos

☐ Discuss *The Clipper Ship Strategy*

☐ Discuss Business Finances

**Notes from Class**

## March Week Three Home

☐ Read "Scheduling"

☐ Fill Out "My Schedule"

☐ Start Reading *Business by the Book*

☐ Complete *Consumer Mathematics Lifepac 8: Business Services* Section III Business Operations

# Scheduling

Time management is necessary so that our business will run smoothly. We can easily be distracted by the tyranny of the urgent. Routine and a predictable schedule provide a framework for all the hard work of running your business.

Even if you are not a "schedule person," I recommend at least a loose schedule to provide structure. Set aside time to plan, do record keeping, make trips to the bank, advertize, and produce your product or do your service. If there is something you want to get done, then schedule it in. Make a decision to be proactive, making changes so that you manage your time rather than time managing you.

Once a day is done, it is lost forever, so make the most of every day God gives! Realize that you are a steward of God's time. Honor him with the way you manage your personal time and business time.

## Business Administration

There is record keeping and financial records to keep. Schedule a time to do your record keeping and make your bank runs.

## Marketing

Set aside time to learn more about your target market and how to serve them. Plan advertizing strategies and keep your website updated. Consider a blog or facebook fan page. All of these require regular updating—schedule it in!

## Making Your Product or Doing Your Service

Set aside plenty of time to do the actual work of your business. The product or service you offer should be excellent. Give your best to this business.

## Appointments

Business requires you to meet people for lunch or at a place of business to get work done. Sometimes, you have to pick up materials or supply a vendor with goods. Be on time to all of your appointments. And if someone is calling to see you, make sure you are where you said you'd be.

## Calendars & Day-timers

A calendar is a wonderful planning tool that gives us a bird's-eye-view of our life month by month. One glance tells us if we are too busy and keeps upcoming events fresh in our minds and sight. We can use a calendar to manage our time on a yearly and monthly basis.

Personal things should be written on the calendar as soon as possible: vacations, weddings, parties, workshops, due dates, and any other company dates. Place your calendar in a prominent place where you can see it. Tentative items should be written in lightly with pencil. If everything is immediately put on the calendar, schedule complications are avoided.

Weekly and daily planning can be done in a day-timer or appointment book. Everyone finds the right scheduling tool for them, usually through trial and error. You may invent your own scheduling tool. This planning is detailed and includes calls to make, things to buy, appointments, errands, banking, etc. Everything on the calendar will be on the weekly and daily planning sheet but with a lot more!

A "typical day" schedule is nice to have in the front of the planner with devotion times, church meetings, family obligations and business hours blocked off. But every week will be different. And additions will sometimes require alterations in your daily schedule. An early appointment may require rising one hour earlier so you don't miss your time with the Lord.

## Schedule & Routine

Routines are simply patterns and daily rituals, things you do without thinking. It is good to get into daily habits such as making your bed upon arising, brushing your teeth after meals, having a daily quiet time, and returning phone calls at a certain time each day. Routine provides a sense of stability and it is a way to make sure that mundane tasks do not fall through the cracks.

While a routine is a pattern of daily habits, a schedule is a timetable that allows you to set aside the time needed to accomplish your goals. The best of intentions won't happen unless time is set aside to accomplish the task!

Some people enjoy a schedule more than others do. If a rigid schedule works for you, then do it! If not, at least come up with a flexible schedule or routine.

My schedule does not have times. From wake-up time until lunch time there are things that I accomplish each day and things specific to a certain day of the week. Then from lunch time to dinner time, we flow through a routine.

Whether you like a flexible schedule or a more rigid schedule, I encourage you strongly to make a schedule and to put it in writing! Better yet, post it in several prominent places in the house. I hang my children's schedules in the homeschool room and also put a copy in their assignment folders. As you can guess, some of my children are more likely to follow it independently than others! But now, all of my children stick to the schedule.

The reality is that time management is a major reason that small businesses fail. Do not let this trip you up. Resolve to manage your time with excellence!

# My Schedule

|  | Sunday | Monday | Tuesday | Wednesday | Thursday | Friday | Saturday |
|---|---|---|---|---|---|---|---|
| Wake up Time | | | | | | | |
| Breakfast Time | | | | | | | |
| | | | | | | | |
| Lunch Time | | | | | | | |
| | | | | | | | |
| Dinner Time | | | | | | | |
| | | | | | | | |
| Bedtime | | | | | | | |

## Alpha Omega Consumer Math Lifepac 8: Business Services

You will continue Alpha Omega's *Consumer Math Lifepac 8: Business Services* this week. You will do the third section on business operations. You will learn about pricing considerations, terms of credit, and markups, markdowns, and discounts. This lifepac will teach you to do some business record keeping. Have fun!

ECONOMICS, FINANCES, & BUSINESS COURSE

# March Week Four Class

☐ Discuss "Scheduling"

☐ Watch *The Ultimate Gift*

☐ Complete Movie Review on *The Ultimate Gift*

☐ Discuss How the Lessons in *The Ultimate Gift* Help Someone Run a Business

**Notes from Class**

# The Ultimate Gift Movie Review

This movie is a great illustration of the gifts that God gives to people so that they can be financially successful. Watch this movie and answer these questions.

Who are the main characters in this movie?

The grandfather requires his grandson to receive several gifts before he receives the actual inheritance of money. Why does he do this?

What are the "gifts" that he receives?

How do these gifts benefit you and me in our lives and financial endeavors?

What gifts has God given you so that you can be successful in life and finances?

ECONOMICS, FINANCES, & BUSINESS COURSE

# March Week Four Home

☐ Read *A Bargain for Frances* by Russell Hoban & Write Your Own Children's Story illustrating the Economic Principle from the Book

☐ Read *Business by the Book*

☐ Complete "Monthly Consumer Price Index Project"

☐ Complete *Consumer Mathematics Lifepac 8: Business Services* Lifepac Test

## Alpha Omega Consumer Math Lifepac 8: Business Services

You have finished Alpha Omega's *Consumer Math Lifepac 8: Business Services*. This week you will take the Lifepace test.

Test Score = _____

# Monthly Consumer Price Index Project

This is an ongoing project for the duration of this class. You will have to go shopping once a month and record prices of each item. Once you choose an item, write it in on your monthly Consumer Price Index Project page. You will need to record the make, model, brand, and size—price the EXACT same item each month. You can go "shopping online." Go to the same store each month. This is a fun project and will provide interesting results at the end of the year.

## Durable Items

(These items are things that you purchase that have life spans of more than 1 year. Examples would be televisions, computers, refrigerators, radios, computers, calculators, washing machines, i-pods, shoes, clothing, chairs, beds, curtains, tables, blenders)

**Durable Item Shopping Bag for Month of** _____

| Durable Item | Store | Brand | Weight or Size | Color | Type/Model | Price |
|---|---|---|---|---|---|---|
| SLR Camera w Lens | Sam's | Nikon | 10 MP 3" LCK 3X Zoom SD/SDHC | | D3000 #23341 | $445.00 |
| | | | | | | |
| | | | | | | |
| | | | | | | |
| | | | | | | |
| | | | | | | |
| | | | | | | |
| | | | | | | |
| | | | | | | |
| | | | | | | |
| | | | | | | |

**Shopping Bag Cost for Durable Item =**

## ECONOMICS, FINANCES, & BUSINESS COURSE

**Non-Durable Items for Month of** _____

(These items are things that you purchase that have life spans of less than 1 year. Examples would be toothpaste, aluminum foil, food, drinks, make-up, gasoline, oil, nail polish, after shave, napkins, fast food, mouthwash, deodorant, candy, vitamins, medicine, contact solution)

**Non-Durable Item Shopping Bag**

| Durable Item | Store | Brand | Weight or Size | Color | Type/Model | Price |
|---|---|---|---|---|---|---|
| Wheat Thins | Target | Nabisco | 10 oz. | | Low-fat Salted | $2.00 |
| | | | | | | |
| | | | | | | |
| | | | | | | |
| | | | | | | |
| | | | | | | |
| | | | | | | |
| | | | | | | |
| | | | | | | |
| | | | | | | |
| | | | | | | |

**Shopping Bag Cost for Non-Durable Item =**

## Service Items for Month of _____

(These are services your family purchases. Examples of services would be haircuts, oil changes, pedicures, lawn mowing, massage, car wash, doctor visit, dental visit, X-ray at hospital, ER visit, gym membership, lawyer consult, accountant consult, taxes, tutoring, college tuition)

Service Items Shopping Bag

| Durable Item | Store | Brand/Kind | Length of Time/Amount | Purpose | Type/Model | Price |
|---|---|---|---|---|---|---|
| Massage | Shear Bliss | | 1 hour | Relaxation | Deep Tissue | $85.00 |
| | | | | | | |
| | | | | | | |
| | | | | | | |
| | | | | | | |
| | | | | | | |
| | | | | | | |
| | | | | | | |
| | | | | | | |
| | | | | | | |
| | | | | | | |

**Shopping Bag Cost for Service Items =**

## Alpha Omega Consumer Math Lifepac 8: Business Services

You will start Alpha Omega's Consumer Math Lifepac 8: Business Services this week. You will do the first section on keeping financial records. You will learn about making a balance sheet and a cash budget. This lifepac will teach you to do some business record keeping. Have fun!

ECONOMICS, FINANCES, & BUSINESS COURSE

# April

How to Make a Formal Business Plan

*Business by The Book* Review

Ministry Fundraising Worksheet

Essay: "Seeking First the Kingdom of God in Finances"

Wisdom from Proverbs

Personalized Consumer Price Index Project

# April Week One Class

☐　Read Stories Aloud in Class

☐　Discuss "Monthly Consumer Price Index Project"

☐　Go Over *Consumer Mathematics Lifepac 8: Business Services* Lifepace Test

**Notes from Class**

ECONOMICS, FINANCES, & BUSINESS COURSE

# April Week One Home

☐ Read "How to Get Your Business Started"

☐ Read "How to Make a Formal Business Plan"

☐ Complete "How to Make a Formal Business Plan" Worksheet

☐ Complete "Wisdom from Proverbs Worksheet"

☐ Read *Business by the Book* by Larry Burkett

# How to Get Your Business Started

First, we are going to brainstorm a little bit about the company you have decided to start.

What kind of business are you starting? A service? Will you sell a product?

Mark decided to start a lawn company. He will cut lawns, edge, weed whack, weed flowerbeds, and trim shrubs. He investigate to find out what other companies are selling before he decides what to charge.

Kim will sell her home-baked bread to friends and neighbors. She is also investigating the possibility of getting a table at the nearby Farmer's Market.

Those are great ideas, but let's start a business that is Christ-centered. Let's choose a business to bless God and serve people.

## Choosing a Business to Bless God and People

You are going to start with your idea. What is it that you are going to sell or offer as a service to your customers? How can you serve your customers? How can you honor the Lord with your business? How can the Kingdom of God be extended through your business? What will your mission statement be?

Here are some ideas that people came up with from my economics class to glorify God and bless people with their business idea.

# Blessing God/Serving People

Zack and Brian made plans to start an **Airsoft Business**. Here are the ideas they had to bless God and serve people.

- Do a fundraiser for Steve Smith, a friend who needed a kidney transplant
- Give discounts for church youth-groups
- Keep the course safe
- Sell good quality products and stand behind them

Another student wanted to start an **Architectural Firm**. Here are his ideas.

- Design good quality homes and stand behind them
- Install high quality appliances that won't break
- Give offerings to the church and charities

Jenny Rose wanted to start a business as a **Vocal Coach**. Here are her ideas to glorify God and bless people.

- Giving quality service for an honorable price, one that people can afford.
- Being honest in all my dealings; not shirking my responsibilities (to customers, the government, family, etc.)
- Keeping God, my family, and my church above my business.
- Being encouraging to my customers, yet being truly helpful to them.
- Tithe with the money the business brings in.
- Sharing the Gospel with every customer in a way that isn't overbearing or rude.
- Taking every chance the Lord gives me to share Him with a customer in a deeper way.
- Being willing to work out a payment plan with people who may not be able to afford the asked price.

Tricia was starting a **Babysitting Service**

- Asking for a reasonable price.
- Doing my task with diligence.
- Being kind to the children even when disrespectful, yet not excusing or tolerating rude behavior.
- Cleaning up after myself and any mess the kids make (with their help, of course).
- Being a godly example to the kids and even the parents (especially if non-Christians).
- Tithing with all the money I receive from babysitting!

These are Laura's ideas for glorifying God and serving people through a **Publishing Company.**

- Provide equipping material to the world
- Provide projects in multiple mediums which will help believers to mature and non-believers to find Christ.
- Provide copying and printing services for churches, books for the needy and could sponsor missions trips to bring printed materials including Bibles to the "10-40 window".

Art Gallery

- Feature Christian artists whose works reflect His Glory and His Creation
- Provide studio work space for Christian artists
- Art classes for all ages and most talent levels.

## Your Company Mission Statement

Before you start your company, you need to clarify your purpose and goals.

Here are some company mission statements.

Starbucks® Mission Statement: "To inspire and nurture the human spirit—one person, one cup, and one neighborhood at a time."

Wal Mart® Mission Statement: "We save people money so they can live better."

Google® Mission Statement: "Google's mission is to organize the world's information and make it universally accessible and useful."

Remember that your mission will have something to do with glorifying God and serving people.

## Create a Logo for Your Company

We have already talked about logos. You may have already designed a logo for your company that you love. Or maybe you want to change it. Or maybe you haven't thought up the perfect logo for your company.

Here are a few things to keep in mind about logos:

- Your logo represents your company. When people think of it, they should think of your company and its product or service. When you see the golden arches, you think of McDonald's.
- Your logo should be simple, clean, and easy to recognize.
- Your logo should stick in people's minds and be easy to recognize.
- Your logo should still be cool in ten or twenty years.
- Your logo should look good big or small, in color or black and white, on fabric or on paper.
- Your logo should be appropriate for your target market.
- Your logo should honor Christ and bless people.

Here are the steps to create your own logo:

- Research logos of companies similar to yours
- Think about what makes you and your company unique
- Sketch, doodle, and experiment with all kinds of ideas
- Get input on your sketches from people in your target market
- Go back and revise the ones that catch your attention but aren't quite what you want

## Market Your Company

Word of mouth is a great way to get new customers. Satisfied customers will spread the news about your company. You can go door-to-door in your neighborhood to distribute flyers if you are starting up a lawn service or babysitting service.

What are some other ways you can market your company?

Marketing has changed so much over the last ten years because of social media. Companies have to have Twitter accounts, Facebook pages, Pinterest boards, and blogs.

Here are some ways to market your company

- Set up a website that is appealing and easy to use
- Maintain a daily presence on social media. Post items that will be helpful for your target market
- Ask for help from other business owners to promote you and offer to promote them
- Maintain regular contact with customers and potential customer through email or another method
- Connect with your customers regularly to make sure they are happy
- Give away freebies
- Post short videos on YouTube with helpful information related to your product
- Join online communities
- Speak at events involving your target market

## Getting your Business Started

Stepping out with that initial step can be frightening. So, my advice is: Just Do It! Think of practical things you can do to get things

Here are some ideas that people came up with from my economics class to get their business started.

Jenny Rose's ideas to get her **Vocal Training** business off the ground:

- Go to a school and get vocal training
- Get hired by school as a vocal teacher
- Work on getting an honorable name through a school
- Break off from the school and advertise on my own
- Work on other things such as being part of a traveling band, being a choir director, making a CD, etc.
- Getting any needed equipment

How to get a **Babysitting Business** off the ground according to Tricia:

- KNOW HOW TO HANDLE KIDS! (especially bratty ones)
- Advertise, advertise, advertise!
- Have a specific price, although allowing it to be flexible.
- Seeing if anyone I know needs a babysitter.
- Preferably, have my own transport, a car, a bike, a sister, etc.

Laura's ideas to get a **Publishing Company** started:

- Acquire projects to produce
- Set up web site(s)
- Purchase ISBN numbers
- Get name recognition through a platform like a class at the community college or a seminar at the home school convention
- Hire an editor, illustrator and cover artist
- Make contact and build relationships with distributors like CBD or Rainbow Resource Center
- Purchase printer & binding machine
- Print, Print, Print, Bind, Bind, Bind, Sell, Sell, Sell

## ECONOMICS, FINANCES, & BUSINESS COURSE

To get an **Art Gallery** started:

- Visit many art galleries and museums
- Study art history – ideally you would study in a school and develop a reputation as an art expert, authority, or connoisseur
- Rent/Buy store-front & build out display areas, office areas and work/studio/class areas (the display areas must be alterable so that different exhibits have a completely different look)
- Set up insurance, utilities, and advertising
- Find artists to display, teach, & rent workspace
- Advertise gallery opening and first exhibit
- Open exhibit

There might be things you need to do to get ready to be successful at running your own business. There is always more to learn. We always want to grow and improve. But, let's move forward and gather together all that we have talked about. You have already put down on paper some of these things, but now you might change your mind and want to have a different logo or a different mission statement. That is great!

I recommend bathing this assignment in prayer. A business can be an opportunity to provide for your family and bless other people. This is a grand adventure!

(Copyright Gospel Communications International, Inc - www.reverendfun.com )

# How to Make a Formal Business Plan

You will be working on a formal business plan this month and presenting to your family and friends the first class time in May.

We are going to talk about the ingredients of a formal business plan first. Next, we will talk about how to brainstorm and get ideas out there.

## Ingredients of a Formal Business Plan

There are nine ingredients in a formal business plan.

## Cover Page

A formal business plan has a cover page with the business name, logo, and owners' names. This should be as attractive as possible.

## Executive Summary

This is a brief message from you, the owner of the company to the reader about your company. This paragraph or two should include the management structure, a description of your product or service, your company goals, financial strategy, and marketing strategy.

## Business Description and Mission Statement

This is a brief description of your business's history and mission statement.

## Product or Service

Describe your product or service and include what makes it unique. Share any plans for future products or services.

## Marketing Strategy

This section allows you to explain how you will get your product or service in front of potential customers.

## Competitors Analysis

Use this section to describe your competitors and how you intend to compete in the market.

## Operations Overview

This section is a glimpse into your company on a daily basic. The building site, the production methods, the management and staffing structure, and the manufacturing details. Since you are starting small businesses, this will be a simple section to do.

## Financial

Include your company's profit and loss statements here. If you are going to sell stock, you can mention that here. Give directions for how people can invest.

## Putting the Package Together

Then type everything up nicely with a title page and table of contents. You might want to take it to a print shop and have it bound.

You can look at a sample business plan here: liveplan.com/features/samples_and_examples

This is a challenging project, but you can do it!

## Brainstorming

Here is the beginning of Jenny Rose's business plan (just a list of tasks). Start with jotting down a list of tasks and ideas. Use the worksheet I made you on the next page. (Jenny Rose didn't have that to work with!)

## Jenny Rose's Business Plan Beginning Notes

- Begin giving voice lessons to friends and family (volunteer)
- Start giving voice lessons for pay
- Choose my legal form: sole proprietorship
- Buy a keyboard (around $500)
- Choose a fictitious name
- Buy fictitious name (around $120)
- Set up a record keeping system for income and expenses
- Set up the place where I plan to run my business (my house, most likely)
- Buy a business license (around $100)
- Advertise (putting ads in the paper, setting up flyers, spreading the word, etc.)

## What Do I Do Now?

First, gather information and fill out the brainstorming worksheet with all the information you need. Be as detailed as possible.

You can download a free business plan form at lawdepot.com/

Customize and download your form here: lawdepot.com/contracts/business-plan/?ldcn=partnership-and-joint-venture#.VuhZ4-IrLIU

# My Business Plan Worksheet

This is a brainstorming session for you. Words are highlighted that are part of the formal business plans so that you can go back to this page and grab the information.

**Name** of my Business


**Mission Statement**


How I will glorify God


How I will serve people


**Description** of my business


**Organization** of my Business (sole proprietor, partnership, S or C cooperation)

**Roles** in my business and who will fill them


**Description of my product or service**

ECONOMICS, FINANCES, & BUSINESS COURSE

**Startup Costs** (list expenses)

**Projected Income**

**Projected Expenses**

My **target market**

My **target market** does/says/likes/dislikes/wants (describe)

How I will let my **target market** know about my product or service

How I will take initiative

What hard work I will do

My **competitors** are



What I will offer that is different from my competitors:



How I will **Market** (advertise and get my name out):

# ECONOMICS, FINANCES, & BUSINESS COURSE

**Logo for my business:**

**Advertisement for my business:**

# Wisdom from Proverbs I

This is a visit to the "Book of Wisdom" in the Bible, Proverbs. Proverbs is full of practical wisdom for running a business. Read a chapter each day (M-F) and choose 1 verse that you really like. Write out the verse and share how it applies to you and your business.

**Monday, I read Proverbs chapter** _____

My favorite verse is: _____
_____

This is how this verse applies to me and my business: _____
_____
_____

**Tuesday, I read Proverbs chapter** _____

My favorite verse is: _____
_____

This is how this verse applies to me and my business: _____
_____
_____

**Wednesday, I read Proverbs chapter** _____

My favorite verse is: _____
_____

This is how this verse applies to me and my business: _____
_____
_____

**Thursday, I read Proverbs chapter** _____

My favorite verse is: _____
_____

This is how this verse applies to me and my business: _____
_____
_____

**Friday, I read Proverbs chapter** _____

My favorite verse is: _____
_____

This is how this verse applies to me and my business: _____
_____
_____

# April Week Two Class

☐ Discuss Biblical Principles from Proverbs

☐ Discuss "How to Make a Formal Business Plan"

**Notes from Class**

# April Week Two Home

☐ Work on Business Plan

☐ Complete "Wisdom from Proverbs Worksheet"

☐ Finish Reading *Business by the Book*

☐ Complete *Business by the Book* Review

ECONOMICS, FINANCES, & BUSINESS COURSE

# Wisdom from Proverbs II

This is a visit to the "Book of Wisdom" in the Bible, Proverbs. Proverbs is full of practical wisdom for running a business. Read a chapter each day (M-F) and choose 1 verse that you really like. Write out the verse and share how it applies to you and your business.

**Monday, I read Proverbs chapter** _____

My favorite verse is: _____
_____

This is how this verse applies to me and my business: _____
_____
_____

**Tuesday, I read Proverbs chapter** _____

My favorite verse is: _____
_____

This is how this verse applies to me and my business: _____
_____
_____

**Wednesday, I read Proverbs chapter** _____

My favorite verse is: _____
_____

This is how this verse applies to me and my business: _____
_____
_____

**Thursday, I read Proverbs chapter** _____

My favorite verse is: _____
_____

This is how this verse applies to me and my business: _____
_____
_____

**Friday, I read Proverbs chapter** _____

My favorite verse is: _____
_____

This is how this verse applies to me and my business: _____
_____
_____

# Business by the Book

A short review on *Business by the Book* by Larry Burkett

Summarize ten principles found in Part I: Business by the Book:

1.
2.
3.
4.
5.
6.
7.
8.
9.
10.

Which of these do not come naturally to you?  Why?


Summarize ten principles found in Part II: Critical Policy Decisions:

1.
2.
3.
4.
5.
6.
7.
8.
9.
10.

What would you do if you hired a close friend and he was a lazy worker? What if his family was dependant on the job and you worked together in ministry, would this affect your decision?




Summarize ten principles found in Part III: Your Business and Your Life:


1.
2.
3.
4.
5.
6.
7.
8.
9.
10.


You start a business with another couple: on-fire Christians! They end up divorcing and the husband backslides. What do you do?

# April Week Three Class

☐ Discuss Everyone's Business Plans

☐ Discuss *Business by the Book*

**Notes from Class**

ECONOMICS, FINANCES, & BUSINESS COURSE

# April Week Three Home

☐ Work on Business Plan

☐ Complete "Wisdom from Proverbs Worksheet"

☐ Read *Principles Under Scrutiny* Section on "Ministries & Scriptural Highlights"

☐ Complete "Ministry Fundraising Worksheet"

☐ Plan an Essay: "Seeking First the Kingdom in the Area of Finances"

# Wisdom from Proverbs III

This is a visit to the "Book of Wisdom" in the Bible, Proverbs. Proverbs is full of practical wisdom for running a business. Read a chapter each day (M-F) and choose 1 verse that you really like. Write out the verse and share how it applies to you and your business.

**Monday, I read Proverbs chapter** _____

My favorite verse is: _____
_____

This is how this verse applies to me and my business: _____
_____
_____

**Tuesday, I read Proverbs chapter** _____

My favorite verse is: _____
_____

This is how this verse applies to me and my business: _____
_____
_____

**Wednesday, I read Proverbs chapter** _____

My favorite verse is: _____
_____

This is how this verse applies to me and my business: _____
_____
_____

**Thursday, I read Proverbs chapter** _____

My favorite verse is: _____
_____

This is how this verse applies to me and my business: _____
_____
_____

**Friday, I read Proverbs chapter** _____

My favorite verse is: _____
_____

This is how this verse applies to me and my business: _____
_____
_____

ECONOMICS, FINANCES, & BUSINESS COURSE

# Ministry Fundraising

A short review based on *Principles under Scrutiny* by Larry Burkett

Describe some ministry/church fundraising that has made you uncomfortable? What Biblical principles were broken?

Why is tithing so important, especially in light of Matthew 6:33?

How can a church/ministry have a balanced view of raising money for the work of the Lord?

Write down a sample of a Biblical appeal for money.

In what financial areas are you seeking the Kingdom first?

In what financial areas are you feeding the flesh?

# Economic Essay: "Seeking God First in the Area of Finances"

We have studied economics and financial management from a biblical perspective. Now, we are studied business from a Christian viewpoint. Think carefully through the year? What have you learned about seeking God first in the area of finances? What would you want to share with other people? Plan your essay this week and write your essay next week. Share your essay with friends and family members.

Here is my Outline

**Introduction**

**First Point =**

**Second Point =**

**Third Point =**

**Fourth Point =** (you may not have a 4th point!)

**Conclusion**

ECONOMICS, FINANCES, & BUSINESS COURSE

# April Week Four Class

☐ Discuss Biblical Principles from Proverbs

☐ Discuss "Ministry Fundraising Worksheet"

**Notes from Class**

# April Week Four Home

☐ Finish Business Plan

☐ Complete "Wisdom from Proverbs Worksheet"

☐ Write Essay: "Seeking First the Kingdom in the Area of Finances"

☐ Complete "Monthly Consumer Price Index Project"

ECONOMICS, FINANCES, & BUSINESS COURSE

# Wisdom from Proverbs IV

This is a visit to the "Book of Wisdom" in the Bible, Proverbs. Proverbs is full of practical wisdom for running a business. Read a chapter each day (M-F) and choose 1 verse that you really like. Write out the verse and share how it applies to you and your business.

**Monday, I read Proverbs chapter** _____

My favorite verse is: _____
_____

This is how this verse applies to me and my business: _____
_____
_____

**Tuesday, I read Proverbs chapter** _____

My favorite verse is: _____
_____

This is how this verse applies to me and my business: _____
_____
_____

**Wednesday, I read Proverbs chapter** _____

My favorite verse is: _____
_____

This is how this verse applies to me and my business: _____
_____
_____

**Thursday, I read Proverbs chapter** _____

My favorite verse is: _____
_____

This is how this verse applies to me and my business: _____
_____
_____

**Friday, I read Proverbs chapter** _____

My favorite verse is: _____
_____

This is how this verse applies to me and my business: _____
_____
_____

# Monthly Consumer Price Index Project

This is an ongoing project for the duration of this class. You will have to go shopping once a month and record prices of each item. Once you choose an item, write it in on your monthly Consumer Price Index Project page. You will need to record the make, model, brand, and size—price the EXACT same item each month. You can go "shopping online." Go to the same store each month. This is a fun project and will provide interesting results at the end of the year.

## Durable Items

(These items are things that you purchase that have life spans of more than 1 year. Examples would be televisions, computers, refrigerators, radios, computers, calculators, washing machines, i-pods, shoes, clothing, chairs, beds, curtains, tables, blenders)

**Durable Item Shopping Bag for Month of** _____

| Durable Item | Store | Brand | Weight or Size | Color | Type/Model | Price |
|---|---|---|---|---|---|---|
| SLR Camera w Lens | Sam's | Nikon | 10 MP 3" LCK 3X Zoom SD/SDHC | | D3000 #23341 | $445.00 |
| | | | | | | |
| | | | | | | |
| | | | | | | |
| | | | | | | |
| | | | | | | |
| | | | | | | |
| | | | | | | |
| | | | | | | |
| | | | | | | |
| | | | | | | |

**Shopping Bag Cost for Durable Item =**

ECONOMICS, FINANCES, & BUSINESS COURSE

**Non-Durable Items for Month of** _____

(These items are things that you purchase that have life spans of less than 1 year. Examples would be toothpaste, aluminum foil, food, drinks, make-up, gasoline, oil, nail polish, after shave, napkins, fast food, mouthwash, deodorant, candy, vitamins, medicine, contact solution)

**Non-Durable Item Shopping Bag**

| Durable Item | Store | Brand | Weight or Size | Color | Type/Model | Price |
|---|---|---|---|---|---|---|
| Wheat Thins | Target | Nabisco | 10 oz. | | Low-fat Salted | $2.00 |
| | | | | | | |
| | | | | | | |
| | | | | | | |
| | | | | | | |
| | | | | | | |
| | | | | | | |
| | | | | | | |
| | | | | | | |
| | | | | | | |
| | | | | | | |

**Shopping Bag Cost for Non-Durable Item =**

## Service Items for Month of _____

(These are services your family purchases. Examples of services would be haircuts, oil changes, pedicures, lawn mowing, massage, car wash, doctor visit, dental visit, X-ray at hospital, ER visit, gym membership, lawyer consult, accountant consult, taxes, tutoring, college tuition)

Service Items Shopping Bag

| Durable Item | Store | Brand/Kind | Length of Time/Amount | Purpose | Type/Model | Price |
|---|---|---|---|---|---|---|
| Massage | Shear Bliss | | 1 hour | Relaxation | Deep Tissue | $85.00 |
| | | | | | | |
| | | | | | | |
| | | | | | | |
| | | | | | | |
| | | | | | | |
| | | | | | | |
| | | | | | | |
| | | | | | | |
| | | | | | | |
| | | | | | | |

**Shopping Bag Cost for Service Items =**

ECONOMICS, FINANCES, & BUSINESS COURSE

# May

Local Church Responsibility Workshop

Personalized Consumer Price Index Project Summary

Essay: "Give & It Will Be Given to You"

Interviews & Resumes

Sample Resumes & Letter

Job Application

Mock Interview

Wisdom from Proverbs

## May Week One Class

☐ Read "Seeking Kingdom First" Essays Aloud

☐ Discuss "Monthly Consumer Price Index Project"

☐ Present Business Plans

**Notes from Class**

## May Week One Home

- ☐ Tweak Your Business Plan based on feedback in class

- ☐ Complete "Wisdom from Proverbs V" Worksheet

- ☐ Read *Principles Under Scrutiny* section on "Church & Sharing"

- ☐ Complete "Local Church Responsibility Worksheet"

- ☐ Finish "Monthly Consumer Price Index Project Summary"

- ☐ Write An Essay: "Give and It Will Be Given to You"

- ☐ Run Your Own Business for the Glory of God and to Serve People

# Tweak Business Plan

You have presented your business plan and gotten feedback from your family and/or homeschool co-op class. Incorporate those changes into your business plan and turn in your final project to Mom or co-op teacher.

# Wisdom from Proverbs V

This is a visit to the "Book of Wisdom" in the Bible, Proverbs. Proverbs is full of practical wisdom for running a business. Read a chapter each day (M-F) and choose 1 verse that you really like. Write out the verse and share how it applies to you and your business.

**Monday, I read Proverbs chapter** _____

My favorite verse is: _____
_____

This is how this verse applies to me and my business: _____
_____
_____

**Tuesday, I read Proverbs chapter** _____

My favorite verse is: _____
_____

This is how this verse applies to me and my business: _____
_____
_____

**Wednesday, I read Proverbs chapter** _____

My favorite verse is: _____
_____

This is how this verse applies to me and my business: _____
_____
_____

**Thursday, I read Proverbs chapter** _____

My favorite verse is: _____
_____

This is how this verse applies to me and my business: _____
_____
_____

**Friday, I read Proverbs chapter** _____

My favorite verse is: _____
_____

This is how this verse applies to me and my business: _____
_____
_____

ECONOMICS, FINANCES, & BUSINESS COURSE

# Local Church Responsibility

A short review based on *Principles under Scrutiny* by Larry Burkett

What are the financial responsibilities of a local church?

Who should receive benevolence?

Who should not receive benevolence?  Why?

Give examples of "fleecing the flock" from real life.

Why are the poor so precious to God?

What does giving do to bless the giver?  Give Scriptures.

# Monthly Consumer Price Index Project Summary

You are finished! Now it is time to tally up your results. List your Shopping Bag Cost from each month.

## September Shopping Bags

Durable Items Shopping Bag Cost for Service Items = _____

Non-Durable Items Shopping Bag Cost for Service Items = _____

Services Shopping Bag Cost for Service Items = _____

Total Cost of Shopping Bags = _____

## October Shopping Bags

Durable Items Shopping Bag Cost for Service Items = _____

Non-Durable Items Shopping Bag Cost for Service Items = _____

Services Shopping Bag Cost for Service Items = _____

Total Cost of Shopping Bags = _____

## November Shopping Bags

Durable Items Shopping Bag Cost for Service Items = _____

Non-Durable Items Shopping Bag Cost for Service Items = _____

Services Shopping Bag Cost for Service Items = _____

Total Cost of Shopping Bags = _____

## December Shopping Bags

Durable Items Shopping Bag Cost for Service Items = _____

Non-Durable Items Shopping Bag Cost for Service Items = _____

Services Shopping Bag Cost for Service Items = _____

Total Cost of Shopping Bags = _____

## January Shopping Bags

Durable Items Shopping Bag Cost for Service Items = _____

Non-Durable Items Shopping Bag Cost for Service Items = _____

Services Shopping Bag Cost for Service Items = _____

Total Cost of Shopping Bags = _____

## February Shopping Bags

Durable Items Shopping Bag Cost for Service Items = _____

Non-Durable Items Shopping Bag Cost for Service Items = _____

Services Shopping Bag Cost for Service Items = _____

Total Cost of Shopping Bags = _____

## March Shopping Bags

Durable Items Shopping Bag Cost for Service Items = _____

Non-Durable Items Shopping Bag Cost for Service Items = _____

Services Shopping Bag Cost for Service Items = _____

Total Cost of Shopping Bags = _____

## April Shopping Bags

Durable Items Shopping Bag Cost for Service Items = _____

Non-Durable Items Shopping Bag Cost for Service Items = _____

Services Shopping Bag Cost for Service Items = _____

Total Cost of Shopping Bags = _____

## Now, answer the following questions.

Which month was the Durable Items Shopping Bag the least expensive?

Which month was the Durable Items Shopping Bag the most expensive?

Which month was the Non-Durable Items Shopping Bag the least expensive?

Which month was the Non-Durable Items Shopping Bag the most expensive?

Which month was the Services Shopping Bag the least expensive?

Which month was the Services Shopping Bag the most expensive?

## May Week Two Class

☐ Share any changes to Business Plan

☐ Present your findings from the "Monthly Consumer Price Index Project Summary"

**Notes from Class**

ECONOMICS, FINANCES, & BUSINESS COURSE

## May Week Two  Home

☐ Read "Job Interviews" & "Writing a Resume"

☐ Write Your Own Resume

☐ Read "Write a Letter of Recommendation" & "Fill Out a Job Application"

☐ Write a Letter of Recommendation for someone in your co-op class or church

☐ Fill Out a Job Application

☐ Complete "Wisdom from Proverbs VI Worksheet"

☐ Run Your Own Business for the Glory of God and to Serve People

# Job Interviews

We have just finished making a business plan. Hopefully, you are operating your own business right now. What if you decided to hire employees for your business? What would you be looking for? Each business owner will be looking for something a little different, depending on his/her business and personal beliefs. I would want employees that would help the business make a profit and represent my company well to the public.

For an employee to help my business be successful, I would look for someone who works hard without complaining, takes initiative, follows directions carefully, interacts well with customers and fellow employees, and produces quality work. Integrity, honesty, good manners, and appearance would matter to me too because this potential employee would be representing my company to the public and I want my company to glorify Jesus Christ.

When you apply for a job, go on an interview, or make a resume, keep this in mind. What is your potential employer looking for to make his/her business successful? Think in terms of how you can meet the needs that your potential boss has and put your best foot forward. What skills, education, volunteer experience, and personal attributes will be a blessing to his/her company?

In all things in our life, we must see ourselves as servants. When we run a business, we are serving God, our employees, and our customers. When we are an employee we are serving God, our boss, our fellow employees, and our customers. With the attitude of a servant, get ready to go on an interview to share why you would be a asset to his/her company.

# Pray

Pray before you go. Ask God to give you favor, to open or shut the door according to His will.

# Dress for Success

What you wear is critical. Guys: suit, tie, dress shoes, clean smelling, and tidy appearance. Gals: suit, pumps, hose, light jewelry, light make-up, conservative hair style, and tidy appearance. Look in the mirror several times from several angles and get input from family members. Pay attention to shoes! And, don't forget to smile.

# Demeanor

Your demeanor is how you present yourself to others. Good grooming, poise, proper posture, eye contact, and a firm handshake all make a difference to employers. Be sure to look your interviewer in the eye, but don't stare him/her down.

# Research the Company

Learn all you can about the company you are applying for: when it started, any newsworthy information, important people in the company, the product or service, sales and profits, innovations, plans for the future, and any potential needs you could fill. Bring plenty of questions with you to ask your interviewer about the company and how you could serve.

# Role Play

If you are nervous about job interviews, try role playing with friends or family members first. Be prepared to be asked lots of questions! Why not role play beforehand with a friend or family member? Have them ask you typical interview questions and see how well you do with the answers.

Here are some things an interviewer might ask or say.

Tell me about yourself.

Why do you want to work for us?

What are your short term goals?

What do you know about our company?

Where do you see yourself in five years time?

Can you do the job?

Do you want the job?

Why do you think you are the best person for this job?

Tell me a little about your experience

What parts of your education do you see as relevant to this position?

What prompted you to study….(law, basket weaving, history)?

Tell me about a significant achievement in your life

Tell me about a time you had to work towards a deadline. Did you meet it?

Tell me about a time you had to communicate information to a group of people

Talk to people about their interview experiences. Learn as much as you can to prepare yourself. Role-play with your family or co-op class some different interview situations.

# Writing a Resume

There are many times in your life when you may want to work for someone else. To be considered for a job, you must fill out a job application and have an interview. It is also helpful to give potential employers a resume and letters of recommendation.

What is a resumè? What is a letter of recommendation?

A resume is a summary of someone's educational and work experience given to a potential employer. The purpose of a resume is to win an interview.

A resume has a listing of all your job experience from the present through the last ten years, starting with the present. Another section has your educational degrees with year graduated. One section has your abilities, achievements, and honors (and any publications).

- Make it pleasing to the eye (font, size of words, layout)
- Use quality paper
- Use bullets—easy to read
- Focus on employers needs, not your own
- Be as brief as possible in your descriptions
- Make sure grammar and spelling is correct
- Focus on the positive, but don't be deceptive
- Give examples of your creativity and innovations on the job
- List jobs in reverse chronological order

The best way to understand a resume is to see samples. Ask friends and family members to look at their resumes. I am including samples here for you to see.

## Write Your Own Resume

Now, it's time to write your own resume. You can model yours after our samples or find more samples to imitate online.

# MEREDITH CURTIS

Jackson Daniel Hendricker
XXXX Steveson Circle
Sanford, FL 32773
xxxxxxxx@gmail.com
(407)999-9999

OBJECTIVE

I desire to find a career with a company I can grow with in order to provide for my family.

SKILLSETS

Management skills in Restaurants
Employee Training in Truck driving and Restaurant atmospheres
Self-taught Mechanic
Self-taught Computer Technician
Trouble-shoot computer soft-ware and hardware

PROFILE

Detailed oriented, highly organized and strong in leadership skills

Assess and solve problems accurately and effectively

EDUCATION

A. A. Degree
Seminole Community College
Truck Driving School
National Training Inc.

EMPLOYMENT EXPERIENCE

| | |
|---|---|
| Autozone, Commercial Driver, Sanford, Fl | 2009-Present |
| Wholesale Trucking Group, Delivery Driver, Orlando, FL | 2006-2009 |
| Qdoba Mexican Grill, Store Manager, Sanford, FL | 2005-2006 |
| Papa John's Pizza, Assistant Store Manager, Orlando, FL | 2005-2005 |
| Transworld Systems Inc., Debt Collections, Winter Park, FL | 2005- 2005 |
| McGilly Trucking, Driver, Groveland, FL | 2002-2004 |
| Danganda, Driver, Orlando, FL | 1999-2002 |

HOBBIES & INTERESTS

Volunteer mechanic for local community
Facilitate small groups in studies
Knowledge base in Windows Applications


References Available

ECONOMICS, FINANCES, & BUSINESS COURSE

Cecil B. Frederick
000 S. Sunshine Dr. Sanford, Fl. 32773
(407) 999-9999 Cell (407) 999-9999 Fx
xxxxxxxxxx@yahoo.com

---

**Experience:**

PROJECT MANAGER Sound it Out, Deltona, FL                 2005-Present

Residential and Commercial * System design (Audio, Video, Control, Lighting, CCTV, Security, Vacuum) * Engineering * Programming * Fabrication * Installation * Writing & negotiating contracts * Coordination of vendors, contractors, & subcontractors * Ordering equipment for projects * Site Supervisor * Customer relations * Troubleshooting * Scheduling * Documentation * Accounting * Inventory control * Training

PROJECT/SERVICE MANAGER Sonic Sound Inc., Orlando, FL     1999-2001

Scheduling and coordinating Service and Retail appointments * Creating an infrastructure for the Service and Retail Departments * Customer walk-throughs to close sales * Engineering systems to suit customers needs and wants * Scheduling and managing seven crews * Overseeing all custom projects * Coordination of vendors, & contractors * Ordering equipment for projects * Customer relations * Trouble shooting problems on projects * Change orders * Infrastructure building * Programming * Service scheduling * Inventory control

INSTALLATION TECHNICIAN Sonic Sound Inc., Orlando, FL     1996-1999

Selling, designing, ordering, installing, programming and instructing of Panasonic phone systems * Installation and servicing of Residential theatres, control systems, phone systems, Lutron lighting control, cameras, CCTV, multi-room music, CATV, and satellite systems * Inventory control

SPECIAL SKILLS:

PC computers * Microsoft Word, Excel, Outlook * Visio * Adobe Photoshop CS4 * Corel Draw X4 * Paint Shop Pro * Adobe Acrobat * Touch Screen Programming software * Innovative * Adaptable * Strong trouble shooting skills * Solid Leadership Abilities * Quick Learning * Ability to read AutoCAD drawings and signal flow charts * Very capable in working with Security systems, Phone systems, Audio/ Video systems, Control systems, Satellite systems, CATV systems, CCTV systems, Intercom systems, LAN systems, Vacuum systems *

EDUCATION:

Recording Arts Specialized Associate Degree: FULL SAIL Real World Education    1995

SPECIALIZED TRAINING:

Completed Alarm System Agent Course # ASA 97-17-001
CEDIA Management and Efficiency courses
Crestron control system training
AMX designer/ programmer training

**Volunteer Work:**

POWERLINE COMMUNITY CHURCH Sanford, FL                 2009-Present

Recording * Mixing * Worship leader * Bass player * Guitar player * Singer * Harmonica player * Special Events coordination * Project management * Evangelism/ outreach * Technical consultant * Sound class * Maintenance of equipment * Hospitality * Men's Discipleship

# Write a Letter of Recommendation

You may be asked to write a letter of recommendation for someone. Maybe you teach a class and a student is applying for a scholarship. You might own a business and one of your employees asks for a letter of recommendation for another job. Your letter will confirm that the person you are writing about can perform a task with excellence or manage people with care and tact. Whatever the reason, a letter of recommendation can affect a person's future. Let's learn to write a letter of recommendation.

Here are things you want to do in a letter of recommendation.

Place your address on the top right of the paper, followed by the date spelled out. After skipping a line, write the address of the letter's recipient's name and address. Skip a line and address the recipient formally.

The body of the letter should be enthusiastic and open with praise for the person who is the subject of the letter.

Follow this up by describing how you know the person and how long you have worked together. Also mention your basic qualifications.

Next, describe the subject's qualifications, successes, and awards. Be specific, not general. Try to give examples.

Make comparisons that will illustrate their success.

Show where and how the person can improve.

Close the letter affirmatively by recommending the candidate once more and inviting the recipient of the letter to contact you if needed.

Use a formal closing before signing your name such as 'Sincerely', 'Yours Truly', or 'Best Regards'.

Sign your name.

I will follow these steps and give you a sample letter on the next page.

## Write Your Own Letter of Recommendation

Now, it's time to write your own letter of recommendation. You can model yours after my sample or find more samples to imitate online.

ECONOMICS, FINANCES, & BUSINESS COURSE

Mrs. Maggie King
111 First Street
Firstville, FL 33333

May 1, 2016

Dr. Stanley Park
777 Creation Center Drive
Long Beach, FL 33333

Dear Dr. Park

I am excited to recommend Mae Smith for the Creation Communication College Scholarship. She is a gifted student and a hard worker.

I have known Mae since she was a little girl as a family friend, Sunday school teacher, and English and history teacher at our homeschool co-op. Being a firm believer in six-day Creation, Mae loves to communicate these truths to the people in her world. Whatever she learns, she passes on to others. As a published writer, speaker, and educator for twenty years, I recognize good communication skills when I see them.

Not only have Mae's essays and writing assignments been excellent, she has asked for extra assignments to grow in this area. When other children, both peers and younger in age, have needed extra help, Mae has volunteered to tutor them in writing. I was not surprised that Mae won the "Best Creation Short Story Award" two years in a row.

In addition to writing, Mae leads the debate team at our homeschool co-op, leading them to victory at the state level two years in a row. The experience of competing on the national level, though the team did not place, was another opportunity for Mae to grow in her communication and leadership skills.

Mae has overcome learning disabilities such as dyslexia to become a fluent reader and skilled writer. When Mae lost a Creation vs. Evolution Debate, she spent weeks researching and reading to grow in her knowledge and understanding of the subject. Obstacles do not deter Mae and I am confident that she will overcome any obstacle to achieve success at the college of her choice.

You will be making a wise choice to award Mae with the Creation Communication College Scholarship. You can contact me with any further questions at my email address below.

Sincerely,

Maggie King

MaggieKing@powerlinecc.com

# Fill Out a Job Application

There are many times in your life when you may want to work for someone else. To be considered for a job, you must fill out a job application and have an interview. It is also helpful to give potential employers a resume and letters of recommendation from people that you have worked for or volunteered with.

Here is a sample application for a government teaching job.

## Fill Out Your Own Job Application

Applications are different because jobs are different. Google a job application for a job you are interested in. For example, if you would like to work at Chick-fil-A, then Google, "job application for Chick-fil-A®" and download that application. Fill it out and bring it to class time next week.

You will also get an application from your mom or co-op teacher to use for the job interview in class time next week.

ECONOMICS, FINANCES, & BUSINESS COURSE

# Wisdom from Proverbs VI

This is a visit to the "Book of Wisdom" in the Bible, Proverbs. Proverbs is full of practical wisdom for running a business. Read a chapter each day (M-F) and choose 1 verse that you really like. Write out the verse and share how it applies to you and your business.

**Monday, I read Proverbs chapter** _____

My favorite verse is: _____

_____

This is how this verse applies to me and my business: _____

_____

_____

**Tuesday, I read Proverbs chapter** _____

My favorite verse is: _____

_____

This is how this verse applies to me and my business: _____

_____

_____

**Wednesday, I read Proverbs chapter** _____

My favorite verse is: _____

_____

This is how this verse applies to me and my business: _____

_____

_____

**Thursday, I read Proverbs chapter** _____

My favorite verse is: _____

_____

This is how this verse applies to me and my business: _____

_____

_____

**Friday, I read Proverbs chapter** _____

My favorite verse is: _____

_____

This is how this verse applies to me and my business: _____

_____

_____

# May Week Three Class

☐ Everyone Share from their Own "Wisdom from Proverbs VI" Worksheets

☐ Turn in Job Applications and Everyone Interviewed by Potential Boss

## Mock Job Interviews

You might need to include more adults in this class to act as "potential bosses" who interview each student after going over their job application.

We had several different kinds of job applications that we downloaded from online. We downloaded a managerial position, a fashion sales clerk position, a lawn care job, and a fast food job applications. Everyone chose their application, filled it out, and turned it in to the person they interviewed with. We used a fashion store owner, a lawn care business owner, a fast food manager, and an executive with Verizon®. They were all people in our church and treated the interview seriously as if they were interviewing potential employees. After the "interview", our interviewers gave the students tips on how to improve their interview skills.

**Notes from Class**

# May Week Three Home

- [ ] Complete "Wisdom from Proverbs VII" Worksheet

- [ ] Complete "Wisdom from Proverbs VIII" Worksheet

- [ ] Plan & Write an Essay: "Give and It Will Be Given to You"

- [ ] Run Your Own Business for the Glory of God and to Serve People

# Wisdom from Proverbs VII

This is a visit to the "Book of Wisdom" in the Bible, Proverbs. Proverbs is full of practical wisdom for running a business. Read a chapter each day (M-F) and choose 1 verse that you really like. Write out the verse and share how it applies to you and your business.

**Monday, I read Proverbs chapter** _____

My favorite verse is: _____
_____

This is how this verse applies to me and my business: _____
_____
_____

**Tuesday, I read Proverbs chapter** _____

My favorite verse is: _____
_____

This is how this verse applies to me and my business: _____
_____
_____

**Wednesday, I read Proverbs chapter** _____

My favorite verse is: _____
_____

This is how this verse applies to me and my business: _____
_____
_____

**Thursday, I read Proverbs chapter** _____

My favorite verse is: _____
_____

This is how this verse applies to me and my business: _____
_____
_____

**Friday, I read Proverbs chapter** _____

My favorite verse is: _____
_____

This is how this verse applies to me and my business: _____
_____
_____

ECONOMICS, FINANCES, & BUSINESS COURSE

# Economic Essay: "Give and It Will Be Given to You"

It is such a blessing to see God bless His people and provide. ☺ This is your last essay for this course. Make it a good one. You will write about God's promise that if we given, it will be given to us!" You can share testimonies in your own and other believers' lives. Be sure to use Scripture verses.

Here is my Outline

**Introduction**

**First Point =**

**Second Point =**

**Third Point =**

**Fourth Point =** (you may not have a 4th point!)

**Conclusion**

# Wisdom from Proverbs VIII

This is a visit to the "Book of Wisdom" in the Bible, Proverbs. Proverbs is full of practical wisdom for running a business. Read a chapter each day (M-F) and choose 1 verse that you really like. Write out the verse and share how it applies to you and your business.

**Monday, I read Proverbs chapter** _____

My favorite verse is: _____
_____

This is how this verse applies to me and my business: _____
_____
_____

**Tuesday, I read Proverbs chapter** _____

My favorite verse is: _____
_____

This is how this verse applies to me and my business: _____
_____
_____

**Wednesday, I read Proverbs chapter** _____

My favorite verse is: _____
_____

This is how this verse applies to me and my business: _____
_____
_____

**Thursday, I read Proverbs chapter** _____

My favorite verse is: _____
_____

This is how this verse applies to me and my business: _____
_____
_____

**Friday, I read Proverbs chapter** _____

My favorite verse is: _____
_____

This is how this verse applies to me and my business: _____
_____
_____

ECONOMICS, FINANCES, & BUSINESS COURSE

# May Week Four Class

☐ Everyone Share from their Own "Wisdom from Proverbs III & IV" Worksheets

☐ Read "Give and It Will Be Given to You" Essays Aloud

☐ Evaluate Course

**Notes from Class**

ECONOMICS, FINANCES, & BUSINESS COURSE

## Being World Changers!
## Raising World Changers!

Powerline Productions exists to serve you! We want you to grow in your relationship with Jesus, experience joy and success in your homeschooling journey, and fulfill the Great Commission with your family in your home, church, and community. We offer Homeschooling books, unit studies, classes, high school classes, ladies Bible studies, God's Girls Bible studies, Real Men Bible studies, audios, and cookbooks just for you!

### Our Websites

joyfulandsuccessfulhomeschooling.com/
jshomeschooling.com/
finishwellcon.com/
powerlineprod.com/
meredithcurtis.com/

E-books Available at powerlineprod.com/
mediaangels.com/index.php?main_page=index&cPath=1_19
currclick.com/browse/pub/247/Powerline-Productions

**Print Books Available @ amazon.com/ (look up Books by Title)**

**Contact Us:** Laura@powerlinecc.com & Meredith@powerlinecc.com & PastorMike@powerlinecc.com

Powerline Productions
251 Brightview Drive Lake Mary, FL 32746

## High School Classes

# ECONOMICS, FINANCES, & BUSINESS COURSE

## Real Men Discipleship Manuals

God calls fathers to impart life to their sons, passing the baton in the race of faith. These Bible studies were created for fathers (or mentors) to go through this material with their sons. Pastor Mike Curtis used these materials to mentor his own son and other young men in the church. These manuals cover tough issues that fathers and sons need to talk about and live out in their lives.

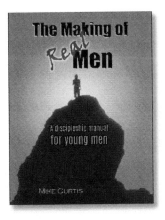  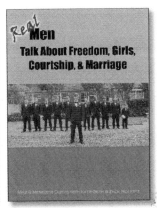

## Real Men Classes

Do you want to prepare your sons to become godly husbands, fathers, church leaders, and pillars in their communities? These one-credit high school life skills classes build character and prepare young men for the future. Using living books, Scripture, and practical assignments, young men will learn to become the man God has called them to be.

   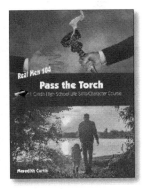

# More Books from Powerline Production

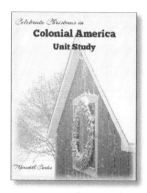

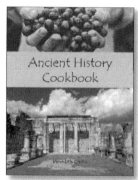

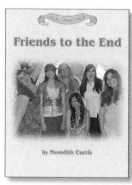
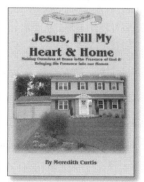

## Maggie King Mysteries

If you like cozy mysteries, you will love this series! Meet Maggie King, a pastor's wife and homeschool mom who keeps stumbling across dead bodies. With her sidekicks, Sophia and Mary-Kate and her curious children, Maggie is on one adventure after another.

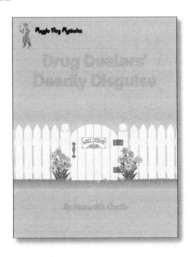
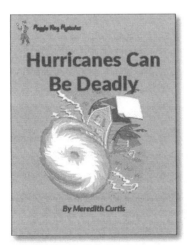

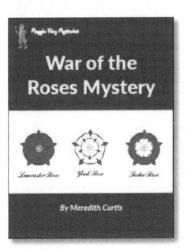
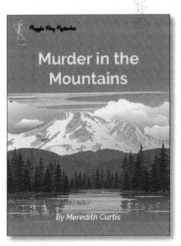

# Economics Test # 1

**True or False (1 point each/30 total points)**

_____ Everything on earth belongs to God (psalm 24:1).

_____ We are just stewards of all our possessions & money; they really belong to the Lord.

_____ Karl Marx wrote Wealth of the Nations.

_____ Karl Marx wrote Communist Manifesto.

_____ Capitalism won't work well apart from a moral framework like Christianity.

_____ Adam Smith wrote Wealth of the Nations to promote mercantilism.

_____ Communism inspires people to work hard so that others can be blessed.

_____ Money is the root of all evil.

_____ The love of money is the root of all kinds of evil.

_____ Inflation is an increase in the money supply.

_____ War is good for the economy because money is spent to replace everything destroyed.

_____ Broken windows help the economy because money is spent fixing the broken window.

_____ The dollar bill in your wallet is backed by gold in Fort Knox.

_____ Hard work should be avoided at all cost—it wastes our time.

_____ God promotes "Get Rich Quick" schemes in His word.

_____ Our economy is built on debt right now in America.

_____ Debt is a good thing.

_____ God's blessing is being debt-free and having enough extra to share with others.

_____ In a market economy, the price is determined by the Law of Supply and Demand.

_____ When the supply is low and the demand is high, the price goes down.

_____ When the supply is low and the demand is high, the price goes up.

_____ When the supply is high and the demand is low, the price goes down.

_____ When the supply is high and the demand is low, the price goes up.

_____ In a command economy, business and economic choices are made by the government.

_____ In a market economy, business and economic choices are made by individuals, not government.

_____ Fascism utilizes a command economy.

_____ Communism utilizes a command economy.

# ECONOMICS, FINANCES, & BUSINESS COURSE

_____ Most countries in the world have a mixed economy, rather than command or market.

_____ Jobs are more important than production.

_____ Coin clipping was a form of inflation.

**Draw and Label the Economic Cycle (5 points)**

**Match each book cover with the description below. Put the letter underneath the book cover. (1 point each/ 7 total points)**

A. This book is "The Book" on free-market economics, explains what wealth truly is for a nation. Rather than based on piles of gold, a nation's wealth is the total of what it produces to make life more enjoyable.

B. This book shares all the biblical principles found in Scripture that dictate how we manage our money in a way that honors Christ.

~ 439 ~

C. This book teaches biblical economics, combining free-market principles with biblical principles. It also gives class assignments.
D. This book makes basic economic principles such as inflation and the economic cycle simple and easy to understand.
E. This book is easy to understand. It is written in the form of letters from an uncle to his nephew and studies more advanced economic principles such as money velocity, how the economy affects society, and why we should learn from our mistakes
F. This book promotes a utopian economic system where everyone does their share of work and shares money equally. Atheism, sexual immorality, and destruction of the family are promoted. In real life application, nations who apply this book end up being ruthless dictatorships.
G. A book on economics that teaches the principle that a good economist looks at the present and future economic effects on ALL people before making a decision.

**Answer the following questions. (2 points/ 44 total points)**

How is government financed?

What are taxes?

What causes inflation?

In what way is the government involved in the banking system?

How does the government being involved in the banking system affect the economy?

What is the difference between Retail and Service?

Are some businesses both Retail and Service? If yes, give 3 examples.

Which is more important: production or work? Why?

# ECONOMICS, FINANCES, & BUSINESS COURSE

What is the difference between stocks and bonds?

What is Credit?

What is Debt?

What is the Law of Supply and Demand?

What is Specialization of Labor?

Give examples of Specialization of Labor?

What is GNP?

What is Capitalism?

What is Socialism/Communism?

Name the 3 kinds of Economic Systems.

What is Wealth?

What is Personal Wealth?

What is Money?

What is Marketing?

**List the Seven Biblical Principles of Economics (1 point each/ 14 total points)**

# ECONOMICS, FINANCES, & BUSINESS COURSE

**Extra Credit (1 point each)**

How did the dollar get its name?

What stock increases its dividend every year?

What year was Wealth of the Nations written?

MEREDITH CURTIS

# Economics Test # 2

**True or False (1 point each/30 total points)**

_____ Everything on earth belongs to God (psalm 24:1)
_____ We are stewards of all our possessions & money; they really belong to the Lord
_____ Debt is okay if you really want to have something and can't afford it.
_____ Stock prices stay the same every day for a year and then they go up or down.
_____ It is cheaper to live on your own in an apartment than to live at home with your parents.
_____ As soon as you file your taxes, you can throw all the financial records from that year away.
_____ When you buy stock, you own a little bit of the company.
_____ When you buy bonds, you lend money to a company.
_____ The love of money is the root of all kinds of evil.
_____ Inflation is an increase in the money supply.
_____ Teens don't need to budget their money.
_____ Car salesmen are always honest.
_____ It is cheaper to buy a new car so that you don't have to pay for car repairs.
_____ Hard work should be avoided at all cost—it wastes our time.
_____ The love of money is the root of all kinds of evil.
_____ Inflation is an increase in the money supply.
_____ Banks make money when you run up a big debt on your credit card.
_____ God's blessing is being debt-free and having enough extra to share with others.
_____ Older people have trouble hearing when there is background noise.
_____ An example of bartering is Sarah cutting John's hair in exchange for John mowing Sarah's lawn.
_____ Scholarships can be based on academic, or other, merit or financial need.
_____ Christians are **never** tempted by advertisements to buy something they don't need.
_____ College, weddings, and vacations are events that families need to save money for.
_____ Tithing is optional for the Christian.
_____ Appliances, cars, and air conditioners last forever. You never have to replace them.
_____ Charge cards have to be paid off at the end of the month.
_____ When you use a debit card, the money you spend is immediately deducted from your bank account.
_____ Credit cards are like a loan with very high interest rates if you don't pay them off at the end of the month.
_____ Families can save money with coupons, sales, and store brands.
_____ Commercials are always truthful and accurate.

# ECONOMICS, FINANCES, & BUSINESS COURSE

**Match each book cover with the description below. Put the letter underneath the book cover. (2 point2 each/ 8 total points)**

   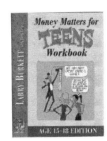

_____    _____    _____    _____

A. This book is easy to understand. It is written in the form of letters from an uncle to his nephew and studies basic principles of managing personal finances and making career decisions.
B. This book teaches teenagers to manage their money including balancing their checkbook, budgeting, buying a car, borrowing, giving, getting a job, keeping a job, and the dangers of borrowing.
C. This is book is not written by a Christian and does promote greed as good, but it also takes about making wealth, investing wealth, and enjoying financial success.
D. This book teaches biblical economics, combining free-market principles with biblical principles. It also gives class assignments.

**Answer the following questions. (3 points/ 54 total points)**

What is a "Get Rich Quick" scheme? Give real life examples.

What is the purpose of advertising?

When does it become unwise to go with the "bargain?"

List ways a family can save money.

Should you ever co-sign a loan for someone near and dear to you, like Aunt Matilda or Brother Cody? Why or why not?

Why is it better to give then to lend? What would be an alternative to both lending or giving to help someone out?

List ten things you would need to buy if you move into your own apartment?

What is bartering?

What is the difference between stocks and bonds?

Mandy owns a house worth $150,000 and $10,000 in stocks, but she still owes $100,000 on her mortgage and $50,000 in credit card debt. What is her net worth?

List 5 home business ideas. (Hint think of people you know)

List events that will require a family to save up money.

List expenses that will require a family to save up money.

How can young people go to college debt-free?

Why do banks offer credit cards to young people?

Is paying a mortgage off early a good idea? Why?

List some financial records or legal documents you could store in file folders.

What is the difference between credit cards, debit cards, and charge cards?

Complete a Budget for Mark who makes $5,000.00 a month, paying $1,000 in taxes. He has a wife and five kids. They live in a 2,000 square foot home. His monthly mortgage payment (includes mortgage, taxes, and insurance) is $1,200 and his auto insurance is $150 a month. Make up the rest ☺

**You will have to estimate. Do your best! Make sure you divide all the money out so there is none left. (8 points)**

# Mark's Budget

**My Monthly Income is:** _____

| Budget Category | Amount |
|---|---|
| Taxes | |
| Tithe (10% of income) | |
| Mortgage & Property Tax & Home Insurance Payment | |
| Utilities | |
| Water | |
| Phone/Cell Phone | |
| Internet/Cable | |
| Car Insurance | |
| Health Insurance | |
| Food | |
| Car Repair | |
| Saving for New Car | |
| Saving for Retirement | |
| Books/Music/Gifts/Entertainment | |
| Homeschooling | |
| Other: | |

# ECONOMICS, FINANCES, & BUSINESS COURSE

**Extra Credit (1 point each)**

Who wrote *Communist Manifesto?*

What is the difference between Free Market and Command Market?

What year was *Wealth of the Nations* written?

Who wrote *Wealth of the Nations?*

What is the "Broken Window Fallacy"?

Is war good or bad for the economy?

List some of the stocks you bought in the Stock Market Game? Which ones were the best investment?

# About the Author

Meredith Curtis, a pastor's wife and homeschooling mom of five children, leads worship, mentors ladies, and, sometimes, even cooks dinner. Her passion is to equip people to love Jesus, raise godly children, and change the world around them with the power of the Gospel. "Lives are changed in the context of relationships," Meredith often says, as well as, "Be a world changer! Raise world changers!" She enjoys speaking to small and large groups.

All inquiries can be made to the author, Meredith Curtis, through email: Meredith@powerlinecc.com or contact her through her websites: joyfulandsuccessfulhomeschooling.com/

meredithcurtis.com/
finishwellcon.com/
powerlineprod.com/

Meredith is the author of several books.
*Joyful and Successful Homeschooling*
*Seven R's of Homeschooling*
*Quick & EZ Unit Study Fun*
*Unlocking the Mysteries of Homeschooling High School* (with Laura Nolette)
*Celebrate Thanksgiving*
*Teaching Writing in High School with Classes You Can Use*
*Teaching Literature in High School with Classes You Can Use*
*HIS Story of the 20$^{th}$ Century*
*HIS Story of the 20$^{th}$ Century for Little Folks*


Meredith is the author of several cozy mysteries: The Maggie King Mysteries series.
*Drug Dealers Deadly Disguise*
*Hurricanes Can Be Deadly*
*Legend of the Candy Cane Murder*
*Wash, Dry, Cut, & Die*
*War of the Roses Mystery*
*Murder in the Mountains*


Meredith is the author of several Bible studies.
*Lovely to Behold*
*A Wise Woman Builds*
*Jesus, Fill My Heart & Home*
*Welcome Inn: Practicing the Art of Hospitality in Jesus" Name*
*Friends to the End*

*God's Girls Beauty Secrets* (with Sarah Jeffords)
*God's Girls Friends to the End* (with Katie-Beth Nolette & Sarah Jeffords)
*God's Girls Talk about Boys, Dating, Courtship, & Marriage*


Meredith is the author of several unit studies, timelines, and cookbooks.
*Celebrate Christmas in Colonial America*
*Celebrate Christmas with Cookies*
*Travel to London*
*Celebrate Thanksgiving with the Pilgrims*
*American History Cookbook*
*Ancient History Cookbook*
*20th Century Cookbook* (with Laura Nolette)
*20th Century Timeline* (with Laura Nolette)
*American History Timeline* (with Laura Nolette)
*Ancient History Timeline* (with Laura Nolette)

Meredith is the author of several "History should be Fun!" books.
*Let's Have Our Own Medieval Banquet*
*Let's Have Our Own Archaeological Dig*
*Let's Have Our Own Ancient Greek Olympic Games*
*Let's Have Our Own Passover Feast*

Meredith is the author of several high school classes.
*American Literature and Research*
*British Literature and Writing*
*Who Dun It: Murder Mystery Literature & Writing*
*Communication 101: Essays and Speeches*
*Foundations of Western Literature*
*Economics, Finances, and Business*
*Worldview 101: Understand the Times*
*New Testament Survey*
*Old Testament Survey*
*Great Commission*


And more…

Made in the USA
Lexington, KY
08 May 2017